Connections

Study Skills for College and Career Success

SHARON K. FERRETT, PH. D.
Humboldt State University, Arcata, CA

with an introduction by
JAN FRIEDHEIM, President
Executive Secretarial School, Dallas, TX

IRWIN
MIRROR PRESS

Chicago • Bogotá • Boston • Buenos Aires • Caracas
London • Madrid • Mexico City • Sydney • Toronto

Irwin Book Team

Mirror Press: *David R. Helmstadter*
       Carla F. Tishler
Marketing manager: *Carl Helwing*
Production supervisor: *Laurie Kersch*
Assistant manager, graphics: *Charlene R. Perez*
Project editor: *Karen J. Nelson*
Designer: *Crispin Prebys*
Compositor: *Graphic Composition, Inc.*
Typeface: *11/13 Times Roman*
Printer: *Webcrafters, Inc.*

**Times Mirror
Higher Education Group**

Library of Congress Cataloging-in-Publication Data

Ferrett, Sharon K.
    Connections: study skills for college and career success/Sharon
K. Ferrett and Jan Friedheim.
      p.   cm.
    Includes index.
    ISBN 0-256-18764-9
    1. Study skills.   2. Critical thinking   I. Friedheim, Jan.
II. Title.
LB2395.F47   1996
378.1'7'0281—dc20   95-37277

To my husband Sam and my children Jennifer Katherine and Sarah Angela for their constant support and love. Nothing is more important to me.

S. F.

PREFACE

Why I Wrote This Book

For many years I have worked with faculty and students in career schools, community college, and universities in developing student success and professional development programs. This experience, in addition to my years in the classroom and as a business and management consultant, made it clear to me that students need to be convinced that the same skills that increase one's success in school also increase one's chance of success on the job. *Connections: Study Skills for College and Career Success* was developed to make this point loudly and clearly. *Connections* goes beyond the singular mission of presenting study skills so as to give students a set of skills and strategies with a lifespan beyond school. Thus, building a strong foundation of study skills, including reading skills, memory strategies, listening skills, writing, notetaking, and speaking skills, as well as time management and goal setting, has double dividends—confidence and success in school, and building skills that employers seek and value in employees.

The Critical Thinking Connection

We hear a lot about critical thinking as *the* most important study skill. But what does this term mean to students and how, exactly, does critical thinking benefit students in school and beyond? In *Connections,* students are encouraged to look at the issues they face in the classroom and the issues they will face on the job as problems to be solved, using sound decision-making skills that will last a lifetime. Thinking critically is presented as the foundation for all effective learning and the foundation for school and job success. Just as academic success will increase through critical thinking, so too will success in today's workplace that values people who reason clearly and think critically.

Through critical thinking exercises in each chapter, called "The Critical Thinking Connection" and as part of the chapter-ending Critical Thinking Resources, students are encouraged to integrate, or connect, critical thinking with their work in all subject areas. "The Critical Thinking Connection" exercises ask students to apply their problem-solving skills to a chapter study skill. **Critical Thinking Resources** are highlighted at the end of every chapter for easy access. These are comprised of Grids, which students can use to tackle recurrent study skills issues such as creating realistic study schedules, preparing for tests, and setting up a practical problem-solving methods, Case Studies in which students use critical thinking to solve issues occurring in school and on the job, and Exercises for more practice.

Connections Across Courses

Study skills are interconnected. Better reading skills lead to better writing skills. More effective listening skills lead to better notetaking. Heightened memory skills boost every study skill, and so on. In *Connections,* students are encouraged to apply effective study skills to various course subject areas. Students learn to transfer study skills from specific applications to more general areas. The strategies learned for success in particularly difficult courses like math, foreign languages, and sciences will benefit study habits in other courses as well. Similarly, the active reading strategies used to analyze the extended textbook reading in Chapter 5 can be used to take better notes in a lecture course. Flexibility and adaptability are key to the transfer of study skills, just as they are key to on-the-job success.

Connections to Attitude, Self-Esteem, and Success

One of the most exciting experiences as a teacher is seeing the energy created by students who are enthusiastic and involved in the process of learning. Study skills alone don't create this energy, however. Successful students connect positive attitudes, motivation, and high self-esteem to study skills to create this powerful energy. Every chapter in *Connections* shows students how to increase their motivation and esteem and build the right attitude to succeed.

Connections to the Real World

Today's students are increasingly aware that what they learn in school needs to pay off in the long term—the time they spend learning skills in class should directly correlate to finding and keeping a job they want. I've stressed this connection throughout the book by emphasizing the link between academic skills and the real world. Clearly, problem-solving skills are just as crucial in school as they are in work. Stress management pays off in better grades and in better job performance. There *is* a connection between this course and a rewarding career. In every chapter, Career Focus boxes make this point by applying chapter study skills directly to a relevant workplace scenario, such as the Career Focus box in Chapter 10 showing how listening skills are crucial to workplace success.

Connection to Diversity

More than ever before, today's students come from widely varied backgrounds in terms of culture, experience, and learning styles. A significant proportion of students do *not* come from the traditional pool of recent high school graduates. Many students are older, some have jobs, and many have children and other adult responsibilities. I've taken care to develop examples, exercises, and case studies that make sense to traditional *and* nontraditional students. The **Instructor's Resource Manual** has been developed to help instructors address the diverse needs of their students. This manual contains information about the course and its purpose, and includes sample schedules and syllabi for using *Connections* in varied course structures. Each chapter includes annotated chapter outlines with teaching suggestions, tips on presentation and focus, and references to transparency masters. Also included are more exercises, quizzes, answer guidelines to all text exercises, and transparency masters.

Make the Connection

Let me know what you think. I am interested in your ideas and suggestions, which will be considered in the next edition of *Connections*. Please write to me and tell me what works and what doesn't work for you.

Sharon K. Ferrett

ACKNOWLEDGMENTS

I would like to express my gratitude to those who have helped make this project a reality: To Jan Friedheim for her advice and introduction. Jan provided me with counsel and real classroom examples. Her dedication to teaching and career education must be recognized. To Carla Tishler, Managing Editor, Mirror Press, for her expertise, discernment, knowledge, and encouragement. To David Helmstadter, President, Mirror Press, for his sense of timing, creative ideas, and championing. In addition I'd like to recognize the entire Irwin Career Education Division for their support and professionalism. Thanks also go to the following reviewers who offered invaluable advice on versions of this manuscript.

Karen Cole, Southern Ohio College, Fairfield, OH
Dorothy Herndon, National Business College, Roanoke, VA
Jeff King, Art Institute of Dallas, Dallas, TX
Jayne Nightingale, Rhode Island College, Providence, RI
Nancey Nightingale, International College, Fort Myers, FL
Barry Stearns, Landing Community College, Grand Ledge, MI
Fran Zaniello, Northern Kentucky University, Highland Heights, KY

S. K. F.

INTRODUCTION

The key to your success in school is the same key to your success on the job. It is your ability to set your sights high and keep your mind focused on those sights. What you will be learning while in school will relate directly to the job you want to do when you graduate. You will be taught all the various skills needed to be successful on the job. There will be a lot of them, to be sure. You will be challenged and stretched in the process.

You will discover that you are somebody different from the person who first enrolled in this institution. If you use the techniques incorporated in *Connections: Study Skills for College and Career Success*, you will find that the road isn't nearly as long as you thought and the hills aren't nearly as high.

The fact that you enrolled in school is a good indication that you want something more out of life than you currently have. You want to achieve something important, something significant. Having made that decision, all other decisions should follow suit.

You will find that in the months ahead you will be challenged by the new material you will be asked to learn. At times this may seem overwhelming and perhaps "too much." But that really is part of the stretching process in which you are asked to reach beyond where you are now. It will require some work, some concentration, commitment, and dedication.

I have spent years in the classroom watching this process take place. My greatest joy comes from seeing a student come alive with the realization that learning can be fun; that learning can help to overcome all kinds of problems or barriers. Once the "learning light" goes on, it is impossible to put it out. Learning, growing, becoming more proficient, will become a way of life, as natural as breathing or sleeping.

It is my hope that the techniques explored in *Connections: Study Skills for College and Career Success* will provide you with a road map to make your travel easier and more fun. Life should be fun; learning should be enjoyable.

When you graduate—not if, but when—you will find that these techniques will serve you well when you go to work. When used consistently, every day, you will discover that you can grow into your job as well as you grew into your class work. Those who grow best and grow most will be those who will be honored best and rewarded most.

Good luck!

Jan V. Friedheim
Executive Secretarial School
Dallas, TX

CONTENTS

▲ CHAPTER THREE   Building Confidence Through Time and Stress Management   57

▲ CHAPTER EIGHT   Test Taking, Evaluation, and Feedback   201

▲ CHAPTER NINE   Expressing Yourself: Research, Writing, and Speaking   223

CHAPTER ONE

SELF-ASSESSMENT AND GETTING STARTED

"We shall not cease from exploration
And the end of all our exploring
Will be to arrive where we started
And know the place for the first time."
            T. S. Eliot

"The pertinent question is not how to do
things right, but how to find the right things
to do."
      Peter Drucker, management theorist

Learning Objectives

In Chapter One you will learn:

1. The connection between school and work.

2. The connection between study skills and school and job success.

3. The connection between learning styles and school and job success.

4. How to show the connection between all your courses.

Becoming a peak performer in school and in life requires taking stock of yourself. Taking stock includes assessing your strengths and weaknesses, discovering what you're afraid of, and finding out how you learn. It also includes setting a goal and mapping out a strategy for achieving it.

WHAT LEADS TO SUCCESS?

Excellence is the ability to create a resourceful and positive state of mind and to develop the skills necessary for whatever task is at hand. It is setting high standards and applying yourself with attentiveness and determination. Successful people achieve excellence in their personal and professional lives by focusing on attitude, motivation, and commitment. For example, film director Steven Spielberg, actress Meryl Streep, former Chrysler Corporation chairman Lee Iacocca, and Federal Express founder Fred Smith are masters at creating excellence by focusing on determination.

Excellence is not perfection. In fact, compulsively pursuing perfection often makes people afraid of mistakes. Thousands of people quietly overcome incredible odds, climb over huge obstacles, and reach within themselves to find inner strength. People from all walks of life set goals and develop appropriate attitudes and behaviors to achieve the results they want. Many are not rich or famous, nor have they reached the top in their careers. They are successful because they know that they possess the personal power to produce results in their lives, overcome setbacks, and find passion in what they contribute to life. They are masters, not victims, of life's situations. They control the quality of their lives.

Being successful involves risk-taking, creative thinking, sound judgment, effective decision making, supportive relationships, skill, confidence, and the motivation to overcome barriers.

Many of the qualities and skills essential for sports, such as a sense of focus and a disciplined practice routine, are necessary for being a successful student and achieving success in your career and personal life. Achieving success can be just as vigorous, stimulating, and challenging as any other vigorous undertaking.

WHAT ARE THE BENEFITS?

There are lots of benefits to learning the strategies presented in this book. Here are a few:

Better grades.

A positive and resourceful state of mind.

More self-confidence.

Healthy relationships.

Effective decision making and problem solving.

Better use of your time.

Improved reading comprehension and, consequently, more enjoyable reading.

Integrating learning styles.

Making stress work for you.

A balanced life.

Feeling connected at school and work.

GETTING STARTED: ASSESSMENT STRATEGIES

To meet any goal, a good place to start is to find out where you are now and where you want to go. Self-assessment sounds like a modern concept, yet people have been measuring their skills and planning their personal and work lives since the beginning of time. The Plotinus of Delphi in the third century A.D. identified three universal concerns:

1. Who am I?

2. What shall I do?

3. What shall become of me?

By facing the truth about who you are and by assessing your skills, abilities, and level of commitment, you can achieve a sense of self-realization. It takes courage to tell yourself the truth. For example, it isn't easy to admit that you procrastinate, miss deadlines, and are often unmotivated. Most of us don't like to admit our faults. Even talking about our strengths can be embarrassing or seem boastful. However, this process of looking honestly at both your current abilities and short-comings can lay the groundwork for making positive changes in your life. This approach can give you the tools to correct your thoughts and behavior—to organize and take charge of your life.

Within you lie wisdom and opportunities. Get to know your strengths, talents, motivators, and desires. Become aware of your habits, learning style, self-talk, and beliefs. Learn about your undeveloped potential. Take time to dream about the contributions you want to make in life. The mark of a successful person is achieving his or her full potential.

Connecting School with the World of Work

The connection between school and job success is the major theme of this book. Successful students know how to connect success in school and success in their careers. They realize that what they learn in school directly correlates with find-ing, keeping, and succeeding in the job they want. Each chapter stresses the link between certain academic skills and life skills. For instance, memory skills are important in school and on the job. Time and stress management pays off in bet-ter grades and in better job performance. Problem-solving skills are just as cru-cial in school as they are in work. Each chapter shows the connection between a specific study skill and a rewarding career. One way to achieve success in any area of life is to use people who are already successful as role models. As you see below, there is a direct connection between your performance in school and your performance on the job.

Peak Performer or A Student

1. Is alert, actively involved, and eager to learn.
2. Consistently does more than is required.
3. Consistently shows initiative, is enthusiastic, positive, and engaged.
4. Demonstrates the ability to solve problems and make sound decisions.
5. Is dependable, prompt, neat, accurate, and thorough.

Good Worker or B Student

1. Frequently does more than is required.
2. Is usually attentive, positive, and enthusiastic.
3. Most work is accurate, neat, and thorough.
4. Often uses critical thinking to solve problems and make decisions.

Average Worker or C Student

1. Completes tasks that are required.
2. Shows a willingness to follow instructions and is open to learn.
3. Is generally involved, dependable, enthusiastic, and positive.
4. Most work is thorough, accurate, and prompt.

Problem Worker or D Student

1. Usually does what is required.
2. Attendance is irregular, often late, or distracted.
3. Lacks a positive attitude or ability to work well with others.
4. Often misunderstands assignments and deadlines.
5. Lacks thoroughness.

Unacceptable Worker or F Student

1. Either will not or does not do the work that is required.
2. Is inattentive, bored, negative, and uninvolved.
3. Is undependable and turns in work that is incorrect and incomplete.

Connecting Personal Qualities and School and Job Success

In addition, there is a connection between the personal qualities or character traits necessary to succeed in school and those that predict job success. Surveys and interviews with top executives indicate that the following personal qualities are most important to employers.

Most Valued Employee Qualities

— Dependable.

— Positive, motivated attitude.

— Honest.

— Good communication skills.

— Good listener.

— Creative problem solver.

— Sound decision maker.

— Team player.

— Willing to learn new skills.

— Open to suggestions and feedback.

— Hardworking.

— Accurate and responsible.

— Ability to follow through.

— Confident.

— Neat and attractive appearance.

— Respectful and considerate (good manners).

— High energy (ability to cope with stress).

Compare the qualities that employers value with the qualities that instructors say are most desirable.

Ten Most Desirable Classroom Attitudes

— Positive attitude.

— Active participant.

— Willing to learn and work hard.

— Responsible for behavior and learning.

— Creative problem solver.

— Dependable.

— Respectful.

— Works well with others.

— Communicates effectively.

— Demonstrates that school is top priority.

Demonstrating Positive Personal Qualities at School and on the Job

As you can see, there is a strong connection between the personal qualities that are necessary for both school and job success. Here are some ways you can demonstrate positive personal qualities at school and on the job. Add to the list.

Personal Quality	School	Career
Positive attitude	Approach each class with enthusiasm	Positive attitude at work
Dependability	Go to every class on time	Get to work on time
Responsibility	Turn in assignments on time	Turn in work assignments promptly
Integrity	Be honest with instructors	Show integrity and honesty at work
Ability to get along	Work well with instructors, roommates	Be a cooperative team player
Respectful	Show respect in class	Use good business etiquette
Enthusiasm	Be a fully engaged learner and active participant in class	Be enthusiastic about your work

Making the Connection between Academic Skills and Job Skills

Think of the skills that help you succeed at school and on the job.

Skill	School	Career
Problem solving	Solving case studies, equations, problems	Solve work problems
Creativity	Choosing a topic for a speech	Original approach to work problem
Time management	Avoid procrastination	Do first things first and achieve goals
Critical thinking	Write a paper logically	Outline a plan of action
Decision making	Decide what to study for a test	Decide what product to promote

Skill	School	Career
Reading	Textbooks	Reports, journals, memos
Writing	Papers	Memos, reports
Public speaking	Speeches in class	Presentations, oral reports, chairing a meeting
Memorizing	Learning course content	Remembering names, learning new job skills
Test taking	Taking tests	Performance reviews, evaluations
Learning styles	Learning how to learn in school	Learn how to learn new job skills

Making Connections with All Your Courses

One stumbling block to learning is the perception that each school course is a distinct entity. For example, you may see your math course as separate from your English course and your speech course or personal development course as separate from your computer course. Successful students see the connection between course concepts. Instead of isolating subjects, events, course content, tasks, and even people into separate and unrelated categories, they continuously ask: How does this concept relate to other areas I am studying? Once you start asking this question, you will discover many areas of similarity.

Find ways to make each subject relevant to other areas of your academic and work life. For example, you can use your writing skills in all your courses—and on the job. Math and science students often find it helpful to write out equations and formulas as English sentences. Some of your papers may be developed into speeches, and a course project may become the topic of a paper. Memory, listening, note-taking, test-taking, and reading skills will help you in all your courses. Learning how to work in teams, give presentations, solve problems, and make sound decisions will help you succeed in various courses and in your job. Learning to concentrate, recall information, use various learning styles, and develop a good working relationship with instructors and other students will help you in all your classes—and in your job. Think of your classes as interrelated and look for connections.

CAREER FOCUS

FOCUS ON CLEAR-HEADED ASSESSMENT

Self-assessment is an important, ongoing career skill in any job. You can learn to take stock of your skills, abilities, attitude, and behavior. Successful career professionals can understand and lead others because they understand and value themselves. They are aware of their strengths and weaknesses, and not only accept them but consciously choose ways to be more effective. They have learned to integrate all types of learning styles to enhance their natural learning preference. For example, they may use tape recorders, flowcharts, visual aids, training films, role-playing, and small task-force teams to accomplish their work. They may combine planning meetings with retreats or combine training programs with after-hour bowling teams or receptions. Peak performers know the importance of positive self-talk and imagery. They choose positive thoughts, see themselves achieving their goals, and create detailed visions of their organization's goals.

Assessment is an ongoing process. Peak performers keep a folder of their successes, awards, letters of appreciation, and projects that they have completed. They keep all their performance evaluations, comments, and a record of informal evaluations; and they see self-assessment and feedback as tools for self-discovery and positive change. Peak performers also keep a folder about areas of their life that they want to improve—relationships, difficult projects, setbacks, and concerns. Let's look at Carol Johnson, who has just accepted an administrative position for a software company. She wants to overcome shyness and give more effective presentations, so she has created a plan based on self-assessment and goal setting.

1. She looks at her present feelings about her performance in these areas and assesses her strengths and weaknesses.

2. She examines the images that come to mind when she thinks about making a speech or meeting someone new.

3. She consciously chooses positive self-talk, such as "I am a good speaker. I am confident and well prepared."

4. She visualizes herself as a confident and successful speaker.

5. She analyzes her style. Since her natural learning style is visual, she tapes herself on video to correct and improve her style.

6. Finally, Carol observes confident, self-assured people and practices adopting confidence in her tone, body stance, eye contact, and behavior.

Carol faces this career challenge head-on and strengthens her self-image. Successful professionals make a habit of analyzing and regularly assessing their work style, habits, and career progress.

Assess Yourself and Your Career Needs, Including:

Characteristics that you would like to improve or reinforce.

Characteristics that you would like to minimize or reduce.

Your personal work style.

Your dependence on authority figures.

Your relationship with your supervisor.

Your ability to work effectively as a team member.

Your goals and objectives.

Your company's goals and objectives.

DISCOVERING YOUR LEARNING STYLE

Self-Awareness, Learning Styles, and Left- and Right-Brain Dominance

Since the purpose of self-assessment is to understand and maximize your learning potential, it is important to explore how you learn best and use this knowledge to work for you. You will be most successful in college and at work when you take responsibility for knowing your learning style and for choosing study techniques that work best for you. In addition, understanding your learning style and determining your left- and right-brain dominance will enhance your self-awareness. No longer will you be asking, What's wrong with me? or Why am I struggling so hard to get organized? Your learning style and preference will be more in tune with your real self, and you will be accomplishing more than you ever have before. Determining and understanding your brain dominance is a powerful tool. We will see throughout the book how integrating your learning styles and left- and right-brain functions can help you increase your memory, energy level, and motivation; improve your concentration and relationships; and give you more control over all aspects of your life. You will be amazed at how much you can achieve when you work in tune with your natural preferences.

Discovering How You Learn Best

visual

auditory

tactile

People process information in different ways. These differences are related to preferences and learning styles. Generally, learning experts highlight three main learning styles: visual, auditory, and kinesthetic or tactile. If you are a *visual learner,* you prefer to see information and read material. You learn more effectively with pictures, graphs, illustrations, diagrams, photos, and any visual design. If you are primarily an *auditory learner,* you rely upon your hearing sense most. Lectures, tapes, music, tone, and verbal messages help you learn. If you are a *kinesthetic learner,* you learn by doing. You like to feel, touch, work with, and actually relate to the material that you are learning. Workshops, teamwork, performing, collecting samples, and role-playing help you learn.

Usually, people have a preferred style, but we all use a combination of styles to help us learn and remember. In Chapter Seven we will be covering learning styles and memory in detail and show you how you can enhance learning by incorporating the different learning styles into one overall style that works best for you. For example, you may be primarily a visual learner and like to see information and rely a great deal on your textbooks. You want to see material on the blackboard and on overheads, and you like handouts. You enhance your learning by using these *visual* tools, and *also* by writing out key words (kinesthetic style) and saying them out loud (auditory style). Using *all* your senses helps you remember information more effectively.

As a self-assessment tool, begin now to determine how you learn best. Your goal is to discover your natural learning and working style and your most effective study habits. First, complete the exercise on page 10 to give you guidance on determining your learning style.

The Critical Thinking Connection

Making decisions, processing information, looking for cause and effect, assessing strengths and weakness, questioning assumptions and excuses, reasoning logically, creating an action plan, and evaluating results are all critical thinking skills involved in assessment. Use critical thinking to answer the following questions. Be prepared to discuss your answers in your teams.

1. Think back on how you learned to use a computer; remembered facts, names, and figures; learned a foreign language; or developed any skill at which you are proficient. Did you listen to directions (auditory), watch others perform the skill (visual), read about it (visual), or practice it yourself (kinesthetic)? Perhaps you used all these methods.

2. What do you think is your preferred learning style? Why do you think so? Give an example of a course that you are taking right now. How does the instructor teach? Is the primary method lecture (auditory)? Are there films, overheads, handouts, or heavy use of the blackboard (visual)? Are there role-playing exercises, hands-on experience, field trips, and emotional stories and examples that help you form connections (kinesthetic)? From which teaching style do you benefit the most? Then describe an instructor that you don't (or didn't) like. Is it because you can't relate to the teaching style?

3. How can you integrate all your learning styles to enhance your comprehension and learning? For example, say you are primarily a visual learner and use pictures and reading as your main method of acquiring information. You can integrate all of the learning styles by playing tapes, collecting samples, reading out loud, and studying with a group. What works best for you? Give an example.

4. Look at the common reasons and excuses that some students use for not assessing their strengths and weaknesses. Add to this list and use creative problem solving to list strategies for overcoming these barriers.

Reasons   **Strategies**

I know what my problems are without self-assessment.

I just partied too much last term, but now I have everything under control.

I know how to study, I just wasn't ready before.

I don't have time for reflection.

I can handle my problems myself.

_____

_____

_____

_____

_____

Why Is Critical Thinking So Important?

Critical thinking is learning how to think instead of just learning facts. It is learning how to connect and integrate ideas instead of just reciting pat answers. Critical thinking is using a systematic process involving facts and logic rather than wishful or irrational thinking. Critical thinking is an important theme throughout this book. Learning to be a critical thinker will help you solve theoretical problems and concepts and also assist you in making life decisions. Making decisions and solving problems are part of your daily life as a student and as an employee. Some of these decisions include the following:

School Life	Work Life
Should I go to school full time?	Should I work full time?
Where should I go to school?	Where should I work?
Which classes should I take?	Which projects should I work on?
What major should I choose?	Which career should I consider?
Is there a penalty for missing deadlines?	Will my career suffer if I miss deadlines?

To be successful, students and employees must know how to solve problems with roommates, co-workers, instructors, and supervisors. Serious mistakes can occur when students and employees act before they consider the nature of the problem, before they clearly define the problem, and before they fully explore the consequences of their actions. Therefore, critical thinking and creativity are essential for success at school and on the job.

Using Both Sides of the Brain

We have just determined that people have different preferences in learning styles, and these differences are related to mental or cognitive preferences. In other words, people differ in which side of the brain they most prefer using for acquiring new information. A case study conducted by two researchers from Johns Hopkins and reported in *Nature* (1992) is a recent example of the relationship between thought and memory and the brain. This study indicates that the brain has two systems by which it classifies information. One is language based (left brain), and the other is visual (right brain). Psychologists and neurologists have long been studying how the brain organizes information. They suggest that some people are left-brain dominant and use a logical, rational, and detailed approach, while others are right-brain dominant and use an intuitive, insightful, and holistic approach to solving problems and processing new information. We all want to achieve goals, and to accomplish that the things we encounter at school and at work must make sense and feel comfortable. By assessing your learning style preference and your brain dominance, you can maximize the effectiveness of your study and work habits. When you integrate both sides of the brain while incorporating all of the learning styles, you enhance learning, memory, and recall, and you achieve a synergistic or whole-brain effect. Knowing which side of the brain you favor makes it easier to understand your natural learning and working style.

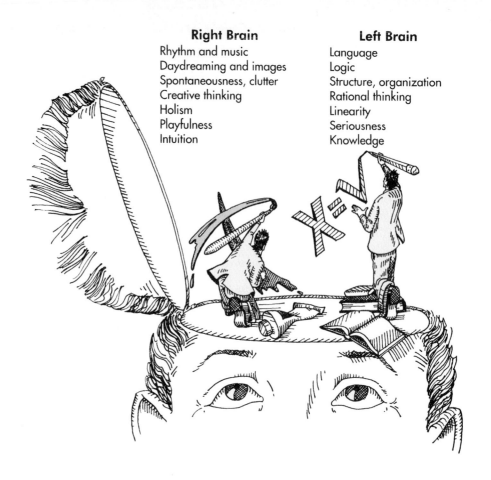

Right Brain
Rhythm and music
Daydreaming and images
Spontaneousness, clutter
Creative thinking
Holism
Playfulness
Intuition

Left Brain
Language
Logic
Structure, organization
Rational thinking
Linearity
Seriousness
Knowledge

Connecting Both Sides of the Brain

"I use my whole brain!" you might answer. And indeed you do. But each side, or hemisphere, of the brain specializes in certain functions. The left side is the center of language, logic, analysis, and the sequencing of information. The right side is the center of imagination, creativity, problem solving, color, and the arts. Everyone tends to prefer one side of the brain to another. For example, if you like quiet and solitude, are very organized, and feel more comfortable in familiar surroundings, you are a left-brain person. If you are stimulated by games and activities, like to take risks, and enjoy socializing, you are a right-brain person. Understanding which side of the brain you favor makes it easier to understand your natural learning and working style.

The next step is to understand how your preference influences your study and work habits. This is a critical step, for studying or working against your natural preference is like writing with the wrong hand. It feels unnatural and can make even a simple task a frustrating and draining chore. For example, suppose you are left-brain dominant. You prefer a highly structured, quiet, and neat study environment, and like to start projects well in advance of their due date. You schedule each step of your project and work steadily until it's completed. Your roommate is right-brain dominant, is surrounded by clutter, noise, books, and papers, and procrastinates until the last minute. She thrives on a flexible, spontaneous schedule and often changes her mind midstream. Unless you can understand and respect each other's style, you could feel frustrated, judgmental, and uncomfortable. Here are some typical studying styles for each side of the brain:

Left-Brain Studying	Right-Brain Studying
Neat, organized study area	Cluttered desk
Daily schedules	Flexible study times
Work on one project at a time	Jump from project to project
Study alone	Study with others
Study consistently	Study in bursts of energy
Plan studying	Cram last minute

If your natural preference is left brain, you will prefer consistency and being alone in your own quiet space. You tend to be serious and like detail, analysis, and facts. If you are right-brain dominant, you like new challenges, spontaneity, and change; work well under pressure; and like a fun, relaxed work area. You come up with lots of ideas while daydreaming but tend to procrastinate and are more comfortable seeing the whole project rather than dealing with details. As you can see, the right-brain list has several negative study habits. Being aware of this, if you are right-brain dominant you can work toward being more organized and working steadily on projects while emphasizing your natural style.

Putting Both Sides of Your Brain to Work

Let's suppose you have a paper due and you have been procrastinating. You are primarily right-brain dominant and tend to be visually oriented. Your left brain is sending you judgmental messages about being lazy and unorganized, and your right brain, although feeling guilty, is resisting this nagging. Instead of feeling as if the two sides of your brain are at war, choose to integrate the best of both. Brainstorm ideas with a left-brain friend and narrow your topic. You will have no problem coming up with many creative ideas. Now engage your left brain to set a time limit and organize one idea into a topic. Outline your paper using a creative mind map rather than the traditional outline form (covered in Chapter Five). Use colored pens and any three-dimensional props to help you creatively pull words into a living project. Hang this large piece of paper on the wall. Talk through your organization, purpose, style, and main points with an organized friend and use visual means (e.g., pictures, blackboard, drawings) to describe your project. Set a time limit (ahead of schedule) for the completion of your rough draft, and reward yourself after finishing each step. These are just a few examples of how you can use your natural preference to enhance study effectiveness. In later chapters we will look at color, self-talk, and imagery as ways to enhance learning.

We become more wide-ranging in our outlook and achievements when we nurture both sides of the brain. Einstein made his breakthrough in physics while engaging in the right-brain activities of imagery and daydreaming. Gary Larson, the famed cartoonist, is both very organized and extremely creative. In Chapter Seven we will discuss how to tap both sides of the brain for effective learning and recall.

Assess Your Self-Talk

The term *self-talk* refers to all the thoughts and messages you say to yourself from when you wake up in the morning until you go to sleep at night. Experts in learning and health care have proven that our thoughts trigger chemical impulses in the brain, which influence attitude, behavior, and physical reactions. Your own thoughts and self-talk—what you say to and about yourself—are affecting your physical, emotional, and intellectual behavior. Throughout the day, countless thoughts, images, phrases, and self-talk go through your brain almost unnoticed, but they have a tremendous influence on your mood and attitude. Learning experts estimate that more than 75 percent of what we say to ourselves is negative. Such negative self-talk takes its toll, making it nearly impossible to become motivated or perform at your peak. The first step, then, is to be aware of your thoughts and assess what you are sending. If they are really negative, you can then choose positive thoughts that will help you to be more confident.

Positive Self-Talk

Positive self-talk is made of thoughts that you consciously choose to reprogram your subconscious to produce a specific result. These are positive messages that you think and say to yourself, such as I feel great today or I feel confident that I can excel on my term paper. These positive words can help "program" you to feel more confident and act in a desired way.

Positive self-talk has the power to energize and support you. Think about a victory in sports, a report you felt good about, or any time you felt confident and motivated. You may have said something like this to yourself: I'm really good at this or I like who I am—I've done a great job! Through deliberate repetition, effort, and attention you can improve your self-image and your overall performance by making a conscious effort to decrease negative self-talk and increase the positive. Here are some examples:

Negative Self-Talk	Affirmations
I'm just not creative.	I have many creative ideas.
I can't remember names.	It is easy for me to remember names.
I am not organized.	I enjoy being organized.
I can't control my thoughts.	I choose to have positive thoughts.
Others make me angry.	I am in control of my emotions.
I have no will power.	I set goals and achieve them.

Assess Your Mental Imagery

How you see yourself can affect your thoughts, behavior, self-image, and performance. Therefore, it is important in our discussion of self-assessment to look at your pattern of imagination—how you visualize yourself. Imagery is what it sounds like: imagining yourself in certain situations, behaving in certain ways. Throughout the day, we all have certain images that run through our mind. Most right-brain people are visual and use imagery a great deal. Left-brain people tend to use imagery less. In fact, many right-brain dominant people say that their imagery is almost like a movie camera with images of themselves, scenes of how they will react in certain situations, and a replay of what has occurred in the past. These images are rich in detail, expansive, and ongoing.

Some people imagine themselves in a positive light and imagine the best occuring in every situation. Positive imagination can produce confidence and enthusiasm. Imagination used destructively can produce fear, worry, and depression.

Imagery can also help increase your memory power and reduce stress, as later chapters will show. In addition, imagery is a powerful aid for improving your attitude and, thus, increasing your motivation. As with self-talk, your mental images often go unnoticed unless you stop and assess them and consciously use them to help you achieve success. Hand in hand with positive self-talk, imagery is a specific action you can take to help overcome self-doubt, increase your confidence, and create a motivated and productive state of mind.

Self-Assessment as a Positive Tool for Lifelong Success

The message of this chapter is that self-assessment need not be a critical judgment about your weaknesses, your thoughts, and your self-image, but a lifetime habit of assessing where you are, who you are, and how you study and work best. Understanding how you learn best, your brain dominance, your natural working style, and being able to assess your self-talk and imagery can give you enormous insight into school, your job, and your relationships. The central theme of this book is that you can empower yourself to learn new skills and adapt the tools necessary to change your thoughts, images, and behaviors. In turn, you can produce the results you want in every aspect of your life. There is a strong connection between positive thoughts, self-talk, imagery, and school and job success.

Grid 1.1
Course Requirements

Make certain you understand the requirements of each course. Use this guide for each course.

COURSE _____

Instructor _____

Office _____

Syllabus

Determine course goals

What am I supposed to get out of this class?

Grading structure

Tests

Projects, papers

Presentations

Special vocabulary and terminology

Instructor's teaching style

Instructor's likes and dislikes

Resources

Tutor

Study teams

Sample tests

Individual help from instructor

Grid 1.2
Connecting With School

For each course, take a minute to think about ways to increase the benefits of your experiences. How can you make sure each course is enriching?

Course

Situation you want to change.

Steps needed to achieve results.

Plan of action for making changes.

Results wanted.

Attitude needed to achieve results.

A.   Pablo is a freshman at a community college. He isn't really sure if he should even be in college. He didn't apply himself in high school and was bored much of the time. He would have liked to travel or work for a while, but his parents really wanted him to go to college. Other students seem to know what they want to be and also seem to have better study habits. Pablo tends to like to get involved with projects and has a hands-on approach to learning. He finds it difficult to sit and read or listen to lectures. He likes the outdoors, is creative, and once he's involved in a project, he is committed. What strategies from this chapter would be most useful to help Pablo understand himself better and gain a sense of commitment? What would you suggest to Pablo to help him find direction and a sense of purpose?

_____

_____

_____

_____

_____

_____

_____

_____

_____

_____

B.   Pablo is a law enforcement officer. He knows that he performs best when he learns by doing. He likes to be active, involved, and physical, and works well on a team. When he is learning a new procedure or writing reports, he bounces ideas off his co-workers.

Pablo enjoys his job and is amazed at how much learning is involved. He also knows he needs to get more education if he wants to advance, but wonders how he'll balance his job, school, and family life. Pablo admits that he didn't like his formal education nor did he excel at subjects that were unrelated to law enforcement. He never really learned good study habits and knows that he will have to be committed to go back to school. What suggestions would you give Pablo to help him do better in school and learn faster on the job?

_____

_____

_____

_____

_____

_____

_____

_____

_____

_____

A. Kristen has just enrolled in a business school, because she thinks she wants a career in business. Except for knowing that she likes math, however, she has not really given much thought to career planning, so she has signed up for a career planning class. She is surprised at the amount of self-assessment involved. She really thought that the instructor would simply review a list of possible careers, give her a vocational test, and help her determine her perfect career. Instead, Kristen has found that she is doing a lot of reflection about her values, beliefs, needs, likes, interests, personal characteristics, and abilities. She is also looking at her level of commitment and at the barriers and poor habits in her life that keep her from being successful. At times she resists doing the exercises and journal entries. Shouldn't the instructor be more helpful and give her direction for choosing a major? What is the purpose of all this writing and assessment?

What strategies from this chapter would be helpful to Kristen to see the value of self-assessment?

_____

_____

_____

_____

_____

_____

_____

B. Kristen is a CPA and has reached a major career crossroad—she has just been offered a position of district manager in a larger branch of a major accounting firm. She is thrilled with the offer. It means recognition of all of her years of hard work and attending night school while working full time. It carries with it a big salary increase and status. However, there are some drawbacks: she would have to move away from family and friends, her husband would have to find another job, and her young children would have to adjust to a new school and community. Can she handle the heavy work commitment and still devote the necessary time and energy to her family? Also, she would be supervising a large staff. She knows she has good mangement skills, but is she ready to supervise so many people?

What strategies from this chapter could help Kristen with all these doubts and questions? How can self-assessment assist her with this major career decision? What would you suggest to Kristen to help her make a decision?

_____

_____

_____

_____

_____

_____

_____

_____

_____

▲ Exercise 1.1 Taking Stock

One of the most valuable skills you can cultivate is not only respect and acceptance of your own needs and abilities, but the ability to recognize them in others. What skills do you have that you need in order to succeed? What is your overall attitude? To help you take stock, complete the assessment scale shown here. For each attitude or skill listed, rate yourself with a score of 1–5, with 1 for poor and 5 for peak. Be honest with yourself. Feedback is a process that gives us information and determines the criteria for measuring our progress. In the long run, information can never hurt you, it can only help you. Accept where you are at this time and be willing to grow and change. (If you are willing to go for a risk, have a good, trusted friend fill out the sheet on you.)

ASSESSMENT SCALE

Area	Peak Performance 5	4	OK 3	2	Poor 1
1. Self-awareness					
2. Motivation					
3. Positive self-talk					
4. Time management					
5. Memory skills					
6. Reading skills					
7. Note-taking skills					
8. Test-taking skills					
9. Writing and public-speaking skills					
10. Creative problem solving and decision making					
11. Stress and health management					
12. Commitment					

▲ Exercise 1.2   Discovering Your Learning Style and Brain Dominance

3. Most like you   2. Sometimes like you   1. Least like you

( ) 1. I learn best when I see information.
( ) 2. I learn best when I hear information.
( ) 3. I learn best when I have hands on experience.
( ) 4. I like pictures and illustrations.
( ) 5. I like to listen to tapes and hear stories.
( ) 6. I like working with people and going on field trips.
( ) 7. I love books, pictures, and puzzles.
( ) 8. I enjoy listening to music for pleasure.
( ) 9. I enjoy sports or gardening for pleasure.
( ) 10. A good textbook and visual aids are important to me.
( ) 11. I learn best in class when hearing, rather than reading.
( ) 12. I learn best when I can take objects apart and put them back.
( ) 13. I retain what I see better than what I hear.
( ) 14. I retain best when I recite information.
( ) 15. I learn best by doing, working on models, or gathering samples.
( ) 16. I have a strong fashion sense and pay attention to details.
( ) 17. I am talkative and love to tell jokes and stories.
( ) 18. I use a lot of gestures, am well coordinated and like activity.
( ) 19. My study space is generally neat and visually attractive.
( ) 20. My study space is generally messy and disorganized.
( ) 21. I don't spend much time sitting in one place to study.
( ) 22. I like logical and rational thinking.
( ) 23. I like creative and open-ended thinking.
( ) 24. I learn best when it's quiet and organized.
( ) 25. I learn best when there is music.
( ) 26. I learn best when there is action and physical activity.
( ) 27. I like structure and work steadily at completing projects.
( ) 28. I like flexibility and often procrastinate.
( ) 29. I like to break problems down and solve them in small steps.
( ) 30. I like to look at the big picture.

Scoring: Add up your score. The highest total indicates your predominate style.
Total your answers to 1,4,7,10,13,16,19,24.   _____ Visual
Total your answers to 2,5,8,11,14,17,20,25.   _____ Auditory
Total your answers to 3,6,9,12,15,18,21,26.   _____ Kinesthetic
Total your answers to 19,22,24,27,29.   _____ Left Brain
Total your answers to 20,23,25,28,30.   _____ Right Brain

My primary learning style is _____.
My primary brain dominance is _____.

▲ Exercise 1.3   Brain Dominance

1. Now that you have read about brain dominance, how will your preference affect your study space? Your relationships (e.g., working in groups, dealing with roommates, working with instructors, etc.)? Describe how you prefer to study and work on projects.

2. List ways you can make the most of your education even if you have instructors who have different learning styles than you do.

_____

_____

_____

_____

▲ ASSESSMENT STRATEGIES ▲

1. *Model the qualities of a high achiever.*

2. *Assess your strengths and weaknesses.*

3. *Commit yourself to excellence in whatever you do.*

4. *Discover and respect your learning style.*

5. *Integrate all learning styles.*

6. *Use both sides of the brain.*

CHAPTER TWO

ATTITUDE AND MOTIVATION

"Nothing great was ever achieved without enthusiasm."

Ralph Waldo Emerson, American poet, essayist, and philosopher

"One of the hardest things a manager is faced with is imparting initiative to employees who lack it. I would 10 times rather have to work hard to hold employees back, redirect them, or say no to unwanted or inappropriate initiatives than have to worry about getting them going."

Andrew S. Grove, President and CEO of Intel Corporation

Learning Objectives

In Chapter Two you will learn:

1. The importance of attitude.

2. The connection between attitude and self-image.

3. The connection between needs and attitude.

4. How to create positive attitudes at school and at work.

5. The creativity connection.

6. How to overcome barriers to positive attitudes.

7. Motivational strategies.

Anyone who has played sports has experienced the excitement and enthusiasm of the crowds, the intense energy, and the feeling of achievement. The Olympics with its pageantry, exhilarating emotions, and worldwide appeal is the crowning achievement, the lifelong dream, and the supreme test for athletes. The Olympics represent our search for excellence and identity. Everyone has a strong drive to excel, as well as a need for uniqueness and accomplishment.

Let's approach motivation as a top athlete approaches and trains for the Olympics. Athletes know that a lack of motivation spells defeat. They realize that a self-generated drive is what is required to be a peak performer.

Can you imagine mustering up the courage and energy for the enormous demands of mountain climbing if you weren't motivated and inspired to achieve success? Mountain climbing is a demanding, potentially dangerous, and passionate sport that requires intense motivation, discipline, and desire to succeed. What is it about people who push the limits of their endurance, who strive for excellence, and who want to test their strength and skill in such a risky sport? What do concert pianists, dancers, or gymnasts have that enables them to practice for hours every day, constantly striving to improve, to compete with themselves, and to excel? It's motivation, driven by a positive attitude. The premise of this chapter is that success in school, and in life, is more dependent on a positive attitude and a motivated state of mind than on innate ability or intelligence. This chapter is full of strategies, suggestions, and tips that will help you create a positive attitude. You will learn the value of affirmations and the power of visualization and imagery.

THE IMPORTANCE OF A POSITIVE ATTITUDE

Nothing is more important for success in school and in your job than a positive attitude. It is your attitude at the beginning of any task that influences the outcome of that task more than any other factor. There is a strong link between attitude and behavior. You are more likely to change your attitude if you see this connection and recognize the value of a positive attitude.

A positive attitude encourages the following:

— Higher productivity.

— An openness to learning at school and on the job.

— School and job satisfaction.

— Creativity in solving problems and finding solutions.

— The ability to work with all types of people.

— Enthusiasm and a state of well-being.

— Confidence and higher self-esteem.

— The ability to channel stress.

— A sense of purpose and direction.

— Increased energy.

— The feeling of empowerment.

A negative attitude can drain you of enthusiasm and energy. Negative attitudes can result in absenteeism, tardiness, and impaired mental and physical health. In addition, people who have a negative attitude tend to

— Feel they are victims and helpless to make changes.

— Focus on the worst that can happen in a situation.

— Blame external circumstances for their attitude.

— Focus on the negative in people and situations.

— Look at adversity as something that will last forever.

CONNECTING VALUES, ATTITUDES, SELF-IMAGE, AND BEHAVIOR

Values

Values are broad beliefs that tend to influence attitudes and behaviors. For example, if you value service to others but enter a program of study or work in a job that values profit and disregards service, you may be uncomfortable with your choice. The more you know about yourself and what is important to you, the better you are able to make choices about school and work that reflect your values.

Self-Image

There is a strong connection between your self-image and behavior. If you see yourself as a successful student at school and a competent, confident professional at work, you will act accordingly. Therefore, if you want to change your attitude and behavior, work on your self-image.

The Behavioral Link

Attitude can influence behavior and behavior can influence attitude. The way you act every day can affect your self-image, and your self-image can affect the things you do. For example, a negative attitude can result in absenteeism from school or work, and being absent can result in feeling disconnected to the class and feeling unmotivated.

You can change your behavior anytime. You don't need to wait until your attitude changes to begin the positive behaviors you'll learn in this book.

Breaking Out of Your Comfort Zone

Other people's expectations of you can create a box that defines who you are and what you are capable of achieving. When you hear messages over and over again, you start to believe them, and in fact, your self-talk mimics these messages. Your behavior is almost always consistent with your self-image. It is difficult to change thoughts, beliefs, values, and behaviors that have become safe and comfortable. Even when you want to change, new thoughts and behaviors feel strange and phony. We become limited in alternative ways of thinking and seeing and lose the acceptance and creativity we were all born with.

Children are good at connecting to many different people, experiences, their bodies, with the earth, and with their emotions. Children link with many different people and choose playmates because they like them, not because of their race, culture, or gender. As we grow older, it takes creativity to break out of a comfort zone and reestablish innovative ways of thinking and relating.

Strategies for Expanding Your Comfort Zone and Widening Your Connections

1. Change Your Self-Image. Without role models, first generation college students may feel uncomfortable and question whether they belong in college. Early messages may not have been encouraging. Cultural minorities, women, people who are disabled, or returning older students may feel that they don't fit the traditional picture of a college student. Perhaps you were told you were not "college material."

2. Own All Your Various Selves. Some people think that if they can disown the ties to their roots, they can overcome debilitating circumstances and become successful. Own all your selves and create a whole from all your experiences. Own and respect your cultural, religious, or economic roots. Refuse to accept definitions that diminish your sense of worth.

3. Reprogram Your Mind. Positive words and images can heal a damaged sense of self. Reprogram your subconscious mind by focusing on your successes. Acknowledge your progress and build on your achievements. Positive self-talk helps you to see yourself as a success, and when you believe something strongly enough, it becomes a reality. Imagine yourself, in great detail, achieving your goals. Your behavior will follow your thoughts and beliefs.

4. Empower Yourself. Empower yourself to get on with your life. Find a mentor who will encourage and coach you. Look for a role model who can serve as an example. These people can be inspirational for you when you feel discouraged. Do something everyday that moves you closer to your dream. Procrastination can damage your self-esteem. Blame and anger only diminish your sense of self. Set goals and priorities and work toward them.

5. Develop Competencies. Continue to learn new skills. Develop your ability in an area that you feel good about—sports, music, acting, computers, working with people, or problem solving. Do something every day that you do well, that you love to do, and do something that stretches you to learn new skills or personal qualities. There are lots of resources that can help you to overcome almost any barrier. Feeling competent is empowering.

6. Connect. Find common bonds with other people. Build bridges of understanding. You will break down walls and create higher self-esteem when you realize that people are more similar than different. Value and build upon the similarities and celebrate the differences in people.

▲ POSITIVE SCHOOL AND WORK ATTITUDES

▲ Positive attitudes can help you be more successful at school and work.

▲ **The Willing-to-Learn Attitude.** The person who is willing to learn is open to new ideas, listens actively, asks questions, and is sincerely interested in learning.

▲ **The Positive Attitude.** A person with a positive attitude is enthusiastic, focused, optimistic, looks at the opportunities in every situation, and likes to explore options.

▲ **The Involved Attitude.** A person with an involved attitude takes an active role in projects, in discussions, and in meetings. This person likes working in teams and focuses on getting the job done.

▲ **The Supportive Attitude.** A person with a supportive attitude listens, shows empathy, works well with others, and is tactful and supportive.

▲ **The Assertive Attitude.** A person with an assertive attitude is problem centered, confident, and communicates in a clear, concise, and direct manner.

▲ **The Take-Charge Attitude.** The person with a take-charge attitude takes full responsibility for his or her attitude and actions, feels empowered to make sound school and career decisions, refuses to be a victim of circumstances, and actively looks for solutions to problems.

These attitudes can validate and increase your sense of worth, help you to be more productive, and improve your relationships at school and at work.

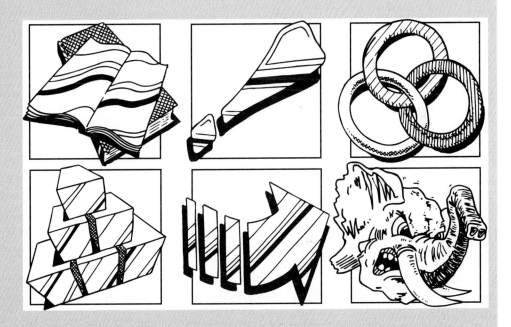

You have the power to overcome the barriers that stand in the way of motivation—and thus achievement. Everyone loses interest in day-to-day activities at times. As a student you will get frustrated, stuck, and discouraged occasionally, but beware of boredom and listlessness that last for more than a few days. If you find yourself overly bored or frustrated, or just plain stalled, try some of the following strategies to overcome boredom, frustration, and an unmotivated state of mind.

1. Focus on the Positive

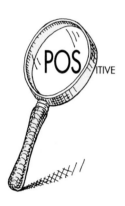

The attitude you bring to class—or to work—is never hidden; it is reflected in everything you do. You may be intelligent, talented, and hardworking, but if you have a negative attitude, you can sabotage your chances at success. Focusing on the positive can help motivate you by enabling you to make the best of any situation. Try to look on the bright side of difficult situations or coursework or other situations. When your mental process—your attitude—is in order, your physical reactions will be easier to direct.

Focusing on the positive extends to feeling positive about yourself. Peak performers are often successful because they have positive self-images. They expect to be successful, and others expect the same of them. The way you behave is a reflection of how you think of yourself and how you think others see you. If you see yourself as a loser, your behavior will reflect it and you will act out a loser script. But if you see yourself as a success, your behavior will show it and you can surmount tremendous setbacks and barriers. Expect the best!

2. Develop High Self-Esteem

A positive self-image leads to high self-esteem, another factor that will increase your motivation. A person with high self-esteem has confidence in his or her personal competence, a sense of dignity, and self-respect. No one can give you self-esteem but yourself. It is based on accepting yourself as you are and assuming total responsibility for your thoughts and behavior. It comes from being able to depend upon yourself to tell the truth and to act from a center of integrity. "Easier said than done," you say. That may be true. Improving your self-esteem doesn't happen overnight. The more skills you acquire, however, the more competent you will feel. The more successes you experience, the more you can stretch your goals and expand your potential. Every time you reach a goal, you will realize the power you have to choose a positive attitude and take actions that produce results.

3. Use Positive Self-Talk and Imagery

As we learned in Chapter One, what you say to yourself all day long and the images that you carry in your head have a powerful effect on your attitude and state of mind. Wise sages have always stressed that if you want to change your life, you must first change your thoughts and mental images. Use self-talk that taps into both sides of the brain, for example, "I like getting organized," "I am creative and have lots of ideas," "I choose to complete this project before I socialize," "I look forward to working with my study group and sharing ideas," and "I have fun when I complete assigned homework—it feels good to achieve." Posi-

▲ It's sometimes hard to feel motivated. You might want to succeed, but something gets in the way. Sometimes you don't really believe that you can succeed. Some of these problems may sound familiar to you:

▲ I've set my goals for the semester and I really want to succeed, but I just lose interest about halfway into the term.

▲ I work full time and also attend school. I just don't have the time to study the way I'd like to, and I always feel behind. There is never enough time to do all that should get done.

▲ I'm busy at school, involved in events, and have a part-time job. My life is full. I just don't know if what I'm working so hard for is really worth it. Will it make a difference?

▲ I'm working full time, going to school every night, and I have a family. I have clear goals, but I worry that they will cost me a close family life. Is all this struggle worth it?

▲ I am 40 pounds overweight, and I really want to slim down. I start a new diet every Monday with great determination, but I fail to stay on it for even a few days. I have no will power.

▲ I've tried time after time to quit smoking, but I feel I have too much happening now, and I'm too nervous. I get myself psyched up, but I just can't see it through. I feel so weak.

▲ I know I could be getting much better grades, but I have a hard time getting myself motivated to attend classes and to pay attention when I'm in class. How can I improve my concentration?

tive self-talk and imagery are powerful aids for improving your attitude and, thus, increasing your motivation.

4. Focus on Your Purpose and Goals

Climbers seldom commit themselves halfheartedly, nor would they climb a mountain without setting goals and having a clear vision of their route. Just as a climber clearly visualizes the final summit, so you must visualize your final goal—to become a paralegal, for instance, or to own your own business. Without a specific goal, it is easy to lack the motivation, drive, and focus to go to classes and complete assignments.

Explore why you're in school and what is important for you to achieve—not only in school but in a career and in life in general. Some students say, "I'm not sure I really want to be in school, but I'll give it a shot." With that sort of attitude, a student would find it hard to be motivated to do the schoolwork. So before you start, think long and hard about your goals; then give it your best effort. Having a sense of purpose and goals does not mean that you have to be absolutely sure of what you want, where you want to go, or what you want to be. You can change paths along the way, but a vision provides the direction to help you climb to the top.

Once you have established your purpose and vision, set realistic, clearly defined goals. If your purpose is, for example, to become a manager of a small com-

▲ WILL YOU BE BUILDING A CATHEDRAL WITH YOUR LIFE OR LAYING BRICKS?

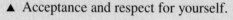

▲ There is an old story about three men who were working on a project in a large city in France. A curious tourist asked them, "What are you three working on?" The first man said, "I'm hauling rocks." The second man said, "I'm laying a wall." The third man said with pride, "I'm building a cathedral." The third man had a sense of vision and high self-esteem. Self-esteem is the core of the self-concept and greatly influences how people perform. Having high self-esteem means knowing you are capable of handling what you're doing right now and that your life has meaning and value for you—even if it's hauling rocks. High self-esteem comes from:

- ▲ Acceptance and respect for yourself.
- ▲ Honesty and integrity.
- ▲ Competence and skills.
- ▲ Knowing you have personal power to make choices.
- ▲ Being connected to a larger group or higher power.
- ▲ Feeling unique.
- ▲ High and attainable goals and expectations.
- ▲ Feeling safe and secure.
- ▲ Being listened to and taken seriously.

pany, your goals might include taking 16 units this semester, keeping up with assignments, and studying every day to get the results you want. Small, specific goals help you see the reasons behind your daily tasks and can help you get through some of the drudgery of schoolwork, officework, and even housework.

5. Acquire the Skills and Habits to Succeed

No one would set out to climb Mt. Everest without the proper training, skills, experience, or equipment. Knowing what abilities and tools you need to be successful for the task at hand is the key to being motivated. If you need training, additional help, or a class to build confidence and skills, take it. This book will help you develop some of the skills you need. If you need additional help, get it. Three of the biggest reasons students fail are lack of skills, lack of good study habits, and procrastination in getting help.

6. Take Responsibility

Peak performers realize that they are responsible for their attitudes and actions, and they know that they have the power to change them at any time. A negative attitude is sometimes the result of not coping maturely with change, conflict, and frustration. Emotional, physical, and social changes are part of being an adult, and learning to adjust to frustration and discouragement can take many forms. Some people may withdraw or become critical, shy, sarcastic, or unmotivated and listless. Blame, excuses, justification, and criticism of others are devices for those who refuse to accept responsibility for their behavior and state of mind. Tune in and acknowledge your feelings and attitude. Decide if they support your goals, and, if not, take responsibility for choosing a state of mind and actions that do. Being responsible creates a sense of integrity and a feeling of worth. For example, if you owe money to a friend, family member, or bank, take the responsibility to repay the loan. It is important to your sense of self-worth to know you are a person who keeps agreements and assumes responsibility.

The Critical Thinking Connection

Determining problems and causes, making decisions, processing information, determining desired results, setting goals, questioning assumptions, reasoning logically, creating an action plan, and evaluating your progress are all critical thinking skills involved in creating a positive and motivated state of mind. Use critical thinking to answer the following questions. Be prepared to discuss your answers in your teams.

1. Describe a time in your life when you were committed. You may have been involved in sports, a club, a play, a recital camp, or some other activity for which you were really committed to produce results. Describe your motivation, the feelings you had about yourself, and your sense of focus and energy. What were the factors involved? Who else was involved?

2. Review a time in your life when you were depressed, could hardly drag yourself out of bed in the morning, and were definitely not performing at your best. What were the factors involved? Who else was involved? What were your feelings?

3. From these experiences, identify your motivators. Are you the type of person who believes you have the power to change your state of mind? Explain.

4. Look at the common reasons and excuses that some students use for not being positive and motivated. Add to this list and use creative problem solving to list strategies for overcoming these barriers.

Reasons   **Strategies**

I'm depressed and lonely because _____.

I can't get up for my morning classes.

I'm shy.

People aren't friendly.

I'm overwhelmed by _____.

I need drugs and alcohol to keep going.

The instructors demand too much.

_____

_____

_____

_____

7. Be in the Present

Being in the present means being keenly interested in everything that is going on around and within you: your thoughts, feelings, sensations, behavior, and reactions. Whether you are playing a sport, climbing a mountain, talking with a friend, working on a hobby, or focusing on a difficult subject, being in the present is a key to success. Worrying about the future and regretting the past are time-wasting behaviors that are self-defeating. It is possible to live in the present and still keep future goals in mind. In fact, making the best of every moment will help you create a motivated state of mind and gain confidence in your ability to do difficult tasks that will help you meet your goals—even if those tasks have no immediate appeal.

8. Be Physically Active

Your mind and body are linked in significant ways. You have control over your posture, breathing, muscle tension, eye contact, gestures, and facial expressions. When your body is energized, you look and act fit and successful. If you are tired and depressed, you tend to slouch and droop. Change your physiology and you will change your mental state. For example, pretend you are trying out for a play. The part calls for a positive, energetic, confident, and intelligent person. How would you enter the room? Would you be smiling? What would your breathing, posture, and muscle tension be like? What kinds of gestures and facial expressions would you use to create this character? Try acting out this part when you wake up in the morning and throughout the day.

9. Focus on Successes, Not Failures

Focusing on successes you have already experienced will create a positive state of mind and lead to more successes. Success breeds success. Focusing on failures might begin a downward spiral. You start to doubt your abilities, reinforce those doubts with negative self-talk, and become depressed—all of which might lead to more failure. Think of all the good things that happen to you, and write them down. Even if it's a small success, like finding a particular book at the library or paying your bills on time or cooking a difficult recipe—write it down. Then review the list at the end of each day. Wake up each morning expecting the best and focusing on the opportunities for success you will have that day. Don't get distracted by little things that go wrong. Visualize yourself being successful.

10. Create a Feedback Loop

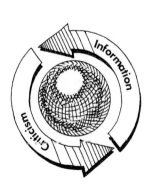

When scaling a mountain, the climber is constantly monitoring the progress of the climb, assessing barriers, checking equipment, and drawing on energy reserves. All successful athletes know how important it is to monitor and measure their technique and vary the training program to improve results. They know that information can only help you, it can never hurt you. Feedback is key for creating and maintaining motivation. Some people think that no news is good news, but you cannot change your behavior unless you are monitoring and measuring your technique. Get to know your instructors. Don't wait for formalized feedback in the form of grades; ask the instructors how you are doing—in class, on quizzes, on papers, etc. Be open to receive criticism and suggestions. Welcome feedback as a way of determining whether you are on the right course. Just like a hiker needs a compass, we all need to check our direction at times.

11. Create a Supportive Climate

One of the cardinal rules of mountain climbing is to never go it alone. Although many climbers are rugged individualists, they readily accept teamwork, companionship, and the support of fellow climbers. Success relies on team skills, faith and trust in each other, and the sharing of skills, knowledge, confidence, and decision-making abilities. So beware of the snags of going it alone or being with negative or unmotivated people. Instead, develop supportive, healthy relationships with friends, faculty, and other students. Associate with people who are positive and have good habits and who support and encourage you. Chapter Three will talk about synergy—the value of working in study teams. Chapter Twelve discusses developing healthy relationships, both with peers and with instructors.

Creating a supportive environment also extends to your physical surroundings. Your study area should be comfortable and well organized. Surround yourself with order, and clear your study area of all distractions, so you can focus on productivity when you work there. Chapter Three will give additional tips on how to make your study area work well for you.

Self-talk can also create a supportive or destructive climate. Consider the following self-talk about public speaking:

Supportive	Destructive
I am self-confident.	I've always been shy.
I am in control and calm.	I'm so nervous.
I am a good speaker.	I can't speak in front of others.
I am getting better each time I do this.	I die every time I do this.
I am well prepared.	I'm too nervous to prepare.
I breathe deeply and am relaxed.	I'm a total wreck.
I face the fear and move forward.	I will avoid this at all costs.

12. Strive for Excellence, Not Perfection

Excellence doesn't mean perfection or working compulsively toward impossible or unrealistic goals. If you strive for perfection, you're setting yourself up for frustration—which can lead to decreased motivation, lowered productivity, increased stress, and a self-defeating perspective. It is all well and good to strive to meet high standards of excellence, but it is important to keep a sense of perspective. Don't fall into the perils of perfectionism. School is not your whole life; it is just a part of your life.

13. Reward Yourself

The simplest tasks can become discouraging without rewards for making progress and for completion. Set up a system of appropriate rewards and consequences. Decide what your reward will be when you finish a project. For a specific task, the reward might be small—a cookie, a hot shower, a 10-minute phone call to a friend. For a larger project, the reward can be larger—listening to a new CD, going out to dinner, or throwing a small party for friends.

Here are a few suggestions for ways to reward yourself:

— Taking a hot bath	— Going to the mountains
— Listening to music	— Buying a tape or compact disc
— Reading a novel	— Having a hot fudge sundae
— Having your favorite meal	— Going to a museum
— Eating your favorite dessert	— Painting, drawing, crafts
— Camping	— Going to the zoo
— Taking a walk	— Taking a nap
— Getting your hair styled	— Gardening
— Taking photos	— Playing sports
— Cooking or baking	— Canoeing
— Watching TV	— Reading fun magazines
— Going to the movies	— Watching clouds
— Renting a video	— Visiting with friends
— Walking on the beach	— Shopping

14. Stay Physically Healthy

It is difficult to motivate yourself if you don't feel well physically or emotionally. If you are ill, you miss classes, fall behind in studying, or both. And getting behind can cause worry, which can cause stress, which can be self-defeating. Eat well, get plenty of exercise, and get plenty of rest. Of course, just doing those things doesn't make you totally immune from cold and flu bugs that make their rounds every school year, but it will help. Chapter Eleven discusses strategies for maintaining your health.

15. Create a Balance of Work and Play

Experienced climbers respect their limits and know not to overextend. Can you imagine a mountain climber who doesn't know when to take time out to rest? Many climbers are driven with a sense of zest and determination, but they know that to stay motivated, they must rest their bodies and their minds.

So watch out for burnout. Create a balance of work and play. Take a break from study—or from work—and rest, see friends, have fun. Add spice to your life so that you're not focused only on your work. Remember, though, that too much partying can leave you feeling frustrated, unorganized, and unfocused. The pivotal word is *balance*.

16. Strive to Be a Self-Actualized Person

Abraham Maslow, a well-known psychologist, developed the theory of a hierarchy of human survival needs. According to his theory, there are five levels of

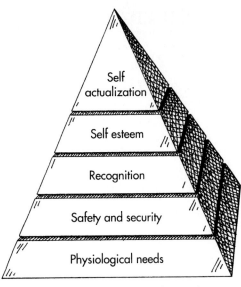

Maslow's Hierarchy of Needs

needs, which are universal: physiological needs, and the needs for safety, recognition, self-esteem, and self-actualization. The lower-order needs must be met before higher-order needs can be considered. For example, it seems obvious that physiological needs, such as for food and shelter, must be met before you can worry about recognition. It is difficult to study or be satisfied at work if you don't have enough money for food and rent.

Once you've attended to your physiologial needs, you can focus on safety and security. You need to feel certain, for example, that you won't lose your job or be forced to drop out of school because of financial difficulties. It is also important that your environment be safe. Do your physical surroundings (heat, light, ventilation, sound, security, furniture) allow you to pursue your goals, or do they distract and concern you?

The next level of needs is recognition. Everyone wants a sense of belonging or recognition, not only at school but also at home and at work. It is critical to have companionship and respect, and to have people around us who share our interests and values.

The next level—self-esteem—is emotional. As we have seen in this chapter, it is vital to believe in yourself and to know that what you are doing is worthwhile. Feelings of high self-esteem are enhanced when you develop the skills that you know are making a contribution to the world.

The highest order of needs is self-actualization. This includes the need to achieve, the joy of mastering new skills, and realizing your full potential. This is what peak performance is all about. Focus on creating a positive image of yourself through positive reinforcement and affirmations and concentrating on skills, competencies, and feelings of worth. People with high self-esteem are able to fulfill their needs for achievement, recognition, and growth in their career and personal lives. As lower needs are satisfied, they cease to motivate. In other words, once your survival and social needs are met, higher needs become more significant. You want to pursue and accomplish significant goals and realize your full potential.

STRATEGIES FOR SUCCESS

1. The Importance of Environment

It's hard to be motivated and maintain a positive attitude about studying if you don't have a study area or space where you can concentrate on your school work. You can take charge of creating a supportive environment that works for you and is in harmony with your learning style and preferences.

Use this space only for study, so that you begin to associate this spot with being alert and producing results. When you eat, take breaks, chat with friends, or write letters, do it somewhere else. This will help your brain connect your study space with concentration and serious studying.

Location. The location should be comfortable and free from distractions. A spare room is ideal. If space is limited, sit with your desk against the wall in a living room or bedroom. This will give you a feeling of privacy.

Temperature. Make certain it's neither too warm nor too cold, but supports your ability to concentrate.

Furniture and Lighting. To create a study area, you needn't buy fancy furniture. Hunt around and see what you already have. The essentials are a flat surface where you can read and write (preferably with a drawer and some shelves), good lighting, and a comfortable chair. The light should be strong enough to keep you from straining your eyes, positioned somewhat overhead to avoid glare and shadows as you work. A real desk chair is probably the most comfortable for sitting for long periods—it is adjustable and provides good back support. But any sturdy chair that you have in the house will do. Try adding a pillow if you feel any strain on your spine.

Learning Style Preference. Use what you have assessed about your learning style preference and left- or right-brain orientation to create a study environment that supports, respects, and energizes you. If you are right-brain dominant, you will be energized by a study area that is unconventional. It may have lots of pictures, bright colors, posters, art work, and music. You probably like to stack your books, papers, and folders so that you can get to them easily. You like your study area, but can also study many different places and still feel comfortable. Go with your natural style, but if you are feeling frustrated because you can't find what you need or are not producing results, choose to adopt a few left-brain tactics. For example, you might want to take the time to organize your study area.

If you are left-brain dominant, you will be energized by a study area that is more conventional. It will probably be neat, quiet, and organized. You dislike clutter, and everything is filed out of sight or piled neatly. You like calendars, a daily task or priorities list, and equipment that helps you stay on course. You work best in an office-like structure that you use daily.

Supplies and Materials. Once you have your furniture assembled in a space free of distractions, clear the desk of all material unrelated to your coursework. Take away bills, stationery, pleasure-reading materials, and the like. Then compile all the supplies you will need for study:

Dictionary

Pens and pencils

Books

Papers

Files

Notebooks

Calendar

Schedule

Names and phone numbers of study team members and instructors

Pencil sharpener

3 × 5 cards

File folder

Scissors and tape

If your preferred learning style is auditory, you might also want to keep a cassette recorder in your study area to play back lectures or listen to tapes. Recite key words, formulas, and summaries of chapters into the recorder and play them back. Read out loud.

If you are primarily a kinesthetic learner, you may want to have a display table or bulletin board with models, graphs, samples, and pictures of your subjects. You may find that you want a computer chair, a stool, or even a drafting table that lets you stand while you work. You may want a learning space that allows you to walk around while you read.

If you are a visual learner, you will want to make your study area as visually appealing as possible. You might want to install a bulletin board so that you can display a calendar, course syllabi, schedules, and a daily to-do list. You also might want to use a project board to list all the projects due this semester.

You'll find that if you keep all your tools in one area, you'll reduce interruptions. Nothing is more frustrating than sitting down to work and being unable to find your favorite pen or your dictionary. So try to study at that space and make it your own private place, where no one else can work.

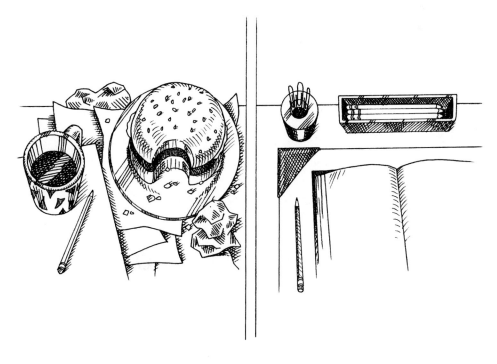

To further organize your materials, make a folder for each class. This folder can hold all class handouts, your schedules, phone numbers of classmates, and returned papers and tests. It can also hold works in process—a draft of a paper, or notes for a speech, for example. You should also have a folder for registration materials, grades, school planning, and a school catalog. To avoid mixing up projects, keep only one on the top of your desk at a time. To reduce distraction from the project at hand, put everything else in a file drawer or on a shelf. After each semester, keep a success file of your best papers, speeches, and tests.

If you have a typewriter, set it on a small table next to your desk. A computer and all its hardware take up lots of space, though, so if you have a computer, you might want to invest in a specialized computer desk or table that has enough space for the keyboard, monitor, printer, disks, and so on. If you enjoy using a computer, you may want to create your semester calendar, redo your course outlines, and write out projects.

When you don't want to study at home or can't find a private space, study in the school or a public library. Most libraries, even public libraries, have carrels that provide some privacy and protection from distractions. Try to pick the same spot each time you go to the library and carry all your essential tools with you. You can invest in an inexpensive backpack or canvas briefcase that has pockets of all sizes for holding pens and pencils, rulers, and different sizes of notebooks. You can carry a pocket dictionary or choose a carrel that's positioned near the reference area of the library, where you can use a larger dictionary. The key again is to keep only one project on the desk at a time, to use the same space if possible, and to pick a quiet place so that you're not distracted or interrupted. It might take some scouting around to find the best place. Some campus libraries have study areas that are quieter than others; check with other students for information, or do your own research. Sometimes the magazine stacks are a quiet area.

2. Form a Study Team: A Great Motivator

The concept of synergy and its effect on learning and motivation is powerful. Synergy means that the whole is greater than its parts. Therefore, studying in a small group can be a creative, resourceful, integrative, and productive experience. Students consistently report that they learn best when they explain a concept to someone else in their own words. Some students have been literally saved from dropping out of school by concerned peers. Many instructors have discovered the value of synergy and use small groups in classes. You can use the power of synergy throughout your education and your career.

Study Team Activities

Here are some of the things a study team can do:

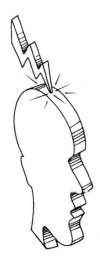

— Brainstorm new ideas and create fresh thinking.

— Teach each other material and lessons.

— Read and edit each others' reports.

— Listen to each others' speeches and oral reports.

— Complete group projects.

— Generate creative alternatives.

— Initiate problem solving.

— Value, affirm, and appreciate different perceptions.

— Quiz each other.

— Build and demonstrate models.

— Role-play, and make slides, plays, or movies.

— Learn to actively listen.

— Learn through play and fun.

— Develop unity and support each other in personal and higher goals.

— Express each others' unique talents, strengths, and abilities.

— Learn from each others' mistakes and experiences.

— Give and receive constructive feedback.

— Create a motivated, supportive, and enthusiastic climate.

CAREER FOCUS

FOCUS ON THE POSITIVE

Having a positive attitude is more than just wishful thinking or seeing life through rose-colored glasses. Your attitude is the single most important factor in job performance and success. As you're becoming aware, a positive attitude can produce success, while a negative attitude often results in failure. Improve your attitude toward your job, your goals, your boss, and your co-workers and you will have taken a major step in improving your working relationships and achieving your goals.

Employees with a positive attitude:

1. Set high standards of excellence.

2. Believe in themselves.

3. Have a sense of enthusiasm.

4. See the best in every situation and in other people.

5. Have a healthy self-image.

Negative employees:

1. Do just enough to get by.

2. Look at the down side of every situation.

3. See the worst in others.

4. Have a poor self-image.

5. Seem indifferent, fearful, and critical.

Motivated, positive people tend to produce outstanding results. Let's look at Dale Everding, a new employee in an automotive company's sales department. He has a list of strategies that he uses every day to get himself into a positive state of mind. Dale spends a few minutes before he gets up in the morning mentally rehearsing his day. He sees himself completing his goals, working well with others, and making sales. He programs his mind with positive self-talk, such as "I am confident and successful. I like to sell quality products."

He pays attention to his appearance and health, since he realizes how these factors affect attitude and motivation on the job. In short, Dale knows that he is in charge of his emotions, thoughts, attitude, and behavior. He creates a positive state of mind that produces positive results.

Motivational Checklist for Starting the Day Positively

— Wake up early.

— Spend quiet moments to vividly imagine a successful day.

— Listen to your favorite music or inspirational tapes while you shower and dress.

— Eat a healthy breakfast.

— Exercise to get you going.

— Use positive self-talk for job success—"I am alert, confident, and ready for the day."

— Plan a relaxing commute.

— Make a review of the day's priorities. ▲

Grid 2.1
Assessing Your Study and Work Climate

At the start of each term, look at the places you study. Do these study areas still support your efforts?

Conditions	Library	Bedroom	Living room	Other
Easily distracted.				
Hear telephone.				
Friends drop in.				
Do household chores.				
Daydream.				
Uncomfortable climate.				
Inadequate materials.				
Tempted to watch TV or listen to music.				
Disturbed by other people.				

COURSE:

Best study area, and why?

_____

_____

_____

_____

_____

Grid 2.2
Setting Goals for Each Course

For each course you take, fill in this chart. Consider what you expect to get out of each course and how you will achieve these goals.

COURSE   **Instructor**   **Expected Grade**

Barriers that I might experience.

Motivators to use to overcome barriers.

Positive habits to get me through course.

Resources that can help.

Positive self-talk.

Visualization.

A.   Joel was excited when he started school, but here it is midway through the term and he is overwhelmed, discouraged, and unmotivated. He is behind in all his reading and assignments, has missed many classes, and is having an especially difficult time taking tests. Joel spends a great deal of free time socializing. It is difficult for him to turn down invitations to parties or not join in when friends stop by to visit.

   1. What would you recommend to help Joel get motivated?

   2. What strategies in this chapter would be most helpful for Joel's situation?

_____

_____

_____

_____

_____

_____

_____

_____

_____

_____

_____

B.   Joel has been a medical technician in a hospital for two years. He really likes his job and has good technical skills. However, lately he feels unmotivated and is having trouble getting to work by 7:00 A.M., when his shift begins. He never liked to get up early for morning classes and now he has to be alert, aware, and motivated from the moment he gets to work. Because he still likes to socialize at night and often has late nights and busy weekends, Joel feels exhausted and can't concentrate. He is also behind in his paperwork. Sometimes the days seem to drag and Joel feels overwhelmed. This lack of motivation is affecting his job responsibilities. What would you suggest to help Joel get motivated?

_____

_____

_____

_____

_____

_____

_____

_____

_____

_____

_____

_____

A. Judy is a drafting major in a business school. She has to work several hours a week and during the summer in order to pay her expenses. Most people would describe Judy as a motivated person since she goes to every class, is punctual, and works hard at school and in her job. Judy wants to get more out of life, though, to feel as if she is really making a contribution to her community. She likes school, but doesn't see the connection with real life. As a result, Judy sometimes feels as if she is just marking time and gets depressed—who wants to postpone life until graduation? What strategies in this chapter could help Judy find a strong sense of purpose and motivation? What would you recommend to Judy to create a more resourceful and positive attitude?

_____

_____

_____

_____

_____

_____

_____

_____

_____

_____

B. Judy is a draftsperson for a small industrial equipment company. She has been with the company for 10 years and is viewed as competent, well liked, and a valuable employee. She has a supportive family, is healthy, and travels frequently. So what is the problem? Judy realizes that she is fortunate and should be content, but somehow she is beginning to feel unmotivated and views the future apprehensively. Unless she gets a degree, she will not be promoted into management, but she doesn't want to take the time away from her family to go back to school. Judy wants to get more motivated on the job or become involved in the community in a stimulating and worthwhile cause.

What strategies in this chapter could help Judy get fired up over work or find new interest in her personal life? What would you suggest to Judy to get her motivated again?

_____

_____

_____

_____

_____

_____

_____

_____

_____

_____

▲ Exercise 2.1   The Attitude Connection

Apply what you've learned about attitude to your other classes. How does your attitude affect your success?

Category	Attitude	Yes	No
Assessment	Do I assess myself in an honest and positive manner?		
Test taking	Am I mentally prepared for taking tests?		
Time management	Do I know how to manage my time?		
Note taking	Do I listen and take notes with a positive and open mind?		
Reading	Do I feel confident and positive about my reading?		
Memory	Do I want to improve my memory?		
Writing	Do I see the importance of writing in all my classes?		
Speaking	Do I approach speaking as an important skill to learn?		
Research	Do I approach research with a creative and positive mind?		
Math	Do I realize that overcoming fear is an important part of learning math?		
Computers	Do I understand the importance of technology for school and job success?		
Instructor	Do I have a positive and supportive attitude toward my instructors?		
Class _____	Do I have a positive attitude toward this class?		

What are your reasons for taking classes? List all your courses and the ways in which they can help you intellectually and emotionally. For example: Math 210 can develop my ability to analyze, synthesize, become more competent with figures, and gain confidence in myself for doing well in a difficult course. These skills will increase my career options. Or: English 101 can help me develop writing, research, reading comprehension, discussion, and evaluation skills. These competencies will be valuable in any job.

_____

_____

_____

_____

_____

_____

_____

_____

_____

_____

_____

_____

_____

_____

_____

_____

_____

▲ Motivational Strategies ▲

1. *Focus on the positive.*

2. *Develop high self-esteem.*

3. *Use positive self-talk and imagery.*

4. *Focus on your purpose and goals.*

5. *Aquire the skills and habits to succeed.*

6. *Take responsibility.*

7. *Be in the present.*

8. *Be physically active.*

9. *Focus on successes, not failures.*

10. *Create a feedback loop.*

11. *Create a supportive climate.*

12. *Strive for excellence, not perfection.*

13. *Reward yourself.*

14. *Stay physically healthy.*

15. *Create a balance of work and play.*

16. *Strive to be a self-actualized person.*

CHAPTER THREE

BUILDING CONFIDENCE THROUGH TIME AND STRESS MANAGEMENT

"Decide what you want, decide what you are willing to exchange for it. Establish your priorities and go to work."

H. L. Hunt, financier

"You need not be a helpless victim. As you learn to recognize stress, you can measure the levels and effects of the several kinds of stress that will commonly occur in your life. You then will have the power to alter your response to much of that which is stressful."

Richard A. Stein, M.D., Director of Cardiac Exercise Laboratory Downstate Medical Center

Learning Objectives

In Chapter Three you will learn:

1. The importance and benefits of time and stress management.

2. To be aware of your energy and physical, emotional, and mental states.

3. To identify your time wasters.

4. How to overcome procrastination.

5. To handle stressful situations.

There seems to be a perception that time and stress are negative energies to be controlled and managed somewhat like a lion that needs taming. The objective of this chapter is to enable you to look at time and stress management with a positive attitude. Instead of controlling, suppressing, or constricting your freedom, time and stress management enables you to achieve the things you really want and frees up time to enjoy life. You will learn to work smarter, not harder, by setting goals and priorities. You will learn the strategies for being effective, not just efficient. Learning to use both sides of your brain will make you a more effective learner, and will thus free up some of your time so that you can focus your energy.

Everyone, no matter how rich or poor, has the same amount of time: 24 hours in each day. You can't save time or steal time. When it's gone, it's gone. You can learn to invest it wisely, however. You will see the value of realizing that you are 100 percent responsible for taking control of your life. This chapter will help you learn *how* to get control of your life by managing your time wisely and by choosing to spend it on your top priorities. You will discover that there is always time to do the things you really want to do and that stress can be channeled and focused into positive energy.

CONNECTING TIME AND STRESS MANAGEMENT

There is a strong link between time and stress management. It is easy to find yourself overwhelmed and stressed by having too much to do and too little time. You can also waste a lot of time by being unfocused, exhausted, ill, or emotionally drained. You will find that once you adopt positive habits for getting organized, you will be able to control your stress and spend your time more productively.

Every business executive, manager, student, or parent knows that time is a valuable resource that cannot be saved but can be used wisely. As a student or a business executive, you must solve the challenge of having too many demands made upon your time. You will find yourself at times in a "time trap," unable to do everything that needs to be done. Too many of us waste time doing things that should be done in a few moments or not at all, and ignore our main goals. So if you don't manage your time well, you might find yourself overwhelmed and behind in your classes.

Let's look at four important questions:

1. Where does your time go?

2. Where should your time go?

3. What are your time wasters?

4. What strategies can help you?

CREATING A TIME LOG

Where *does* your time go? Where are you spending your energy? Are you trying to accomplish too much at one time? A good way to find out is to do a time log. Use the log shown on page 60, or devise your own, to record your activities throughout the day. If your activities vary a great deal from day to day, you may want to do a log for several days or even a week. It often takes several days of logging for patterns to become clear.

Get Started

Record how much time you spend sleeping, grooming, eating, commuting, sitting in classes, studying, working, socializing, running errands, and all the things that you do but don't think about. Every hour jot down what you have done. After a week, you will have a good idea of where your time is really going and how this differs from your estimate. Also indicate when your energy level seems high or low.

Next, try to figure out how much of your time is committed, how much is maintenance time, and how much is discretionary.

Committed Time. This is time devoted to school, labs, studying, work, commuting time, waiting for the bus, and other activities involving your main goals.

Maintenance Time. This is the time you spend in maintaining yourself (eating, sleeping, bathing) or your home (cooking, cleaning, shopping, laundry, and so on).

Discretionary Time. This is time that remains yours to use as you please. Separate the discretionary commitments from your discretionary time, and put all your activities into certain categories. For example, grooming may include showering, styling your hair, cleaning your contact lenses, getting dressed, etc. Don't spend too much time trying to determine which category an activity fits in. For example, time spent in cooking a gourmet meal could be classified as discretionary time rather than maintenance. House cleaning might fit into committed or maintenance time. The point is to determine how you use your discretionary time. Are the discretionary activities conscious choices, or do you just allow them to happen? What can you do to increase your discretionary time?

Now take a look at your log to determine your peak energy time. Are you a morning or evening person? When does your energy lag? How do you tend to spend your time during those high and low periods? It is important to be aware of your body's rhythms in order to plan your time wisely. If your peak time is in the morning, don't waste that time by answering mail, socializing, cleaning, checking out books at the library, or routine work. Use your high-energy time for concentration, thinking, writing, difficult mental work, and completing projects. Use your low-energy time to do mindless physical work, chores, or easy reading. And, if possible, schedule your classes for high-energy times.

Monitoring your time helps create a cycle of success. Your awareness of where your time goes becomes a continual habit of assessment, planning, and choosing things in the order of their importance, and this leads to success.

		Activity	Notes	Energy level (high or low)
	6:00 — 7:00			
	7:00 — 8:00			
	8:00 — 9:00			
	9:00 — 10:00			
	10:00 — 11:00			
	11:00 — 12:00			
	12:00 — 1:00			
	1:00 — 2:00			
	2:00 — 3:00			
	3:00 — 4:00			
	4:00 — 5:00			
	5:00 — 6:00			
	6:00 — 7:00			
	7:00 — 8:00			
	8:00 — 9:00			
	9:00 — 10:00			
	10:00 — 11:00			

The Critical Thinking Connection

Determining problems and causes, making decisions, processing information, determining desired results, setting goals, questioning assumptions, reasoning logically, creating an action plan, meeting deadlines, and evaluating your progress are all critical thinking skills involved in time and stress management. Use critical thinking to answer the following questions. Be prepared to discuss your answers in your teams.

1. What are the major activities and tasks that take much of your time?

2. What activities cause you to use your time ineffectively?

3. What activities could you eliminate or reduce?

4. When is your high-energy time?

5. When do you study?

6. Look at your committed time. Does this block of time reflect your values and goals?

7. How can you increase your discretionary time?

8. Look at the common reasons and excuses that some students use for not being organized and focused. Add to this list and use creative problem solving to list strategies for overcoming these barriers.

Reasons   **Strategies**

I ran out of time.

I overslept.

I'm easily distracted.

People interrupt me.

Instructors put too much pressure on me.

I feel overwhelmed and panic at deadlines.

I forgot about an assignment.

_____

_____

_____

_____

WHERE SHOULD YOUR TIME GO?

Sometimes it's hard to know how to spend time because there are so many things to spend it on. It can be overwhelming. One of the first steps is to think about your goals. Then you can set priorities and go from there. This is clearly portrayed in the conversation between Alice and the Cheshire Cat in Lewis Carroll's *Alice in Wonderland.*

"Would you tell me, please, which way I ought to go from here?" asked Alice.
"That depends a good deal on where you want to go to," said the Cat.
"I don't much care where," said Alice.
"Then it doesn't matter which way you go," said the Cat.

You can avoid Alice's plight by determining what it is you really want to accomplish and your specific destination.

1. Set Goals

The first rule of time management is to set goals: to determine what you want to accomplish. Goals help clarify what you want and give you energy, direction, and focus. Goal setting often isn't quick or even easy. You need to take the time to go inward and think about your deepest values and desires. Even though change is inevitable, goal setting helps align your everyday actions with your life's purpose.

2. Make a Schedule

To help you decide how to spend your discretionary time, make a calendar or write a schedule so you know what your commitments are for the next week or month. You can make up your own schedule or mark up a printed calendar. If you use a printed calendar, find one with spaces large enough for each date, so you can fill in all fixed activities, classes, work hours, project due dates, and the like. Include exercise time and social events, too.

Once you have recorded your committed time, add in study time and other daily activities such as shopping, eating, and commuting. Make sure you allow for free time, and realize that you can't schedule every minute of the day.

Follow this schedule for two weeks and see how accurate it is. Bear in mind that the schedule should be flexible. It is merely a guide and should allow for unexpected events.

In addition to a weekly or monthly schedule, you might find it helpful to make a schedule for each important project you have. It works best to start with the due date and work backward, allotting plenty of time for each step. For example:

PROJECT BOARD

Project: Term Paper for Business Class 110

Today's Date: January 23   **Due Date:** April 23

Key Activities:

Activity	Date Completed
Paper finished and turned in.	April 23
Type final draft and proof.	April 15
Proof second draft, revise.	April 10
Additional research, spell-check.	April 5
First draft.	March 27
Detailed outline.	March 15
Detailed library research.	March 10
Library research.	March 5
General outline.	February 22
Initial library research.	February 8
Mindmap outline.	February 4
Finalize topic.	February 28
Explore topics.	January 23

Weekly Activity Schedule	Instructor		Office #		
	Monday	Tuesday	Wednesday	Thursday	Friday
7:00 — 8:00					
8:00 — 9:00					
9:00 — 10:00	Business 110				
10:00 — 11:00					
11:00 — 12:00					
12:00 — 1:00					
1:00 — 2:00					
2:00 — 3:00					
3:00 — 4:00					
4:00 — 5:00					
5:00 — 6:00					
6:00 — 7:00					
7:00 — 8:00					
8:00 — 9:00					
9:00 — 10:00					

3. Write a To-Do List

Once you have established your goals and priorities and established a schedule, it is time to write a to-do list.

First brainstorm: what are all the projects, activities, and errands that you can think of for the month? Write them all down. Narrow that list to what you want to accomplish this week, including routine tasks, projects, and deadlines. Finally, boil that list down to a daily to-do list. Write down all the things you want to do today, even small or routine items such as shopping, paying bills, making photocopies, cleaning, attending a meeting, seeing an instructor, taking books back to the library, and so on. Put a number 1 next to the item with the highest priority. Assign numbers to the rest of the items, with the highest number going to the least important item. Then rewrite the list, starting with number 1 at the top and listing the rest of the items in descending order of importance.

Some people like to write a to-do list for the next day, taking some time before they leave the office or their desk for the day. Others like to write theirs in the morning, at breakfast, or when they first sit at their desks. Try writing your list at different times and determine what works best for you.

After you've written your list, get going! Begin your day with number 1. Don't go on to the bottom items until the most important ones are done. Resist the temptation to do mindless things to avoid more weighty ones. Check off each item as you complete it. When you see all the items checked off, you'll get a feeling of accomplishment.

4. Revise and Modify, Don't Throw It Out

If goal setting is so important for achieving success, why do so few people have written goals or abandon them? Some people do not know how to write goals that are realistic, and others give up too quickly before they can see results. Many are afraid someone will tell them they can't achieve their goals, or they're afraid to fail. Some people don't like to set goals and priorities or write out lists because they know that circumstances change and they will need to adapt. Unexpected things do happen—the best plans sometimes have to be changed, but it is still important to plan. Goals empower you to be in control of your life and to change direction, just as using a map and planning your route are integral parts of mountain climbing.

WHAT ARE YOUR TIME WASTERS?

Refer to the time log you filled out earlier. Try to identify wasted time: time spent on low-priority, often unplanned activities. If you spend an hour and a half early in the morning drinking coffee and chatting with a good friend, you're not necessarily wasting time unless your top priority that day was to study, while your energy was high, for an exam. Wasting time is letting activities take up much more time than necessary, more than was planned, or even more than you enjoy.

To avoid wasting time, take control! Don't let endless activities and other people control you. Every day, set priorities that will help you meet your goals. For instance, if your friend calls you for coffee, set a limit of 20 minutes or postpone it until later in the day, after you have previewed your Business 101 chapter and outlined your speech. If you don't want to miss a favorite TV program, turn the set off right after that show. Set the answering machine if you are studying, or tell the caller that you will call back in an hour. When you do, chat for 5 minutes instead of 45 minutes. The essence of time management is taking charge of your life.

CAREER FOCUS

FOCUS ON TASKS, NOT TIME

Being known as a "doer" can greatly enhance your career. Successful professionals know it is important to plan, set goals, prioritize their tasks, and achieve results. Therefore, they set realistic and worthwhile goals. Career professionals are more concerned with achieving results than with frantic activity. Successful employees have learned not to procrastinate. They use their natural style and energy to achieve their goals in a flexible way. Let's look at Bob Dickerson, a real estate associate. He is a primarily visual learner who uses slides, charts, and overheads

DO SHEET

URGENT	Priorities	TO SEE OR CALL		
CONTINUING ATTENTION		AWAITING DEVELOPMENTS		
		What	**Who**	**When**

as a way to organize information and set goals. He likes to work with people and uses small teams to accomplish his goals. He tends to be creative, so he plans his day to tap his most creative periods. Bob works when his energy is high, which is often late mornings and evenings. He takes frequent breaks to discuss his projects with co-workers, visit new developments, and read reports of new market trends. Bob knows that paying attention to his commitments and interests outside work help him create a balanced life and enable him to set realistic goals in all aspects of his life. One tool used by many effective employees is a "to-do" time management list like the one shown above.

CONTROLLING INTERRUPTIONS BEFORE THEY CONTROL YOU

Interruptions steal your time: they cause you to stop and start projects, they disrupt your thought pattern, divert your attention, and make it difficult to build up momentum again. The first step in managing interruptions is to identify them. There are annoying interruptions that are obvious, such as drop-in visitors, the telephone, roommates who play music, and a variety of everyday demands for your attention. If you live with other people, you know how distracting these interruptions can be.

Successful students and effective managers know how to live and work with other people and yet limit and manage interruptions. It may require a bit of creativity to get control of the interruptions in your life. Try the following strategies to reduce interruptions and noise, increase your study time, and help make you more effective.

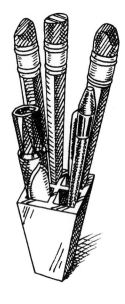

1. Work in a Supportive Study Area

It is important to create a private, quiet study space. Find a time when it is most quiet, such as early mornings, lunch hours, late afternoon or weekends. Study when most people are out. If it is difficult to study at home or in the dorm, study in a library. (Perhaps this is the location you have chosen for your study area.) Many students swear by going to a library for quiet time. Once you enter, your brain responds to a serious study mode. Sitting in a quiet place and facing the wall can reduce interruptions and distractions.

2. Keep Your Study Space Organized

With all your study tools—a dictionary, pencils, pens, books, papers, files, notes, calendar, semester schedule, and study team and instructor names and phone numbers in one place, you won't waste time looking for items you need. Keep only one project on your desk at one time and file everything else away or put it on a shelf.

3. Set Guidelines and Review Expectations

Discuss study needs and expectations with your roommates or family. Work out agreements, and respect and honor them. You might establish certain study hours or agree on a signal to let each other know when you need quiet time, such as closing your door or hanging a quiet sign. If one of you likes loud music, invest in ear phones or find a roommate who appreciates your style. Discuss and devise a workable agreement about responsibilities regarding overnight visitors and drop-in friends. You can waste a lot of time cleaning up after someone else or feeling resentful when they have friends over too often.

4. Have a Clear Purpose

Having a clear purpose of what you want and need to do makes it easier to say no to distractions. If someone wants to talk, party, or have friends over when you need to study, be assertive and say no. Don't blame others if you don't have enough courage to directly decline offers to socialize that interfere with your set priorities. If you live with someone, learn to read each other's signals when it's time to get back to the books or your projects. Developing friendships is an important part of life, but it has to balance with other demands and priorities. Try setting aside some time each day to visit with your family or roommates, such as during dinner, a walk, or a snack. It is important to be assertive when you need to study or go to class. Don't let anything interfere with your purpose.

5. Know Your Rhythms

When you completed your Time Log on page 60, you also determined the time of day when you have the most energy. Review this log to see your energy pattern.

As mentioned previously, use your high-energy time to do serious studying, work that requires concentration, and to attend classes. Guard against interruptions, and don't do mindless tasks or socialize during your peak energy periods.

For instance, if you are a morning person, plan your most demanding work for the morning hours. In the late afternoon and evening, open your mail, visit with friends, go on field trips, and do low-level tasks.

WHAT STRATEGIES CAN HELP YOU?

We've already discussed some basic strategies, such as establishing goals, writing a to-do list, and saying no to interruptions. Here are some others that will help.

1. Take Time to Plan and Set Priorities

It takes time to write out your goals and objectives, set priorities, establish action steps, write down due dates, organize your work space, and plan your course of action each day.

Tackle the most difficult tasks first. Start your day with a high-priority item and work through your list. Your energy level will be high and you will feel a sense of accomplishment as you tackle your tough jobs or boring projects first. Start out with your most difficult subjects, while you're fresh and alert. Know your body rhythms and study your hardest subjects during your peak energy times. For instance, if you are avoiding your statistics homework because it is difficult, get up early and do it before your classes begin.

2. Manage Your Life in Sync with Your Left- or Right-Brain Style

You will find that you can manage your life and your time much more effortlessly when you understand your brain dominance. As we discussed in Chapter 1, you will accomplish more in less time when you *support* rather than work against your natural preference. If you tend to be left-brain dominant, the traditional time management strategies work best for you. You are organized, consistent, and self-directed, want a quiet place to study alone, and like to work step by step to complete your projects. If you have a strong right-brain tendency, you may find that you accomplish more when you focus on the whole picture instead of the parts. You may need more visual cues, work better with a flexible schedule, prefer to juggle several projects throughout the day, and get energized by working with people.

You will also save time when you support your natural learning style. If you are primarily a visual learner, create lots of pictures, images, diagrams, examples, and illustrations. If you are primarily an auditory learner, invest in cassettes, tape your notes, and play them back—that way you can listen to all lectures as much as you need. Many executives say that their biggest time saver is a dictating machine. You can dictate ideas and outlines for papers, practice speeches, plan your day, and record formulas, definitions, key words, and class notes. Play them back and listen again to your voice. If you are primarily a kinesthetic learner, adapt a hands-on approach, stay active and involved, learn by doing, and join a study team. Increase your productivity by using your natural learning style and tapping into other styles as well.

"Perhaps the most valuable result of all education is the ability to make yourself do the thing you have to do, when it ought to be done, whether you like it or not; it is the first lesson that ought to be learned. . . ."
T. H. Huxley
Technical Education

3. Study during "Down Time"

Be prepared for all the idle time that is part of every day—the 5 or 10 minutes of waiting between classes, for the bus, or for appointments. Carry notecards with you to review formulas, dates, definitions, facts, and important data. Bring class notes or a book with you and study while waiting. Tape record important material and lectures and play these tapes while commuting, exercising, dressing, walking, or waiting for class to begin. Avoid, if possible, crowded times in the library and computer labs. Don't shop on Saturdays or do laundry on weekends unless you have to. But even if you plan well, you will occasionally get stuck in lines.

4. Study in Short Segments throughout the Day

Study during the day instead of waiting until evening to sit down and tackle all your work. Most students are more effective if they consider school as their main job, get up in the morning as if for work, and study during daytime hours. You will be surprised how much you can accomplish by consistently using short periods of study. Actually, studying in short segments is much more effective than in marathon sessions—your brain is much more receptive to recall when you review at various times in short sessions.

5. Break Projects Down and Consolidate Similar Tasks

We all get discouraged if we face a large task, whether it's cleaning a closet or beginning a major term paper. Getting started is half the battle. Spend just 15 minutes before you go to bed to begin outlining your chapter for next day or mindmapping the main ideas for your term paper. If your paper is due on a certain date, make a plan of all the steps necessary prior to that date. Break down the task and start doing something on each step every day. Self-discipline is important in dealing with procrastination. You will find inspiration with just a small investment of your time, and the task will be less overwhelming.

If you group similar tasks, you can maximize your efforts. For example, if you need to make several calls, make them all at a specific time and reduce interruptions. Set aside a block of time to shop, pay bills, go to the post office, and run errands. Don't make unnecessary trips. Save your energy and utilize your resources by planning and combining similar activities, such as taking a walk with a friend, thus combining exercise with socializing.

6. Be Assertive

Learn to confront your concerns and problems and act to resolve them in a constructive way. Find creative solutions by defining the problem, approaching the person in a calm manner, and expressing your needs. Stomping into your instructor's office and demanding a better grade is no more effective than swallowing or ignoring your hurt or anger and passively hoping things will improve on their own. It takes courage to practice being assertive, but you will not waste valuable time on angry, resentful feelings.

Being assertive also means being responsible, fair, and making certain that everyone does their share. Make certain that your workload is evenly distributed in your study groups. Don't volunteer to type the report or do the research unless the assignment is shared by everyone. Discuss expectations and household chores with your roommate or family. It is easy to feel resentful and overwhelmed if you are doing more than your share.

▲ SCHOOL IS YOUR CAREER; MANAGE IT LIKE A PRO

▲ The management process is a key business concept. Well-run organizations use the management process to ensure efficiency. Every effective manager uses planning, organizing, staffing, directing, and evaluating to meet the organization's goals. You can apply the same principles to your education.

The Management Process

Planning Specify what goals you want to achieve. Visualize the end results you want. Break these large goals into semester goals and weekly and daily priorities. Keep these posted by your study area. Detail the steps you need to take to get to your goal. Be prepared for frustrating barriers and deal with them in a calm manner. For example, attending college includes registering, waiting in lines to pay fees, finding classrooms and parking spaces, getting a library card, obtaining ID, etc. This is just "stuff" that everyone has to go through. Don't let the little irritations discourage you, or distract you from your goals.

Organizing Organize your activities to achieve your goals. Organize your office or study area for effective and efficient concentration. Post charts of major projects, due dates, and class schedules. A project board is very important for keeping you on track. Prepare for the really busy weeks and reduce your other commitments. Ask yourself, "What do I need to do to get the results I want? How organized do I have to be?"

Staffing You play the major role in your school career. Build a solid commitment to disciplining yourself and carving out the time you need to meet your goals. Delegate whatever you can and build independence in others. Don't take on other people's problems. Do, however, join a support group of other students who will encourage, listen, and support each other. Form study teams that will help maximize study time. Know how to reach at least two students in each of your classes. You can take notes for each other in an emergency, share information, ask questions, and study together. Your instructors are key staff in your school career. If you have a choice, pick the best instructors and build supportive relationships with them. Know their names and expectations, take an active part in class discussions, and view them as supportive, helpful people. Become familiar with support services for students. If you are a reentry student, there are resources available that can help.

Directing Use positive reinforcement to motivate yourself. Keep a list of all the ways you can reward yourself. Take frequent short breaks for walks or exercise. Keep a list of your goals on your desk. Reward yourself and others. Treat yourself to a night out once a month for pizza and a movie. When you are with family or friends, enjoy them totally. Reward yourself after each project and for small tasks. Example: "I will have a dish of ice cream after I complete this chapter."

Evaluating Monitor your attitude and behavior. Detach yourself, and in a nonjudgmental way, measure your results. Be honest and don't allow excuses or blame to distract you from finding solutions to achieving the results you want.

7. Focus on Results, not Activity

All the time-management strategies in the world will not help if you don't make a commitment to achieve results. After you analyze your time log, review your time wasters, and monitor your peak energy times, you will be aware of where you want to make changes. Don't try to make too many changes at once or get discouraged if a strategy doesn't work for you. Change certain aspects until it fits your style. Be flexible. If it works, do it. If not, try something new. Just make sure you've given yourself at least 30 days to develop new habits. It often feels strange and uncomfortable to do any new task or vary your system of daily events. For example, you might discover that you have a habit of getting a donut and coffee every morning and spending an hour or so socializing before your morning classes. Changing this habit will feel strange for a while.

8. Make Learning Physical

Physical activity gets your blood flowing throughout your body, including your brain—which is why physical activity often enhances academic performance. When you feel your energy dip, take a walk (even if it's up and down the hall), jump rope, do deep knee bends, or go for a quick jog. Exercise also helps relax the body, so it is a good way to reduce stress and increase your effectiveness.

Too often we think of learning as a mental process, but clearly the body can be an important tool in helping you to learn. Try the kinesthetic learning style: act out scenes from your books, draw a diagram, or build a model to illustrate a problem. Albert Einstein talked about the importance of using the physical body to reinforce learning by combining the visual with muscular elements.

You'll also find that if you use alert body language—that is, sit up straight rather than slouch—you'll act more alert and learn better. For instance, you may remember more when you read out loud, or when you read and write standing up.

9. Do First Things First

Lack of organization is a common reason that students fail, become unmotivated, and procrastinate. Top executives know it is important to plan their day, prioritize their goals, and work to achieve results in each project. Going to school demands no less a commitment to stay on track, focused, and prepared for the day. Nothing is quite as unsettling as rushing in the morning, skipping breakfast, and arriving late and scattered for class. Spend 10 minutes before class reviewing your notes, scanning the chapter, and getting your mind in a calm, receptive state. Keeping up with assignments on a daily basis eliminates cramming and is much more effective. Of course, to know what to do first, you need to be organized. Having an organized study area will help, but there's more to it than that.

10. Pay Attention to Details

Pay attention to details and appearance. Written work is impressive when it is clear, concise, and neat. Yes, neatness counts. So does paying attention to due dates and extra-credit work. Often the only difference between an A and a B grade is an extra-credit assignment. Turn in homework assignments even if they are only worth "a few extra points."

11. Develop a Positive Relationship with Your Instructor

Develop a relationship with your instructor just as you would your supervisor at work. Make certain you understand the objectives and expectations of the course and the style of the instructor. Most instructors will give you extra help and feedback if you take the initiative. For instance, before a paper is due, hand in a draft and say, I want to make sure I am covering the important points in this paper. Am I on the right track? What can I add to make this an A paper? If you don't understand or you disagree with a grade you have received on a test or paper, ask for an appointment with the instructor. Approach the situation with a supportive attitude. "I like this course and want to do well in it. I am unclear as to why I got a B on this paper because I thought I had met the objectives. Could you show me exactly what points you think should be changed? Could I make these corrections for a higher grade?" Make certain you are respectful and appreciative of your instructor's time and help. Effective relationships will help you be more efficient and effective.

12. Just Do It!

Stop talking about it, complaining about it, worrying about it, resisting it, and simply do it! Work on your top-priority task and move on. Getting started is the hardest part. You already know what projects need immediate attention. Jump in early each day, give yourself a specific priority, and reward yourself for completing it. Combine fun and discipline. Color your notes, calendar, and mind map. Fun and discipline are the keys for achieving results. Measure your everyday behavior against your mission statement. Are your actions aligned with your life's purpose? There is a sense of commitment and excitement when you know you are in harmony with your deepest self-expression.

MANAGING STRESS

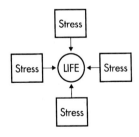

Stress is a natural reaction of the body to any demand, pleasant or unpleasant. Stress is not the result of an event, but simply your body's *reaction* to external events (taking an exam or giving a speech) or internal events (fear, worry, or unresolved anger). Everything you experience stimulates your body to react and respond. Stress is normal and, in fact, necessary for a vital life. With too little stress, many people are bored and unproductive. The key is to find out your optimal level of stress.

Life is a series of changes, and these changes require adaptive responses. The death of a close family member or friend, a serious illness, exams, divorce, financial problems, being fired, or moving are all examples of changes that require adjustment and cause stress. It is important to emphasize, however, that it is your perception of these inescapable life events that significantly affects how they affect you. Public speaking may be exciting and fun for one person and cause an anxiety attack in another. Stress isn't "out there"—it is something you create and can manage. Personality traits such as being a perfectionist or a pleaser may also govern how you respond to stress.

Stress is not always negative. Even positive events such as marriage, a promotion, going away to school, a new romantic relationship, a new roommate, graduation, even vacations and Christmas may be disruptive and demanding for some people and therefore stressful.

STUDENT STRESS FACTORS

Home Life

For students going away to school, separation and loneliness can be major stress factor. Learning to live with roommates can be a major source of enjoyment or conflict. For students who have never lived away from home, learning to cook and take responsibility for themselves is a major adjustment.

For students living at home, becoming adults with new friends and activities can require an adjustment in roles and expectations.

For returning students, juggling the demands of a family with school and often a job can be very difficult.

Social Life

It can be difficult to balance school with an active social life. Parties, clubs, activities, and late-night gab fests are all important parts of school, but can also cause students to miss classes, sleep, and deadlines. Peer pressure to drink, try drugs, and engage in sexual activity can also be confusing and stressful.

Balancing a social life with a demanding full-time job is also stressful.

Deadlines

Increased pressure to meet deadlines and excel in courses can be a source of stress. Competition for grades, financial aid, scholarships, student work programs, internships, and jobs can also add to feelings of isolation. Students often spend hours studying alone in order to compete and achieve good grades.

The stress of meeting deadlines is also part of most jobs.

Finances

For the first time students may be paying their own bills and finding that they are always short of money. Financial pressure can cause stress even for students who hold full-time jobs. Few people ever think they have enough money to live well.

Job

Many students now work and go to school. Balancing the demands of a job, school, activities, and a personal life can be stressful. Getting to work on time, working effectively with others, clarifying expectations, learning new skills, and completing tasks can add pressure.

Career Decisions

Deciding on a major and choosing a career can be confusing. This can be especially stressful if your parents want you to become an accountant but you want to be a graphics designer or journalist.

Once students start working full time, there are still many career decisions—Is this the right job, career, location, company? Should I continue for an advanced degree?

Freedom

The new freedom a student feels can be exciting and overwhelming. No one is setting curfews or limits, enforcing a dress code, making class attendance mandatory, or tracking down students who get into academic trouble. Students can choose what to eat and drink, whether to exercise, and study, and when and how much to sleep and to play. Students have to make their own friends and may have trouble bridging the diversity of cultures. It is also hard to say no to such an array of classes, clubs, activities, and parties and an overload of choices and freedom can create new stresses.

Being on time for school and work and being responsible for meeting deadlines and completing projects are additional sources of stress.

Relationships

Working with academic advisors, instructors, administors, supervisors, co-workers, and other students can be enjoyable, but also stressful. Some students avoid these relationships but won't be able to on the job. Forming effective working relationships can be a real benefit for school and job success.

External and Internal Barriers

Everyone has barriers or issues that can cause stress. Some are more obvious than others. Prejudice, misunderstandings, or perceived barriers may be felt by multicultural, disabled, elderly, homosexual, international, or overweight students; members of religious groups; and women (especially pregnant women). Some students who are first-generation college students have told me that changing their self-image and other people's expectations of them was a major barrier to overcome. Students who face discrimination or barriers, or who have a limiting or negative self-image, may withdraw or feel highly stressed.

STRESS-REDUCTION STRATEGIES

Research has indicated that too much change for too long a period of time can cause excess stress. Too many negative or positive changes stimulate the production of certain hormones and chemicals that can affect the body. Attempts to eliminate or escape stress through drugs or alcohol only result in lower self-esteem. The solution is not to avoid stress, but to face it directly and learn to manage and channel it. You must find your own way to dissipate stress. The following strategies not only reduce stress but also increase your productivity and effectiveness.

1. Tune In to Your Body and Emotions

Many of us have been taught to deny emotions or physical symptoms and ignore stress. Listen to your body. Stress produces physical symptoms that warn us we are under pressure.

The transition to college or professional school is a major life transition and forces you to become more self-reliant and self-sufficient. Give yourself permission to feel a variety of emotions.

▲ The following symptoms may be early warning signs that your body is pushing too hard, too long, and may be on its way to burnout. If you have more than four of these symptoms, you may want to consider getting help for dealing with stress overload.

Stress Symptoms

1. Frequent headaches, backaches, neck pain, stomachaches, or tensed muscles.

2. Insomnia or disturbed sleep patterns.

3. No sense of humor; nothing sounds like fun.

4. Feeling fatigued, being listless, feeling hopeless, and having low energy.

5. Increase in alcohol intake, smoking, or taking drugs.

6. Depression, moodiness, or a hopeless feeling.

7. Heart racing.

8. Appetite changes (eating too much or too little).

9. Frequent colds, flu, or other illnesses.

10. Feeling "wired," anxious, nervous; having difficulty in concentrating.

11. Irritability or losing your temper and overreacting.

12. Lack of motivation, energy, or zest for living.

13. Feeling that you have too much responsibility.

14. Lack of interest in relationships.

2. Exercise Regularly

Experts say that exercise is one of the best ways to reduce stress, relax muscles, and promote a sense of well-being. Interestingly enough, most people find that they have more energy when they exercise regularly. Students often find it difficult to take the time to exercise. Sometimes the best way is to make it a daily habit and make exercise a top priority in your life.

3. Rest and Renew Your Body and Mind

Everyone needs to rest; not only through sleep, but also through deep relaxation. Too little of either causes irritability, depression, inability to concentrate, and memory loss. Yoga is a great way to unwind, stretch and tone the muscles, and focus your energy. Many people find that meditation is essential for relaxation and renewal. You don't have to practice a certain meditation; just create a time for yourself when your mind is free to rest and quiet itself. Other people find that a massage relieves physical tension. Visualization is another powerful technique for relaxing your body. At the end of this chapter, try the visualization process for focusing your attention and reducing tension.

4. Develop Hobbies and Interests

Hobbies can also release stress, focus your energy, and spark a passion for living. Sports, painting, quilting, reading, and collecting can add a sense of fun and meaning to your life. Mental exercise can refresh and stimulate your mind and body.

Many find satisfaction and focus by developing an interest in the environment, the elderly, politics, children, animals, or the homeless. Investigate volunteering opportunities in your area. Every day, do at least one thing that you really enjoy.

5. Use the Power of Breath

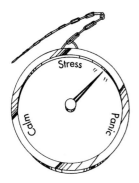

Deep breathing reduces stress and energizes the body. If you are like many people, you breathe in short, shallow breaths, especially when under stress. Begin by sitting or standing up straight, breathe through your nose, fill your lungs completely, and push out your abdomen and exhale slowly and fully. Deep breathing is an effective tool to reduce stress and focus thoughts.

Meditation is the act of focusing your attention so completely that you are only conscious of your deep breathing. Research has shown meditation to be effective in lowering blood pressure, heart rate, and respiration. Find a quiet spot and still your thoughts. Focus on a word, a sound, or your breathing. Give this your full attention for about 20 minutes. You can do a variation of this any time during the day, even if you can't escape to a quiet spot. When you find yourself in a panic, tell yourself to stop, and breathe deeply. Stop the negative chatter and slowly breathe in and exhale. Stopping your thoughts for a moment and breathing deeply increases your self-control and calms you down. Remind yourself that you can choose your thoughts and behavior. You are in control. You can choose to create a positive mindset by using positive thoughts and affirmations. Biofeedback training can be helpful, but you can also learn through practice to create a deep state of relaxation by awareness and breathing techniques.

6. Develop a Support System

Talk it out. The support and comfort of family and friends can help you clear your mind, sort out confusion, and make better decisions. Express your feelings, fears, and problems to people you trust. Make friends with nonworriers. Negative, chronic complainers who worry but don't act to solve their problems, are stressful. Surround yourself with people who are flexible, hopeful, and positive.

7. Take Minivacations and Have Fun

Next time you are put on hold or kept waiting in line, pull out a cartoon book and enjoy a few moments of laughter. Or practice a series of exercises such as deep breathing, head rolls, or visualizing the tension flowing out of your body. Get up and stretch periodically while you're studying. These "minivacations" can keep you relaxed and expand your creative side.

When you find yourself overreacting or getting angry, ask yourself, How can I see this differently? Take a minibreak, a deep breath, and approach the world with a more forgiving and loving view. Count to 10 before you react with an angry reply or say something that puts up a wall. You can take a minivacation every time the stress starts to build.

8. Rehearse the Feared Event

In a sense, when you mentally rehearse beforehand, you are inoculating yourself against a stressful event. Your fears become known and manageable. Visualization is an excellent technique for rehearsing an event. For example, you may feel stressed at the thought of giving your speech in class. Visualize each step in the experience. Imagine what you are wearing, what your audience will be like, your key points, and see yourself giving an excellent presentation. When you actually give the speech, it will seem like "old hat." You will have reduced your stress and anxiety. Rehearsing, practicing, and reviewing are keys to success.

9. Exercise and Stretch Your Mind

Mental exercise can refresh and stimulate your entire life. Reading, doing crossword puzzles and playing challenging board games renew the spirit and stretch the mind.

Attend guest lectures, take workshops and seminars, and brainstorm creative ideas or current subjects with well-read friends. Think of all the ways that you renew and expand your thinking. Make friends with creative people who inspire you and renew your perspective.

10. Create Balance in Your Life

All work and little relaxation produce burnout. Successful people recognize the importance of balance between work and play in their lives. Set a time limit on work, demands from other people, and study. Say, "I will study hard and consistently this week, but I'll take off Friday night for a movie and Sunday afternoon for a long hike."

When you feel mentally drained, try some useful physical work like washing your car or cleaning your closets. Or unplug the phone and disconnect from life for an hour or so. Go to the zoo, play with the dog, or take a child to the circus. Above all, take time to play and rediscover the child that still is within you.

11. Develop a Sense of Humor

Nothing reduces stress like a hearty laugh or spontaneous good fun. Discovering the child within helps us release our natural creativity and kicks our brain into the right hemisphere. People who validate play see innovative solutions, explore new ideas, and transform work into fun. Play releases built-up tension, helps us to relax, and puts everything in perspective.

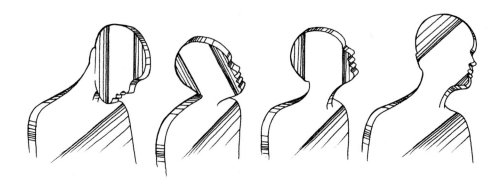

PREPARATION: THE BEST ANTIDOTE TO STRESS

Being prepared will certainly help to relieve stress. The following strategies will help with every class.

1. Go to Every Class

Woody Allen once remarked, "Eighty per cent of life is just showing up." This is such an obvious tip—but somehow people overlook its importance. You cannot be successful in a career if you miss work or meetings, or show up late for work or leave early. Your education is your career, so make it a rule that unless you are very ill and contagious to others, you will go to all your classes on time and stay the entire period. For one thing, it makes good financial sense. Your education is costing you on an average of $100 per class session. Get the most from this investment. If you arrive late, you may miss the tone of the class or valuable information, and you interrupt the class. Often an instructor reviews due dates for assignments, explains term papers, and answers questions at the beginning and ending of class. Arriving early and staying to the end also demonstrate that you are interested, respectful, and have good organizational skills.

2. Sit in the Front Row

Chapter Two talked about the importance of being in the present. It is easy to get distracted, daydream, finish your homework, talk to other students, and mentally check out while sitting in class. To keep yourself alert during lectures, sit in the front row. You will be more attentive there, more likely to ask questions and get involved in the lecture. You will also hear better and see the board more clearly. Peak performers know it takes time and energy to discipline the mind, to bring it back to the moment, and to keep it alert and aware.

3. Get Help Early

A common mistake many students make is waiting too long to get help. Don't wait until the end of the term to go to your instructor. Stop in occasionally during office hours, ask questions in class, and get feedback about how you are doing. At the first sign of trouble—if you have concerns about the material, or get a low grade on a test—talk with your instructor. Ask what you can do to improve your understanding of the subject and whether there are supplemental materials that you can use.

Assess where you are every few weeks. Do you understand the material? Are you keeping up with the reading? Can you answer the chapter questions? Do you do well on the tests? Do you turn in assignments? Ask your instructor before midterm what grade you have earned to that point.

You are responsible for your education, but there are lots of resources to help you: tutors, study teams, extra credit, sample tests, learning skill labs, and different books and learning resources.

4. Develop a Plan of Action

Sometimes students who feel they are being discriminated against become withdrawn and depressed. Others become angry and aggressive or become suspicious of anyone who is not part of their group. Others passively accept the prejudice just to fit in. None of these are positive reactions to stress. Instead, it is vital that students find out what resources are available to help them cope and to obtain equal rights and treatment.

The college and school environment is a safe place to learn coping skills and to advocate diversity. Speaking out in a calm and constructive manner will help students acquire confidence and courage about expressing needs and advocating tolerance. Once students with diverse backgrounds become acquainted, they will often feel less discomfort and develop the empathy to support other people's needs. Some people just don't know how to act around people whose backgrounds differ from theirs. It is everyone's responsibility to help eliminate discrimination in schools and in the workplace. Be assertive and work for constructive changes.

SPECIAL CASES: BUILDING CONFIDENCE IN DIFFICULT COURSES

Building Math Confidence

The general study skills and stress reduction techniques that are covered in this book can be used to learn any subject and overcome any type of stage fright or fear. The following strategies offer some extra help for overcoming math anxiety.

1. Be Aware. You can free yourself from past attitudes, myths, and fear by facing them and accepting your feelings. Realize that your feelings are not unusual. People from all walks of life suffer from math anxiety. Become aware of how your body responds to anxiety. Keep a journal of your reactions. How does your body respond when you do math problems or take a math test? Do you panic at the thought of a word problem? What attitude do you bring to this subject? Where did this attitude come from? Do you tend to blame yourself for some personal deficiency?

2. Take Control of the Situation. Become aware of how you relax and take control of other fearful situations. Most people are fearful and experience anxiety when they feel they have no control of a situation. They are anxious because they know that panic behavior is inappropriate for successfully completing the task at hand. What value is a pounding heart, shallow breathing, tense muscles, negative thoughts, and sweaty palms? Anxiety merely interferes with your ability to concentrate and think clearly. Take control by learning how you create a resourceful and calm state of mind. Use relaxation and deep breathing as discussed earlier.

Watch for negative self-talk, which causes anxiety and stress. Replace these statements with positive self-talk.

Negative	Positive
I am just not good at numbers or formulas.	I patiently learn what is needed.
Other people can learn math and science, but I can't.	I am good enough to succeed.
I'm simply not a logical person.	I will use my imagination to solve problems.

1. With your feet flat on the floor, close your eyes and completely relax your body.

2. Use positive self-talk to relax each part of your body. "My forehead is relaxed. My eyes are relaxed. My eyelids are relaxed. My jaw is relaxed." Drop your shoulders. Clench your fists and then relax them. Go through this process with your entire body several times a day.

3. Focus on your breathing. Consciously breathe deeply. Each time you exhale, feel your body relax and your mind become calm and centered.

4. Use positive words and phrases to relax your mind.

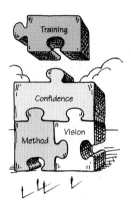

3. Recognize the Benefits of Excelling in Difficult Courses. It is important to approach difficult courses with a positive attitude. They are not just courses to "make it through" or avoid, but have value and offer many benefits. More majors in college and jobs are available to you if you have a background in math, science, foreign languages or technical subjects. An array of careers in retailing, banking, insurance, business, and government require people who have skills in math and who can think analytically. Don't eliminate potential careers for lack of a math or science background. Don't limit yourself. Many schools offer courses on overcoming math, computer, and science anxiety.

4. Be an Active Learner. People who experience writer's block use active writing to overcome their anxiety. They write about anything that comes into their minds, unconcerned about subject order, spelling, or composition. You can overcome your math anxiety by jotting down ideas, formulas, drawing pictures, and writing out the problem. Find and write out a similar problem that you can do and examine the similarities and differences. When working on homework or test questions, always do the easiest problems first—success builds success. Get rid of your anxiety by focusing on the task instead of on your feelings.

5. Be Persistent. Mathematics requires discipline and focused effort. You need to give it your full attention. Be realistic about the time required to finish your homework and always use the full amount of time available to complete a test. Often students become discouraged because a problem is difficult to solve or requires more than one step. It takes time and patience to learn any new skill. Don't look for quick, easy answers. Stay with the problem and give it intense concentration.

6. Evaluate Your Progress. Get feedback and assess your progress. It helps if you can review your problems or test results as soon as possible so you can see your mistakes and look for patterns. Look for what is working and what isn't. You can also use feedback while you are working a problem. If you get stuck, take a break. Sometimes it helps to take a quick walk or relax for a few minutes and come back to the problem refreshed.

Be flexible and creative. Unconscious work is going on even when you are not actively working on a problem. Approach the problem from a different direction. Remember, mathematics is not just a logical skill. Intuition, estimation, and going with your first ideas are important. Don't erase your work. Think intensely for a while and then get away from it and assess how you are doing.

7. Adjust, Correct, and Practice. Use corrective strategies to get back on track. Review study sheets and correct mistakes. Most of all, practice, practice, practice!

Dealing with Difficult Mathematics Instructors

It would be great if all instructors were well prepared, organized, available, motivating, entertaining, supportive, explained concepts clearly, and used a variety of teaching and learning styles. However, you may find yourself having to take a mathematics course with a less than inspiring instructor. It is your responsibility to learn math and make the best of the stituation. Here are some tips that may help:

Take Responsibility for Your Own Learning. Don't reinforce your negative perception with negative self-talk and behavior. Instead tell yourself, "This instructor is doing the best job at this time. I am supportive and positive and committed to learning mathematics. I attend all classes and have developed an effective working relationship with my instructor." There is a tendency to cut classes when you don't like your instructor. This is the worst thing you can do. You miss valuable class discussions, question-and-answer sessions, explanations, reviews of concepts, expectations about tests, contact with students, and structure to help you stay focused.

Adopt Positive Study Habits. This is the time to follow all the study skills presented in this book. Make certain you go to every class. Show up for class on time, prepared and motivated, and sit in the front row. Preview the chapters, listen actively, take good notes, ask questions, review your notes right after class, keep up on your reading and practice exercises, and do homework and end-of-chapter problems every day.

Form a Study Group. The first week of class, get the names and phone numbers of three or four students who will be in your study group. Meet regularly to practice solving problems. Explain concepts out loud to each other. Make up practice tests and give them to each other. If none of you understand a concept, go to the instructor.

Get Help Early. At the first sign of trouble, talk to your study team and then your instructor. Review your homework, sample problems, and tests and determine why you missed questions. Check out resources on campus such as tutorial labs, tutors, different textbooks, and resource manuals. Don't wait until midterm to see your instructor or advisor. Get help the minute you don't understand a concept.

Use Your Math Checklist. Use the math checklist at the end of this chapter to review your progress and give you direction. Make certain you are approaching mathematics in a systematic and positive approach. If you are persistent, motivated, and resourceful, you will learn math even if your instructor is less than perfect.

Use a Tape Recorder. Ask permission from your instructor to tape the lectures. Play them back to pick up main points and examples. Also, use the tape recorder to explain concepts in your own words, and to list formulas, definitions, and new words. Play your tape back throughout the day. You are using the auditory method of studying, plus hearing yourself repeat main words and concepts. This is especially important in learning foreign languages.

Schedule Frequent Breaks. Schedule your time so that you can really concentrate for about 45 minutes or so and then take a short break. Exercise, eat, stretch, take a brief walk, or complete a task. Most students find that shorter study periods are more effective.

Get Help Immediately. Don't wait until you're frustrated and behind. The instructor, other students, tutors, and the learning skills center can all offer you help. Don't be afraid to ask questions, request concepts be repeated or further explained, or ask for materials to stay on the board longer. See the instructor if you have any problem with understanding a new concept. You also might tape lectures to augment notes.

Do All Assignments, Problems, and Homework. Work out sample problems, make up test questions, and get new problems from different textbooks and other students. Practice doing lots of problems—write formulas and definitions on note cards and practice throughout the day.

Explain Again and Again. Summarize the material in your own words, out loud. Write out formulas using words, illustrations, drawings, or any other method that can help you see the problem. Reading out loud is a great way to increase recall and sort through confusion. Explain the problems to others.

Review Right before Each Class. Review your notes and skim the chapter so that your brain is open to new information. Your success in these classes depends a great deal on adopting an orderly, precise, and correct attitude toward your reading assignments, homework, and lab projects. Read ahead, practice, and summarize. Since broad concepts are so important, familiarize yourself with them ahead of time and ask questions in class on integrating the material. Reading ahead promotes a sense of familarity, offers a general understanding of what you are studying, and gives you a sense of control of the material.

Study Actively. Use your body to help you learn. Write down formulas, take notes, work out problems, and ask questions. Take more breaks (as mentioned above). Reduce interruptions and concentrate fully for 45 minutes. Discipline your mind to concentrate for short periods. Time yourself on problems to increase speed, and make the most of short study sessions.

Use Your Study Teams. As has already been discussed, studying in a team maximizes your effectiveness. Have each team member explain a problem on the board so that everyone can understand. Working in a small study team is an effective way to really understand difficult subjects. Have timed study drills to practice and reduce the anxiety of exams.

Use an Analytical Approach.

— **Define the problem.** First, define what is being asked for and what is unknown.

— **Analyze the problem.** You have to understand the problem in order to solve it. Analyze the data and conditions, and decide if it is possible to determine the unknown or satisfy the conditions. Restate the problem in your own words.

— **Devise a plan and gather information.** Gather facts and find the connection between the known and the unknown. Set up a plan to solve the problem. Have you seen similar problems? What formulas could help?

— **Use your plan to solve the problem.** Go through each step. If you have trouble, stop and think of related problems. What formulas did you use? Can you solve part of the problem? Did you use all the data, conditions, and known factors in the problem? Rewrite the problem. Think of a more general problem and a more specific problem. How do they relate?

SPECIAL STRATEGIES FOR MANAGING LANGUAGE COURSES (INCLUDING ESL)

1. Practice Exercises. As with math and science, practice exercises are critical in learning another language.

2. Keep Up with Your Reading. You must build upon previous lessons and skills. Therefore, it is important to keep up your readings, preview chapters so you have a basic understanding of any new words, and then do your practice sessions several times.

3. Carry Note Cards with You. Drill yourself on parts of speech and verb conjugation through all the tenses, and practice vocabulary building.

4. Recite Out Loud. Recite new words to yourself out loud. This is especially important in a language course. Tape record yourself, and play it back.

5. Form Study Teams. Study in a team, and talk only the language you are studying. Recite out loud to each other, explain verb conjugation, and use words in different contexts. Recitation is an excellent strategy when studying languages.

6. Listen to Tapes. Play practice tapes while commuting, jogging, exercising, before going to sleep, etc.

7. Visualize. During an exam, visualize yourself listening to a tape, see the diagrams you have drawn, and hear yourself reciting the material.

8. Model and Tutor. Invite to your study team or out for coffee a student whose primary language is the one you are studying. Talk only his or her native language. Offer to teach your language in exchange for tutoring you. You can find foreign students in classes where English as a second language is taught, usually in local schools and communities.

9. Focus on Key Words. Study words, meanings, tenses, and pronunciation. Keep these drilling exercises on 3×5 cards.

10. Have Fun. Do research on the country of the language you're studying. Make the language come alive for you. Have your study group over for an authentic meal, complete with music and costumes. Invite foreign students and your instructor.

GRID 3.1
Creating a Semester Calendar

At the start of each semester, take the time to map out your week. Planning reduces stress!

WEEK OF:	Sunday	Monday	Tuesday	Wednesday	Thursday	Friday	Saturday

GRID 3.2
Setting Personal Goals

PART A

List goals that you want to accomplish in the next five years. For instance, "I will graduate," or "I will go to Europe."

Goal 1:

Goal 2:

Goal 3:

Goal 4:

PART B

List goals that you want to accomplish within the next year. For instance, "I will jog 45 minutes, three times a week."

Goal 1:

Goal 2:

Goal 3:

Goal 4:

PART C

List goals that you want to accomplish this term in school. For example, "I will preview chapters for 10 minutes before each lecture," or "I will go to all of my classes on time."

GRID 3.3
Checklist for Mathematics

— Have you approached math with a positive attitude?

— Have you built math confidence by changing your self-image, relaxing, and getting involved in the problem?

— Have you clearly defined the problem?

— Have you discovered what you want to know and what you are asked to find out?

— Have you separated and broken down the essential information from the unessential and the known from the unknown?

— Have you determined how to best approach the problem? Have you devised a plan for solving the problem?

— Have you gone from the general to the specific? Have you used your intuition and known information to guess and speculate?

— Have you illustrated or organized the problem?

— Have you made a table, a diagram, drawn a picture, or summarized data? Have you written out the problem?

— Have you discovered a pattern to the problem?

— If stuck, have you done a similar, but easier problem? Have you alternated intense concentration with frequent breaks so you can approach the problem creatively? Have you tried working backwards, completing similar problems, solving small parts?

— Have you corrected problems immediately so you can determine if you make careless errors or do not understand the concepts?

— Have you practiced mathematics as you would any skill that you want to learn? Do you think, apply, do, reflect, and practice?

— Have you sought help at the first sign of trouble?

— Have you been persistent in working on the problem and not expecting a quick and easy answer?

— Have you analyzed the problem? Was your guess close? Did your plan work? How else could you approach the problem?

— Have you rewarded yourself for facing your fears, overcoming anxiety, and learning valuable skills that will increase your success in school, your job, and in life?

4

A. Judy is a returning student. Not only is she going to school part time, she also works full time and has a family. Her husband supports her goal of becoming an accountant, but does little to help her with the children or housework. Her children are 12 and 14 years old and have depended on Judy to help them with their homework, drive them to various activities, clean their rooms, and even bake homemade cookies. Judy prides herself on keeping a spotless house and loves being a mom and wife. However, now that she is in school, she has trouble keeping up with classes, homework, job responsibilities, and housework, let alone finding time for herself. Judy has dropped her early morning exercise, is getting less sleep, and is feeling exhausted and resentful. What would you suggest Judy do to get more control over her life? What strategies in the chapter would be most helpful?

_____

_____

_____

_____

_____

_____

_____

_____

_____

_____

B. Judy is a court reporter. She has always had a very busy schedule, but expected that she would have more free time after she graduated from business school. Instead, she finds she is just as busy as ever. Her children are active in school and she wants to be involved in their activities and school work. Judy is also in two important community organizations, does volunteer work at the local hospital, and is active in her church. Lately, she has found herself late for meetings and rushing through her day.

Because she knows her health is important, Judy promised herself that she would return to a regular exercise program after graduation. So far she has had difficulty finding time for herself. What strategies could you suggest to help Judy gain conrol over her time and her life?

_____

_____

_____

_____

_____

_____

_____

_____

_____

_____

A. Brian is an industrial technology student. He does well in his technical classes, but finds himself getting behind in his report writing and reading for other classes. His basic problem seems to be procrastination. Brian has trouble saying no to friends who stop by to chat or who want him to go to a party. He puts off his reports until the night before they are due, and delays choosing a topic for speech class until the last moment. All of a sudden Brian finds himself hopelessly behind, overwhelmed, and discouraged. He can't wait until he finishes school and has just a job to deal with.

What suggestions would you give Brian to get organized? How can he meet deadlines and take control of his time?

_____

_____

_____

_____

_____

_____

_____

_____

_____

B. Brian is a department head of technology for a plumbing supply company. His life is busier than ever. He has several meetings almost every day, reports to write, presentations to give, and problems to solve. He doesn't know how to deal with the constant flow of interruptions. He often feels behind, frustrated, and rushed. He also has three children, and his wife also works full time. He spends much of his free time, and even some of his work schedule time, attending parent-teacher conferences, athletic games, and taking care of sick children. In addition, he is active in his local Rotary Club and feels that it is important to contribute to his community and to network with other professionals in the business world. Between work, family, and community demands, Brian has little free time. He would like to take computer software classes to add to his effectiveness at work, but doesn't feel he has the time.

What strategies in this chapter would you recommend to Brian to gain control of his life and his time? What would you suggest to get him to control interruptions and to deal with the issue of procrastination?

_____

_____

_____

_____

_____

_____

_____

_____

▲ Exercise 3.1 ASSESSING YOUR TIME LOG

Take a close look at your log. Then fill in the following chart to determine how much time you spend on certain activities. Typical activities are listed here; you may, of course, alter or add activities to the list. Remember, the total number of hours should be about 24.

Activity	Time Spent	Activity	Time Spent
Attending classes	_____	Eating	_____
Work	_____	Sleeping	_____
Commuting	_____	Cooking	_____
Studying	_____	Shopping	_____
Attending meetings	_____	Running errands	_____
Grooming	_____	Socializing	_____
Exercising	_____	Talking on the telephone	_____
Doing household chores	_____	Doing hobbies	_____
Waiting in lines	_____	Watching TV	_____
Other	_____	Other	_____
		TOTAL HOURS	_______

Think over the last few months and reflect on the stress items on the lists below. What items give you the most stress? Indicate the factor of stress on the right.

Stress Performance Test			
Stress Factors	Severe (3)	Moderate (2)	Little (1)
Lack of time to accomplish goals.			
Lack of money.			
Uncomfortable living and study areas.			
Long working hours.			
Boring, uninteresting job.			
Conflict with roommate, family, etc.			
Conflict with instructors, etc.			
Too many demands or responsibilities.			
Deadline pressures.			
Boring classes, irrelevant to goals.			
Too many changes in life.			
Lack of motivation for school.			
Difficulty finding housing.			
Poor grades.			
Parents have set too-high standards and expectations.			
Unclear on goals and priorities.			
Too many interruptions, too noisy to study.			
Health problems, difficulty sleeping.			
Dependency on alcohol, drugs.			
Too much socializing.			
Lack of career/life goals.			
Speaking/test-taking anxiety.			
Lack of relationships, friends.			
Low self-esteem (feeling I'm not good enough to do what is expected).			

Results

24–36: High Achiever (you have learned how to function effectively under stress).
37–48: Persistent plodder (you handle stress in most situations, but have some difficulty in coping and feel overwhelmed sometimes).
49–60: Stress walker (you have frequent feelings of being overwhelmed and exhausted, and it affects your performance).
Over 60: Burnout disaster (you need help coping—stress is taking its toll on your health and emotions and you are facing real burnout).

▲ TIME MANAGEMENT STRATEGIES ▲

1. *Take time to plan and set priorities.*

2. *Manage your life in sync with your left- and right-brain style.*

3. *Study during "down time."*

4. *Study in short segments throughout the day.*

5. *Break projects down.*

6. *Consolidate similar tasks.*

7. *Delegate.*

8. *Be flexible.*

9. *Just do it!*

CREATIVE PROBLEM SOLVING AND CRITICAL THINKING

"A problem is a picture with a piece missing; the answer is the missing piece."

John Holt, educator and author

"Take time to make creative and sound decisions. A rushed decision can mean more work and more grief for everyone if it turns out to be a wrong move and you have to undo it."

Josie Natori, president of Natori Company

Learning Objectives

In Chapter Four you will learn:

1. The importance of creativity in problem solving and decision making.

2. Strategies to enhance creativity.

3. The importance of critical thinking.

4. Strategies to improve critical thinking.

5. Strategies for problem solving and decision making.

Have you ever noticed how people are obsessed with finding the "right" answer to questions? Perhaps this is why quiz shows and parlor games are such popular entertainment. However, real-life decisions are often not clear cut, and there is not usually one absolutely right answer to a particular problem.

Solving problems and making decisions are part of life. Let's approach problem solving and decision making as a climber approaches a difficult mountain. A mountain climber is faced with problems and decisions at every level of the climb: which mountain to climb, what equipment to take, what team to put together, whether the weather and timing are right, whether the skills and training are adequate for the challenge, what alternate routes are available, how to proceed on difficult terrain, and so on. Similarly, students face many day-to-day decisions and problems: which courses to take, how to find a job, where to live, how to resolve problems with roommates, choices about alcohol or drugs, and how to generate creative ideas for speeches and papers. Making sound decisions and solving problems are important skills for school, career, and life.

When an experienced climber gets stymied by a difficult climb, creativity and critical thinking are available. A climber also knows how important it is to guard against wishful thinking, faulty perception, and other fallacies. When you get stuck or are overwhelmed by the problems facing you, you can draw upon the same creative resources and critical thinking methods to expand your awareness and open up new possibilities and alternatives. In this chapter, you will learn to use creativity and critical thinking to help make effective decisions and solve problems. You will also learn to see alternatives instead of searching for the absolute answer, to imagine the consequences for each decision, and to weigh the risks involved in each choice. Effective decision making and problem solving are essential skills that use sound judgment, personal responsibility, and creativity. We'll explore how to be more creative by integrating play into your lives, your work, and your studying.

USING CREATIVITY TO ENHANCE DECISION MAKING AND HELP SOLVE PROBLEMS

Successful people have an abundance of inventiveness and imagination. They tend to get very involved in the task at hand and are totally absorbed in the moment. They are almost childlike in their vitality, curiosity, and enthusiasm. In fact, observe how creative and expressive children are. They seem to have boundless energy to explore, search, and dream, and are passionate in their approach to

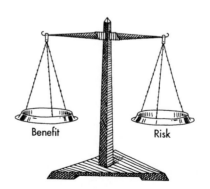

Benefit   Risk

the serious business of play. We are all born creative. That is, we all start life with the ability to think about objects and situations in original and creative ways. Unfortunately, for many people, growing up meant learning to "stop acting foolish" and learning to "act your age." Thus, one of the first steps in unlocking your natural creativity is to realize that you have control over your thinking—it doesn't control you.

Creativity is coming up with something different; using new approaches for solving problems. Roger von Oech, founder and president of Creative Think, is a well-known creativity consultant. He contends that as we grow up, we often lose a lot of our willingness to be creative. In a sense, your attitudes form mental blocks that keep you from being creative. If you find yourself imprisoned by routines, afraid to look foolish, and reluctant to challenge the rules or allow failure, you may be in a rut. Before long, you may abandon your dreams, ignore your intuition, deny problems, and follow the practical, safe, no-risk path. Can you change your perspective and learn to unlock the natural innovation that you had as a child? Researchers say yes, and indicate that most people use only about 10 percent of their brain's potential. The studies also indicate that there is almost no limit to what the brain is capable of.

One thing is certain. It is much easier to make decisions and solve problems in a creative climate where ideas are welcomed than in an environment that won't tolerate failure or divergent approaches to decision making. Many inventions involved a breakthrough in traditional thinking and resulted in an "Aha" experience. Buckminster Fuller experimented with shapes until he invented the geodesic dome. Einstein broke with tradition, tried many unusual approaches, and, as a result, revolutionized thought. You will find that you too can solve problems and make decisions more creatively once you use your imagination. Problem solving and decision making become more effective when you discipline your mind to see events and people in fresh ways, explore new ideas, and look for relationships between seemingly unrelated events. Try the following strategies to unlock your mind's natural creativity.

STRATEGIES TO ENCOURAGE CREATIVITY

1. Use Creative Games, Puzzles, and Humor. Reframing an assignment as a puzzle, a challenge, or a game instead of a difficult problem allows an open frame of mind and encourages your creative side to operate. There is a myth that school should be hard, serious work and that difficult tasks shouldn't be fun. Creative people know that they often get fresh ideas when they are having fun and performing an unrelated activity. When your defenses are down, your brain is relaxed, and your subconscious is alive, creative thoughts can flow. Children spend much of the day playing and turn even routine jobs into a game. Approach your studying in this same way. Turn problems into puzzles to be solved.

2. Challenge the Rules. Habit often restricts you from trying new approaches to problem solving. There is more than one solution and often more than one right answer. Develop the approach of listing many alternatives, choices, and solutions and imagine the likely consequences of each. Empty your mind of the "right" way of looking at a problem and strive to see situations in a new, fresh way. How many times have you told yourself that you must follow certain rules and do things a certain way? If you want to be creative, you must try new approaches, look at things in a new order, break the pattern, and challenge

▲ SHIFTING YOUR PERCEPTION

▲ Describe what you see in the picture here. Do you see an attractive young woman or an old woman with a hooked nose? Most people see the young woman. Once they see the young woman it is very hard to see the old woman. It is really difficult to see another frame of reference once your mind is set. This is one of these "Aha" exercises. It is exciting to experience the light that goes on when people really "see" the other picture. There is enormous power in shifting your perception and gaining a new way of seeing things, events, and people. Perceptual exercises of this kind clearly demonstrate that we see what we focus on. You are conditioned to see certain things, depending upon beliefs and attitudes. Rather than seeing "the facts," you see your interpretation of reality. Perceptual distortion can influence how you solve problems and make decisions. To do so effectively, you will need to see things objectively, not through perceptual filters.

the rules. In the movie *Star Trek II,* Captain Kirk solves a problem by refusing to follow the rules. Faced with a no-win decision, he rewrites the program that allows him to win.

Try your hand at challenging the rules by completing the nine dot exercise. Connect the following nine dots by drawing only four straight lines (or fewer, if you can). Do not retrace any lines and don't lift the pencil from the paper. Don't give up too quickly. (Answer is on page 102.)

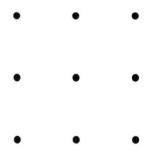

Your previous experiences may have influenced your expectations with how the problem was to be solved. You probably assumed that you had to stay within the square. How else could you solve this problem?

3. Brainstorm. Brainstorming is a common creativity-enhancing strategy that opens up the imagination. Using this strategy, a group throws out many ideas for papers and speeches and many answers to test questions. Brainstorming encourages the mind to explore new approaches. It does this by encouraging even silly and irrelevant ideas. While brainstorming ideas for a speech, one study group started making jokes about the topic, and new ideas came from all directions. Again, humor generates ideas, puts you in a creative state of mind, and can make work fun. There is much in life that is not logical or practical. The brain processes information, but it also stores memories and experiences, makes comparisons and contrasts, and uses analogies and metaphors to gain a better understanding. Play the game "What if . . ." with your study team.

Top executives, scientists, doctors, and artists know that they can extend the boundaries of the known by allowing themselves to probe and unfreeze their limits. They ask, what if? In the 1950s the United States was building faster and faster military jets and investigating what would happen when the jets went fast enough to break the sound barrier. Test pilots such as Chuck Yeager, made famous in Tom Wolfe's book (and Phillip Kaufman's subsequent movie) *The Right Stuff,* called it "pushing the envelope."

4. Change Your Routine. Go to work a different way. Order new foods. Read different kinds of books. Become totally involved in a project. Stay in bed and read all day. Spend time with people who are very different from you. In other words, break away occasionally from your daily routine and take time every day to relax, daydream, putter, and renew your energy.

Look at unexpected events as an opportunity to retreat from constant activity and hurried thoughts. Perhaps this is a good time to brainstorm ideas for your speech or outline your paper. Many creative people need an incubation period in which ideas have time to develop. Occasionally, flow with the disruption that unexpected experiences bring and joyously welcome these gifts of time, space, and a break in routine.

5. Allow Failure. We learn early in school not to make mistakes and to avoid failure. Fear of failure undermines the creative process by making us play safe. Creative people know that if they don't fail occasionally, they are not risking. Mistakes are stepping stones to growth and creativity. When you take away the fear and shame of failure, you will learn to joyously admit mistakes. Look at mistakes as stepping stones and opportunities for growth. Ask yourself, "What did I learn from this mistake? Did I jump into this venture too quickly? Did I overlook obvious concerns? Was I inattentive to important detail?"

Also don't be afraid to look foolish occasionally. Creative people aren't afraid to look foolish at times, to generate unusual ideas, and to be nonconformists. They tend not to take themselves too seriously. Being creative has a lot to do with risk taking and courage. It takes courage to explore new ways of thinking, to risk looking different, foolish, impractical, and even wrong.

6. Expect to Be Creative. If you think you are a noncreative person, you will act like one. Just look at the excuses you come up with for why you don't study or accomplish projects you say you want to. You *have* to be a creative person to make up such original and diverse justifications! Everyone is creative and inventive. See yourself as a creative person and take full responsibility for being an innovative and positive person. In other words, don't blame others for holding you back. Use affirmations that reinforce your creative nature:

I am a creative and resourceful person.

I have many imaginative and unusual ideas.

Creative ideas flow to me many times a day.

I live creatively in the present.

I act upon many of these ideas.

When in the action stage, I act responsibly, use critical thinking, check details carefully, and take calculated risks.

7. Support, Acknowledge, and Reward Creativity. Reward enthusiasm, new ideas, and creative approaches. Plato's advice "What is honored in a country will be cultivated there," is just as true today as it was over 2,000 years ago. If you honor new ideas, they will grow. Get excited about new ideas and approaches and acknowledge and reward yourself and others for creative ideas. Give yourself many opportunities to get involved with projects that stretch you and encourage you to explore and be creative. Monitor your daily life as well. How often do you put your creative ideas into action? Are there certain things

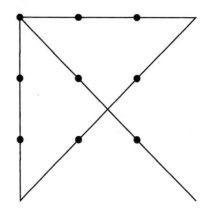

you want to change but keep putting off? What new hobby or skill have you wanted to try? If you find yourself getting lazy, set a firm deadline to complete a specific project. If you find yourself running frantically, then take an hour or so to review your life's goals, review the big picture, and set new priorities. If you are feeling shy and inhibited, clear some time to socialize and risk meeting new people. Reward your creativity and risk taking by acknowledging it. Of course, the biggest reward of all is to see yourself grow.

8. Use Both Sides of the Brain. You use the logical, analytical side of your brain for certain activities and your imaginative and multidimensional side for other activities. When you develop and integrate both the left and the right sides of your brain, you become more imaginative, creative, and productive. Learn to be attentive to details and to trust intuition. Don't force yourself to work in a straight, logical mode; allow yourself to wander, explore, and piece together patterns.

Mapping is one way of using both sides of the brain. When you have an idea, sketch it on a piece of paper, using subtopics, color, and drawings. This can help you break out of rigid thinking patterns and open up your imagination. It produces a creative way of thinking by stimulating associations. This gives abstract ideas a concrete focus and allows you to see the interrelationship between ideas.

9. Keep a Journal. A journal is a great way to catch the beginnings of creative thought. Keep a journal of creative ideas, dreams, and thoughts and make a commitment to complete journal entries in this book. Explore the first stirrings of a new idea and jot it down to develop and explore later. Get to know your colorful, expressive, and imaginative self. Write down dreams, draw pictures, and include jokes and cartoons. A journal will help you shape your thoughts and take action. Make time for writing, for reflecting, and for recording creative hunches. Collect stories of creative people. Write in your journal about the risks you take and the ideas you have that are imaginative and different.

The Critical Thinking Connection

Stating the problem clearly, exploring alternatives, reasoning logically, choosing the best alternative, creating an action plan, and evaluating your plan are all critical thinking skills involved in making decisions and solving problems. Use critical thinking to answer the following questions. Be prepared to discuss your answers in your teams.

▲ CREATIVE IDEAS CHECKLIST

▲ Use a Creative Ideas Checklist to challenge usual thought patterns. A list can free the thinking process and help generate fresh ideas. When exploring alternative approaches to problem solving, you can put each category on separate cards. For example:

- ▲ What other idea does this suggest?
- ▲ How can I modify?
- ▲ What can I subtract?
- ▲ What can I streamline?
- ▲ What can I rearrange?
- ▲ Can I combine, or blend?
- ▲ What are other uses if modified?
- ▲ What could I model?
- ▲ Can I use another approach?
- ▲ Can I interchange components?
- ▲ How about opposites?
- ▲ What are the positives and negatives?

1. Describe a recent time when you were creative. What did you do? Do you consider yourself to be a creative person? Explain.

2. Where were you when you came up with your last creative idea?

3. Look at the common reasons and excuses that some students use for not solving problems creatively or making sound decisions. Add to this list and use creative problem solving to list strategies for overcoming these barriers.

Reasons   **Strategies**

I'm not a creative person.

Facts can be misleading. I like to follow my emotions.

I avoid conflict.

I postpone making decisions.

I worry that I'll make the wrong decision.

I let time take care of my problems or decisions.

My mind is made up from past experience.

_____

_____

_____

_____

CRITICAL THINKING

In his book *How We Think,* John Dewey defined the core of critical thinking as having "healthy skepticism and using suspended judgment." Richard Paul, in his book *Critical Thinking,* describes a critical thinker as someone who "not only explores alien, potentially threatening viewpoints, but . . . also desires to do so." Critical thinking, then, is not just a skill to help us learn to analyze, criticize, and reason inductively and deductively to reach sound, factual decisions. It is also an attitude; a willingness and passion to explore, probe, and search out answers and solutions. Shallow, illogical, and biased thinking is a major barrier to sound decision making and problem solving. As a student you are well aware of daily struggles with problems, issues, and decisions, and these challenges continue on the job. As a career professional, you will be valued if you can examine, question, analyze, and struggle with real problems to come up with creative solutions. School is an excellent opportunity for you to become a truly educated person—a critical thinker. It is living, as Socrates urged, "an examined life."

As children, we had a natural curiosity about life. With great diligence and desire we learned to speak, explored the environment, and asked "why" and "how" hundreds of times. Children have an innate ability to think, categorize, and solve problems. Unfortunately, by the time students reach high school, many have stopped discovering, exploring, or questioning, and simply remain silent rather than risk being wrong or embarrassed. As a result, too many of us cling to our cherished beliefs and points of view and refuse to put them to critical scrutiny. It is easy to become mentally lazy, and thus confuse facts with opinions or beliefs. Illogical thinking plays a big part in drug and alcohol abuse, child abuse, eating disorders, sexual problems, miscommunication, and failing classes. It is easy to rationalize or justify our beliefs or behaviors with attitudes like "Well, that is my point of view and it is just as valid as yours."

Attributes of a Critical Thinker

— A willingness to ask pertinent questions and assess statements and arguments.
— The ability to suspend judgment and tolerate ambiguity.
— Enough humility and confidence to admit a lack of information or understanding.
— A sense of curiosity and an interest in seeking new solutions.
— An ability to clearly define a set of criteria for analyzing ideas.
— A willingness to examine beliefs, assumptions, and opinions against facts.
— An ability to listen carefully to others and give appropriate feedback.
— An ability to see critical thinking as a lifelong process of self-assessment.

Shallow, illogical, and biased thinking is a major barrier to sound decision making and problem solving. There is the tendency to confuse facts with opinions or beliefs. Illogical thinking plays a big part in drug and alcohol abuse, child abuse, eating disorders, sexual problems, miscommunication, and failing coursework. Critical thinking is purposeful, conscientious, and logical. It is creative in that it explores many options rather than settling for a few obvious ideas. Critical thinking and creativity go hand in hand as tools for decision making and problem solving.

Critical thinking and creativity have a lot to do with perception and attitude. In fact, your attitude as you approach a problem or decision, to a large degree, determines the outcome. There's an old saying, "If I hadn't seen it, I wouldn't have believed it." Based on research involving perception, perhaps a truer statement would be, "If I hadn't believed it, I never would have seen it." We all see things differently, and the way we perceive events is based on our values, beliefs, and attitudes. In *The Road Less Traveled,* Scott Peck writes ". . . we all have mental maps of how we see the world, and some of our maps have not altered for years and no longer serve our best interest. They don't represent the territory but are a subjective view of how we see the territory." Faulty perception can lead to errors in judgment, rationalization, illogical decisions, and ineffective problem solving.

As you can see, critical thinking is not just an idealistic, abstract perspective, but a learned skill that we can use in school, our jobs, and every aspect of our lives. It involves continuous self-assessment of our thoughts, beliefs, attitudes, and behavior. Critical thinking can make us better listeners and enhance our reading, note-taking, test-taking, memory, writing, and speaking skills. It can help make sense of our classes, jobs, relationships, and the world around us.

One of the best ways to promote critical thinking is to allow space, silence, and time for reflection. Journal writing encourages quiet pondering and self-assessment. As John Dewey said years ago, "All reflection involves . . . stopping external observations and reactions so that an idea may mature."

LINKING PROBLEM SOLVING AND DECISION MAKING

When things go wrong, people generally react in one of three ways: (1) they blame other people, (2) they throw up their hands in despair, or (3) they face the problem squarely and solve it. All problem solving involves decision making; that is, you have to make decisions in order to solve the problem. In addition, some problems are a result of the decisions that you have made. For example, if you decide to drink alcohol or smoke cigarettes, you may later face the problem of addiction. If you decide to drive even though you have been drinking, you may create a serious, life-and-death problem. So you can see that many of your problems do not just "happen" but are the result of your choices and decisions.

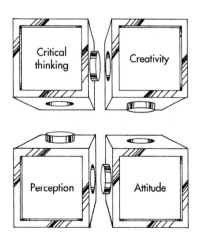

- ▲ **Stereotypes** are judgments and overgeneralizations about a person based on the observations of the group. For example: All instructors are absent-minded intellectuals and wear tweed jackets. Learn to see individual differences between people and situations.

- ▲ **Snap judgments** are decisions made before information or facts are gathered. Too often people attempt to solve a problem before it is even determined exactly what the problem is.

- ▲ **Unwarranted assumptions** are beliefs and ideas that are taken for granted: My business instructor allows papers to be turned in late, so I assume that my real estate instructor will allow the same thing.

- ▲ **The halo effect** is the tendency to label a person good at many things based upon one or two qualities: Serena sits in the front row, attends every class, and gets good grades on papers. I bet she is really smart, organized, nice, and a great student in all her classes.

- ▲ **Projection** is the tendency to attribute to others some of our own traits: Everyone else cheats on their tests, so why shouldn't I?

Even though problems and decisions are a part of everyday life, many people have trouble making decisions. They agonize, worry, and fret that the wrong decision will forever ruin their lives and deprive them of all the good things in life. Others spend little time thinking through decisions, preferring to make quick, spur-of-the-moment decisions based upon immediate needs and desires. Still others prefer to avoid making decisions by hoping the problems will go away. Making effective decisions, however, requires that you clarify the nature and causes of the problem before you decide on an alternative solution to it. At other times, decision making involves choosing among a number of alternatives or opportunities. For example, should I take Retail 101 or Financing 112? Should I go to a business college or a community college? Should I have corn flakes or a bran muffin for breakfast? Every day we make a number of minor and important decisions, and some days, problems and decisions seem overwhelming and endless.

Peak performers don't have fewer problems than other people, they simply choose to face problems directly and solve them in a creative and effective way. They accept that decisions are a part of life. They have learned to use good judgment, anticipate outcomes, weigh the risk, look ahead, and take full responsibility for the consequences of their decisions. You, too, can learn to solve problems effectively.

The following is a modification of the widely followed 12-step system, or logical approach, to problem solving. It is far more effective to follow a systematic approach to problem solving than to let emotions filter your judgment and cloud your thinking. Use your creativity at each step to explore alternatives, look for relationships among different items, and develop imaginative ideas and solutions. Use critical thinking skills to raise questions, separate facts from opinions, develop reasonable solutions, and avoid self-deception.

1. Identify the Problem

The way you perceive a problem defines the problem. Just as a rock climber sizes up the territory, you can think about the problem from several different angles before you start making decisions. It is important to be as specific as possible about what the problem is. Ask yourself: is there a core belief that affects the way I see this problem? Am I blaming the other person based on past events or perceived hurts? How can I see the problem more clearly? Whose problem is this? Is it necessary to make a decision at this time? Am I creating a problem where none exists?

Part of identifying and clarifying the problem is to determine whose problem it is. Sometimes people get involved with other people's problems or make decisions that are not required. Distinguish between your responsibilities and unnecessary involvement. You own the problem if the situation interferes with your needs or happiness. It is important to take responsibility for your own problems and realize that you have the wisdom and power to make effective decisions.

To identify the problem clearly, *state the problem in one or two sentences.* Be as specific about the problem as possible. For example, instead of saying, "I'm disappointed about my grade," say, "I received a B– on my paralegal paper. I think I deserve an A."

2. Gather Information

The next step is to make certain that you have all the necessary information to solve the problem. Don't go off the deep end and flare up in anger or make a snap decision. Use critical thinking to uncover objective information that is relevant to your problem. Is there anyone else that this problem affects? Do you know how others perceive the problem? Should you consult with them before you gather more information? Clarify your aim. What is the purpose of this problem? What is it you want to accomplish? Is your intent improved communication, peace, conflict, or resolution? Whose problem is this? Who is responsible for it? Who is involved in this problem? How do you feel about the problem? Is there a time limit?

Critical thinking is required to see the situation as it really is and not how you think it is or wish it would be. Too many students drop out of school, quit jobs, and sever relationships because they acted in haste, wrongly defined the problem, had insufficient information, or came up with a snap solution. For example, "this is my problem because I am the one responsible for my education. My instructor is also involved. I think it is an A paper, but if I want a higher grade, I must own up to the problem and take the first step. I will read the directions again, review the comments on the paper, and see if I can determine what I did wrong."

3. Take Action

Many people have the tendency to allow procrastination, mental laziness, and the need for a quick fix to undermine their ability to solve problems. As with many things in life, perseverance, discipline, and the ability to delay gratification is imperative if you are to solve problems effectively. Rather than take the time necessary to work through problems, you may be tempted to sulk, blame, become frustrated or angry, or ignore the problem and hope it will go away. Problem solving requires action. Problems do not just go away. It doesn't help to wish things were different. Everything is the way it is and wishing it were different does not help. The mark of a healthy person is the ability to take full responsibility for confronting problems and working through them.

Take action by developing solutions to the problem. Brainstorm lots of creative alternatives. These may include doing nothing, removing the problem, finding a way around the problem, or changing the objective. For example, "I have several options in dealing with this problem. I could just forget it. I could just study harder and do a better job on the next paper. I could give the instructor a scathing teaching evaluation or go see the department chair. I could talk to other students and see if they think the instructor is too hard. I could drop out of school. I could join the Peace Corps. Or I could go and talk with my instructor." Again, use critical thinking to avoid illogical thinking.

4. Have a Positive Attitude

Your attitude has a lot to do with how you approach and solve a problem or make a decision. Approach problem solving and decision making with a positive viewpoint. You can reframe the problem and see the positive qualities in a person or situation rather than focus on the negative. Negative thoughts trigger emotions, and you may overreact to a situation when you are imagining the worst. Stop for a moment and observe your thoughts. Are they based on the reality of the moment or on the past? Are your feelings a result of the problem, or are they a symptom of something deeper? Are you jumping to conclusions or making false assumptions? As you observe your thoughts and emotions, you may see that you misinterpret or exaggerate another person's behavior or assume that it is offensive. This can cause a negative view of the situation, and you draw in every past offense to add weight and justify your interpretation and behavior. When you become angry or confused, take time out to think through the situation. Ask yourself: What is my intent? What is it I want to accomplish? Do I want to prove I am right? What deep meaning do I attach to this behavior? Am I choosing to look at this in a negative way? Sometimes it is these automatic negative thoughts that trigger emotions, not the situation itself or the person. If you are upset, it may influence your ability to think clearly. For example, "At first I was really angry, confused, and frustrated at my instructor for giving me a B. I put a lot of time into this paper. I worked very hard on the paper and felt that the directions were unclear. Now that I have thought it through, I realize that I'm actually angry at myself. I'm disappointed that I didn't read the instructions over again or ask for clarification. I am also having problems with my roommate, so it seems as if everyone is picking on me."

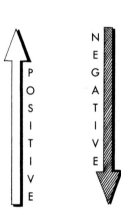

When you are upset, you might try sleeping on the issues and asking for guidance in your dreams. Your subconscious mind never sleeps, and many people work out their decisions while they sleep. In addition, everything looks brighter and clearer after a good night's sleep.

5. State the Consequences of Alternatives

This is a very important step. Before actually choosing an alternative, you would do well to consider the likely consequence of each alternative. Some alternatives may create more problems than they solve. For example, "I could just forget the B grade on my paper, but then nothing would happen. If I see the instructor, I will know exactly what I can do to improve my paper and have a clearer understanding of expectations. The best case: I may get an opportunity to redo the paper for a higher grade or do extra-credit work and still earn an A−. The worst case is that I would not be allowed to redo the paper or do extra-credit work."

6. Clarify Your Purpose

Before you select the best alternative, take a moment to review your purpose. In one sentence state your intention. What do you want from the other person or what kind of solution would you like?

You may also find yourself dealing with the same kind of problems over and over again. Has a similar problem occurred before? Certain problems can be anticipated and avoided. For instance, since miscommunication concerning classroom assignments and directions can be expected, reviewing the syllabus carefully, clarifying the assignment with the instructor, asking questions, and talking with your instructor on a regular basis may help resolve many of them. For example, "My intention is to resolve this problem, get a better grade, and understand what I should correct. I want feedback and another chance. I do not want to argue with my instructor, prove I'm right, or get defensive."

7. Select the Best Alternative

After evaluating each of the alternatives, anticipating the likely consequences, and clarifying your purpose, it is time to select the best one. Use critical thinking to choose the alternative most likely to help you reach your objectives. Which solution seems best for this particular case? Be careful that you don't just react as you have to similar situations or choose solutions because they have worked for friends. Each situation is different, and you must be prepared for contingencies should you have to alter your choice. For example, "Having the courage to be assertive with my instructor is the best choice. I want the instructor to tell me specifically why I was given a B − on this paper and what I could do to earn an A −."

8. Review the Pros and Cons of the Best Alternative

Take a moment to review the positive and negative consequences of the best alternative. You might try listing the pros and cons of the top alternative in a form like the one on page 110. Draw a line down the middle of a paper. List all the opportunities that this choice would bring. Ask, what are the advantages of this choice? What are the disadvantages? For example, "I will receive valuable information that will help me in this class and others. I will have better expectations of what is required, and I will have created a common ground for effective communication between my instructor and me. I will have tested my courage and assertive communication skills. The negative consequences for this solution are embarrassment, fear, and time. I may worry, fret, and be stressed at the thought of having to confront my instructor. I might be too forward, get angry, and even say something I'll regret. It also may be a waste of time and energy that could be better spent in studying."

9. Use a Decision Tree

A decision-making tree, (an example is shown on page 111), can be most helpful in illustrating various decision points that you may face when solving problems, and the possible consequences of each choice. In the business world, a decision tree is often used as an effective graphic tool for helping people make choices and decisions. You can see the alternatives and possible outcomes of your decision. From beginning to end, you must use your best judgment, and no one solution is usually the best for everyone. However, your probability of choosing the best solution for you may be enhanced if you use a systematic method such as a decision tree. For example, see the accompanying decision tree.

10. Act on the Best Alternative

At this point, make the best choice that you can, and put all your energics into making it work. There are few things in life that are irreversible (having a child is one of them), and you can almost always choose again. Once you make a deci-

PROS	CONS
Consequences	Consequences
Risk	Risk

sion, do everything you can to make it work. What details need your attention? What can you do to make this decision a success? What attitude will help you accomplish your purpose? List the steps that need to be taken. For example, "I will make an appointment to see my instructor this week. I will be calm, centered, confident, and straightforward. I will not be defensive, and I will listen carefully to what is said. I will ask for clarification and specific information. I will be assertive and respectful."

11. Use Critical Thinking

Use critical thinking and avoid the common stance of "Don't confuse me with the facts. I already have my mind made up." At this point, stop and ask yourself if you are using critical thinking to evaluate alternatives, consequences, feelings, and actions. Critical thinking is a logical, controlled, and disciplined mental activity. Can you support your plan of action based on logical thinking? Have you fallen into faulty perceptual traps or common fallacies? Daydreaming, rationalization, and clinging to illogical beliefs are all examples of shallow, illogical thinking. Critical thinking is based on reality, not your interpretation of reality. Question your beliefs and assumptions. What are your opinions based on? Seek additional information, evidence, and other viewpoints, and make a reasonable decision in light of that evidence. Critical thinking means you can support your conclusion. By using critical thinking, you can prevent many decisions from becoming problems. For example, "Instructors are all alike. They love to trick students and don't want to answer questions. Besides, my instructor didn't review the guidelines for the paper, which shows thoughtlessness and disorganization. It's useless for me to try and work this out." Instead, try seeing things as they are: "My instructor is a reasonable person. I am a serious and committed student. I have the skills and confidence to discuss the paper and redo it for a better grade."

12. Evaluate

The problem-solving script is not complete until you follow up and consider if your actions helped you to accomplish your objectives. Examine the objectives, the situation, and the results of your action. If your objectives were not met, modify and adjust your actions. For example, "I resolved the problem by seeing my instructor and getting feedback. The session was most helpful. I received an A on the revised paper, I learned a lot, and I have a better relationship with my instructor."

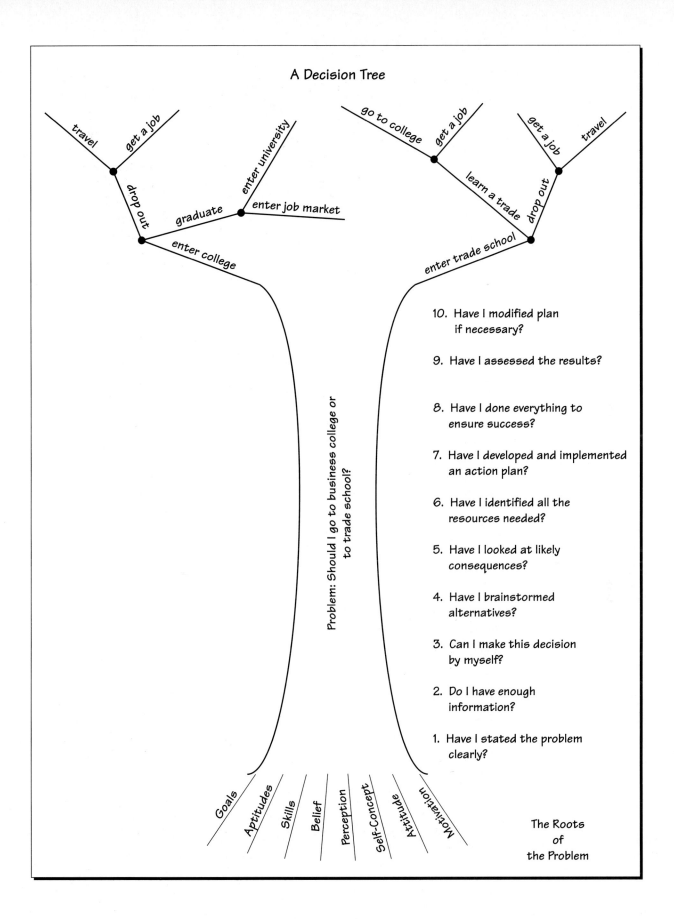

A Decision Tree

travel
get a job
drop out
enter university
graduate
enter job market
enter college

go to college
get a job
learn a trade
get a job
travel
drop out
enter trade school

Problem: Should I go to business college or to trade school?

10. Have I modified plan if necessary?

9. Have I assessed the results?

8. Have I done everything to ensure success?

7. Have I developed and implemented an action plan?

6. Have I identified all the resources needed?

5. Have I looked at likely consequences?

4. Have I brainstormed alternatives?

3. Can I make this decision by myself?

2. Do I have enough information?

1. Have I stated the problem clearly?

Goals
Aptitudes
Skills
Belief
Perception
Self-Concept
Attitude
Motivation

The Roots of the Problem

CAREER FOCUS

FOCUS ON CREATIVITY

Creativity is a trait often associated with artists, writers, and performers. We can all see how important creativity is for a cartoon writer or a standup comedian, but it is also important in most jobs. Fast-food workers are creative when they come up with new ways to be efficient and have an edge on a competitive industry. Manufacturers are creative when they raise productivity and reduce costs. Salespeople are creative when they design ways to increase customer satisfaction and increase sales. Creativity is exploring different alternatives to make decisions and solve problems.

Creativity is, of course, a valuable job skill. Too often employees fall into the "We've always done it this way" trap, which leads to burnout and negative thinking. The employee who is able to see situations and problems in a fresh way, explore many alternatives and options, and come up with innovative ideas and thoughts is certain to be sought after and promoted.

Let's look at one approach to creative problem solving in the job. John Knowles, an assistant manager at a pizza parlor, realizes that competition is stiff and many small pizza businesses are failing. He considers what extra touches his business could offer while maintaining a good profit. Since the business is located in a college town, John has decided to create a college night, when both movies will be shown and popcorn will be offered free at the restaurant. Saturday, he will feature special movies and prizes for small children. There will also be a special senior's night, when he will show old movies.

After a few weeks, John's scheme has worked superbly. With a little creativity, his business now makes a bigger profit and keeps customers interested and loyal.

John also uses creativity and brainstorming to solve workload issues. His staff agrees that production and service cannot be kept at a high level unless additional work hours are added to the regular schedule. Should John hire new employees, or ask regular employees to work overtime? An example of his brainstorming notes are shown below.

▲

Production Department			July 17, 1995
Brainstorming Session			
Problem: Should we hire temporary employees or increase overtime			
of our regular employees to meet new production schedule?			
Ideas	Evaluation	Plus + or Minus –	Selection
hire temp. employees	may lack training	–	1. hire temps
	additional benefit	–	
Work regular employees			
overtime	may result in fatigue	–	
	Extra $ for employees	+	
	possible advancement	+	
	save overhead/benefits	+	
turn down contract	not possible		2. work overtime
reduce hours store is open	not feasible		explore further
reduce product line	not acceptable		

GRID 4.1
Preparing for Critical Thinking

Brainstorm alternative approaches and solutions to the problems that come up in your day-to-day activities. By using critical thinking, you will be able to explore new ideas.

Issue/Problem

Criteria

	Benefits	Limitations	Consequences	Costs	Timing
Alternative A					
Alternative B					
Alternative C					
Alternative D					
Alternative E					

GRID 4.2
Overcoming Barriers to Creativity

Keep an ongoing list of what gets in the way of creative thinking and how you can overcome these barriers. A few examples are shown to get you started.

Creativity Builders	Creativity Stoppers
Bright colors Music Creative, fun people	Fear Worry People who say, "you act silly."

A. Craig has just graduated from high school and wants to decide between two alternatives: (1) business college or (2) trade school. Suppose Craig decides to go to business college. There are certain events that are likely to occur: (1) he may graduate, or (2) he may drop out. He will then be faced with additional decisions. If he graduates, he may go on to graduate school to get an MBA, or he may get a job.

1. Using the decision tree as a guide, write out the consequences of Craig's choices if he decides to go to trade school instead of college. What are the likely consequences of this decision?

2. What other strategies in this chapter would you suggest to Craig to help him make creative, logical decisions?

_____

_____

_____

_____

_____

_____

_____

_____

_____

B. Craig is a manager in a small electronics business. He went to trade school and became an electrician, and now is taking evening classes toward a business degree. Craig is keenly interested in the the electronics field and loves to solve problems. He has received promotions quickly, but knows that he needs further training. Since he is faced with daily issues to solve and decisions to make, he is getting practice predicting consequences and using critical thinking for making sound decisions. When he received his last promotion, Craig knew he needed to make a major decision about school and work. Should he take a semester's leave from his night classes and enroll at the nearby university that also offers an MBA, or continue going to school in the evening at the local college? What strategies in this chapter could Craig use to help him make a sound decision? What problems may he encounter with each alternative? How would you suggest that he solve this problem?

_____

_____

_____

_____

_____

_____

_____

_____

_____

A. José is a computer student at a career school. He takes a full load of classes, and works full time as well. He could handle this during his first year, but now he has more demanding classes and a valuable internship. José faces a decision. Should he stay in school full time, really concentrate on getting good grades, and give his all to the internship? This would mean he would have to reduce his work hours or work on campus as a work-study student. Or should he go to school part time and continue to work full time? Going to school full time would get him out into the work force earlier, but he really needs the money for a car, clothes, and social expenses. If he only worked part time on campus, he could sell his car and take the bus.

What suggestions could you give José that would help him make a sound decision?

_____

_____

_____

_____

_____

_____

_____

B. José had one of the most outstanding sales records ever achieved at a small computer company. Two years ago he founded a small computer firm of his own. Now he has to decide if he should expand or streamline his product line. If he is to serve the needs of local businesses and colleges, he must diversify. If José expands his company, he will need to add more staff and move to a larger building. Most of his employees like the small and informal atmosphere of the small company. He would have to establish new work patterns and perhaps deal with lower morale.

What suggestions would you offer to help José make a sound decision based on critical thinking? What problem-solving strategies from this chapter would help José?

_____

_____

_____

_____

_____

_____

_____

_____

▲ Exercise 4.1   Get Involved

1. Using a decision tree as a guide, work through a problem you are having at this time. Go through each step and determine how you can best resolve the problem.

2. Choose a controversial topic, such as abortion, saving the environment, or affirmative action. Write a one- or two-sentence thesis that supports your viewpoint. Examine and test your beliefs using critical thinking strategies. Are there other ways to look at the issue?

▲ Exercise 4.2   Get Creative

1. Give each group a cup or saucer. You are to brainstorm all the possible uses of the cup or saucer. One person should serve as a recorder and jot down answers. Share your ideas with other groups.

2. Write down a problem for which you want some creative solutions. (Examples: how to get better grades, increase income, meet more friends, get along better with a roommate.) List as many creative solutions as you can. Discuss your solutions in small groups.

▲ PROBLEM-SOLVING STRATEGIES ▲

1. *Identify the problem.*

2. *Gather information.*

3. *Take action.*

4. *Have a positive attitude.*

5. *State the consequences of alternatives.*

6. *Clarify your purpose.*

7. *Select the best alternative.*

8. *Review the pros and cons of the best alternative.*

9. *Use a decision tree.*

10. *Act on the best alternative.*

11. *Use critical thinking.*

12. *Evaluate and modify.*

ACTIVE LISTENING AND NOTE TAKING

"He listens well, who takes notes."
Dante

"I only wish I could find an institute that teaches people how to listen. After all, a good manager needs to listen as much as he needs to talk . . . real communication goes in both directions."
Lee Iacocca, former chairman of Chrysler Corp.

Learning Objectives

In Chapter Five you will learn:

1. The difference between listening and hearing.

2. The importance of listening.

3. Active listening strategies.

4. The connection between listening and note taking.

5. Effective note-taking strategies.

The notebook is an essential item in school. Attending lectures, listening, taking notes, and gathering information are such a daily part of school that few people give much thought to how we best process and record information. Active listening and note taking are not just handy tools for school—they are essential job skills. Throughout your career you will be processing information. We live in a computer age where the volume of new information is exploding, and the career professional who can listen, analyze, record, and remember information will be sought after. Note taking is a way to order and arrange thoughts and material—it saves time in the long run, because it is a way to learn something thoroughly. Essential parts of effective note taking are listening, analyzing, and asking questions. Before you can be an effective note taker, you must become an active listener. Active listening is one of the most valuable skills that you will use in school, in your job, and in relationships. Therefore, this chapter will focus on strategies for being an active listener in all areas of your life. We will then look at ways to highlight main ideas, organize key points, and compare and contrast relationships while taking effective notes.

ACTIVE LISTENING AND HEARING

Most people think of themselves as good listeners. After all, listening to the world around us is the way we all learn new information and assess our skills, behavior, and attitude. Research, however, indicates that most people use less then 25 percent of their listening potential. Listening should not be confused with hearing—unless you have a medical problem, you can "hear" the message, but you may not be "listening" to the intent. Listening, on the other hand, is a mental effort to observe details, be fully attentive, and be in the present. Active listening is a focused, consuming activity that requires energy, concentration, and discipline. Active listening means focusing on the whole message, observing body language, and seeking to understand the intent. As you can see, active listening requires much more than just "hearing" the message.

A good listener is highly valued. Good listeners make good students, friends, roommates, parents, teachers, managers, employees, and co-workers. In fact, think of a person whom you consider a good listener. A name may not just pop in your mind, for good listeners are rare. Once you do have a person in mind, think about your feelings toward this person. Do you like him or her? Most people respond "Yes." It is usually difficult not to like someone whom you consider to be a good listener. Active listening shows respect and caring and is one of the best gifts one person can give another person.

LISTENING AS A LEARNING TOOL

Not only is listening fundamental to taking good classroom notes, but it is directly related to how well you do in school and in your career. As a student, you can spend more than half your waking hours listening. Indeed, listening is a major part of information processing. Students take in information from lectures, books, films, and various visual, verbal, and nonverbal mediums. Career professionals attend meetings, follow directions and orders, take notes from professional journals and lectures, and give and receive feedback. All through our lives, listening continues to be a key in the ongoing assessment process that we begin as infants. By listening to others we get a sense of how we come across, and feedback about our skills, attitude, and behavior. Through listening we assess what information we know and what is new, and then we form associations. We listen to ourselves to gain a sense of who we are and what we want. Therefore, listening is an essential part of self-assessment. Most people agree that listening is important for learning, for improving communication, for assessment, and for taking better notes. Yet few people have been taught how to listen well. Let's begin by looking at ways we can break down the barriers that keep us from being effective listeners and improve the way we sort out, record, and remember information.

ACTIVE LISTENING STRATEGIES

1. Apply Yourself

The first place to start is with your intention. You must want to be a better listener and see listening as an active, rather than a passive, process. The best strategies in the world won't work unless you have the desire to apply them. As we learned in Chapters One and Two, assessing your listening skills and observing your state of mind and your intention are key for improving listening. Effective listening can also prevent rumors and misunderstandings from occurring in school, organizations, and our personal lives. Once you see the value of listening for reducing misunderstanding, gaining information, increasing morale, and processing information, you will want to become a better listener.

2. Be Open

Students sometimes have problems listening to lectures because they already have their minds made up or they want to prove the instructor wrong and mentally challenge everything that is said. If your intention is to prove how smart you are, how wrong the other person is, or to impress, argue, or embarrass the other person, your real purpose will show through. It is easy to misinterpret the meaning of a message if you are defensive, bored, or emotionally upset.

3. Be Alert and in the Present

Paying attention is vital for active listening. It's true that everyone's mind wanders during a long lecture, but being mentally preoccupied is a major barrier to effective listening. It's up to you to focus your attention, concentrate on the subject, have a positive attitude, and bring your mind back to the present. Really look at the instructor and notice the energy, tone, style, and intent of the message.

Notice your thoughts, feelings, internal judgments, and then let go of them while you concentrate on the message. Imagine a picture in your mind of what is being said—increasing your observation and awareness skills are key for becoming an active listener. Observe your own thoughts, your physical and mental states, and the speaker's body language, eye movements, gestures, and choice of words. Every so often, ask yourself, What is the instructor's main point? Listen with empathy and the intention to understand. Active listening requires that you be attentive and live totally in the moment. If you tell yourself that you can read the material later or copy your notes over, you won't be attentive.

4. Postpone Judgment

There is a tendency to judge an instructor's dress, mannerisms, and voice and make assumptions based on these perceptions, or to prejudge an instructor as a result of other students' comments. Don't let your negative judgments about an instructor's appearance or style filter out the positive qualities or turn you off to information and get in the way of your class performance. Be careful that you don't judge your instructor or others based on clothes, reputation, style, voice, and such, or judge the message too quickly. Acknowledging your judgments and letting them go will help you stay tuned to the topic.

5. Be Open to New Information

This step goes hand in hand with postponing judgment. Be aware of the resistance you have to learning new information. Many students resist change, new ideas, or challenged beliefs. This gets in the way of actively listening and learning. Be open to different points of view, different styles of lecturing, and new ideas. If you have a strong disagreement, write it down and clarify it with the instructor after class. Don't challenge the instructor in class or attempt to show that you know more about the subject.

See if you can apply these active listening skills to out-of-class situations. Not only will improved listening heighten your learning at school, you'll probably notice that you'll also learn more from your friends and family. Write a list of daily situations where active listening is a must. Some situations could include talking to your child about his or her day at school, listening to your spouse's views on politics, or meeting with a community group to plan a fundraising event. Hold this list against our active listening tips. Would some of these tips and hints increase your attention and responsiveness in the situations you've listed?

Think of someone you consider thoughtful and receptive. Does he or she appear to be an active and open listener?

6. Predict Questions

Predict what questions your instructor will ask. Since listening is an active process, try getting involved by asking yourself questions as your instructor lectures. Is this story supporting the main topic? What are the main points? How does this example clarify the readings? What questions could be asked of these main points?

Ask your instructor to elaborate or explain certain points if you need it. Jot questions down in your notebook. Unless the lecture is formal, most instructors want you to ask questions. Make certain you have previewed the chapter and done your homework, so that your questions can be thoughtful and you do not ask about material that has already been covered and reviewed. Note what questions you correctly predict.

7. Observe and Pay Attention to Details

A large part of listening and note taking is observing. Observe your instructor and watch for obvious verbal and nonverbal clues as to what information is important. Some clues may be obvious. If your instructor talks a great deal about a concept or gets very involved in the subject matter, it is probably important. If your instructor writes information on the board, pay attention. Overheads or handouts may also include important diagrams, lists, drawings, facts, or definitions.

Watch for questions, examples, and stories, and listen for key words. As well, such phrases as "one important factor is," "in contrast," "don't forget," "furthermore," and "a definition of" are clues that the information is important.

8. Listen for the Intent of the Speaker

Students sometimes jump to conclusions when listening to lectures. Try to weed out extraneous factors (e.g., voice, style, reputation) and focus instead on what the actual message is. Keep on the same train of thought as the speaker until you have really heard the message. Don't jump to conclusions. Listen with understanding. Having a sincere intention of understanding the person speaking can overcome many barriers of communication. Listen to nonverbal messages and what is not being said. "Listen" to the speaker's body language and tone of voice and check to see if they match the message. If not, ask for clarification. For example "Mr. Jones, you said that the section on group dynamics was important for the understanding of group think. Could you clarify the interrelationship between the two topics and give a few examples?"

9. Sit in the Front Row

You will have more energy and create more of a relationship with your instructor if you sit in the front of the class. Sitting in front gives you the feeling that you are actively communicating with your instructor, rather than passively sitting back. Research shows that students who sit up front take better notes and do better in classes. Sitting in the front row makes it easier to hear, see the blackboard and overhead material, and stay alert. You are not likely to doze off, do your homework, be distracted, or talk with your neighbor if you are close to the instructor. You are also more likely to get involved with the class, ask questions, be more interested, and take part in exercises. Finally, by sitting in front, you are able to maintain eye contact with the instructor and be alert to verbal and nonverbal clues.

10. Listen, Don't Talk

Students sometimes talk to other students during lectures or to other team members while their team leader is talking. The fundamental rule of listening is, be quiet while the speaker is talking. As the listener, your role is to decode the sender's message with the sincere intent of comprehension and understanding. The speaker's role is to encode the message with the intent of making the message clear and comprehensible. Don't confuse the two roles. When you are listening, *really* listen until the sender is finished. Don't interrupt to ask questions or talk to a classmate, even to ask for clarification.

11. Show Interest

Act as if you are listening and understanding the message. Sometimes students will sit in the back row, thinking that the instructor will not notice if they are doing homework or dozing and won't call on them for questions. Since they are in a lecture, not engaging in a personal conversation, they don't feel that they have to look at the instructor. Such behavior is passive learning, and is not effective. Instructors can tell who is paying attention and who is not mentally present. Even in a large class, it is important to acknowledge the instructor with good eye contact, nods, and a smile when appropriate.

NOTE TAKING REINFORCES LEARNING

Learning active listening skills will help you develop concentration, attention, and discipline—all of which are key to effective note taking. Now that you have sharpened your listening and observation skills, let's look at the structure and format of your notes. The following strategies can help you record notes that enhance learning and recall. On page 133 you'll see many note taking strategies put into action.

NOTE-TAKING STRATEGIES

1. Integrate Different Learning Styles

Many people view note taking not only as a passive activity, but primarily as an auditory activity. Actually, you will find note taking more effective if you integrate learning styles and use *all* your senses. If you are primarily an auditory learner, listen attentively and capitalize on this style of processing information. You might want to tape certain lectures or recite your book notes into a tape recorder and play it back several times. Explain your notes to your study group so you can hear the material again.

If you are primarily a visual learner, supplement your lectures with drawings, illustrations, and pictures, and take special note of material on the blackboard, overheads, and handouts. Read your notes right after class to reinforce your learning, and compare your notes to material in the textbook. Use imagery to form pictures in your mind.

If you are primarily a kinesthetic, or tactile, learner, you will learn more from writing and rephrasing than from just listening. You may want to leave extra spaces in your notes for samples of material, examples, stories, and diagrams. Use notecards and carry them with you. Summarizing material and working with a study team are also effective modes of learning for the kinesthetic learner.

View note taking as a way to process information that reinforces other ways of taking knowledge in and of making connections with existing knowledge.

2. Summarize—Don't Duplicate—by Focusing on Key Words

The essential element in taking effective notes is to jot down only main points. A common mistake is to attempt to write down everything the instructor says. Listen for and highlight main points, and isolate this information from filler data. If you have prepared for the lecture by previewing the chapter and are listening attentively, you should be able to take accurate notes in your own words that are understandable. Reviewing your textbook chapter first also helps you create a synthesis of the material and may provide helpful examples. Your goal should be a set of clean notes that you can understand and from which you can study.

Practice selecting key words and phrases that link concepts, associate words for recall, and emphasize main ideas. Focus on key words that highlight the main ideas, facts, theories, and comparisons. Illustrations, filler statements, stories, introductions, and transitions are important for depth and interest, but you don't have to write down every detail.

Separate the Essential from the Nonessential. Typically, students take lots of notes, and as much as 90 percent of the words are unnecessary for recall and association. Previewing the chapter before class will allow you to listen for key ideas and understanding, rather than frantically trying to write everything down. Compare your preclass notes with your class notes and fill in details.

3. Organize and Structure Your Notes According to Your Learning Style Preference

Almost no one speaks in an organized manner, not even instructors. Lectures tend to detour from the main points with stories, questions, side comments, explanations, and filler material. That's why it is so important to structure what you hear in an organized manner *that works for you*. You will be most effective if you create a structure that supports your brain dominance.

Use an Outline (Left-Brain Dominance). As we discussed in Chapter One, if you are left-brain dominant you probably feel most comfortable with a traditional outline form for note taking. You like to use this sequential format following the order given by the instructor. This style helps you recall what was said in a lecture and when it was said. The outline form ranks main points and supporting ideas and, thus, forces you to organize them as you write them down. Left-brain dominant people like neat, orderly notes. See page 130 for a sample outline.

Create a Map—Creative Outlining (Right-Brain Dominance).
If you are right-brain dominant, you may naturally feel more comfortable with a creative outline. You can simply divide the paper and use the left side of the paper for key words, illustrations, questions, graphs, definitions, stories, dates, or formulas. Use the right side to take notes. You can also use the creative outline style that is often called mapping. Mapping starts from a key idea placed in the center of a page and branches out with subtopics through association. If you are right-brain dominant, you will find that a mapping format helps you boost your comprehension, creativity, and recall. The main idea is clearly defined and focuses on key words and main ideas. Subpoints are linked to the main concept, and the result is an effective and easy system of note taking and review. The map grows as ideas are developed. Try using different-colored pens for different categories and drawing symbols, illustrations, diagrams, pictures, and any other image that will aid your memory and help you have fun. Mapping provides a mental framework for relating main ideas to associated areas and logically organizes material in a graphic and visual manner. Since it is not sequential, a right-brain person feels less constricted and finds it easy to see the big picture. These notes do not have to include all the main ideas, but can summarize main points, link key points, and show relationships among chapters. You can do one for each chapter and put them all on your bulletin board, or you may want to use a combination of maps and a traditional outline.

A left-brain dominant student may have trouble mapping because the outline is not sequential, it is difficult to get a sense of the instructor's train of thought, there is little space for corrections or additions, and the notes must be shortened to key words and only one page. An option for a left-brain dominant student is to use a map to illustrate the whole chapter, but also use the traditional outline for daily notes. A creative outline is shown in the middle of page 130. A mind map is shown at the top of page 131.

1. Effective strategies for taking notes
   A. The traditional outline for notetaking
      1. Advantages
         a. totally occupies your attention
         b. organizes ideas as well as records them
      2. Disadvantages
         a. too structured for right-brain person
         b. time consuming
   B. The mapping system for notetaking
      1. Advantages
         a. presents a creative and visual model
         b. you can start anywhere on the page
      2. Disadvantages
         a. too busy for a left-brain person

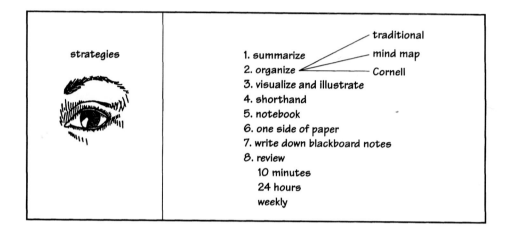

4. Visualize and Illustrate the Material

Form a mental picture of what the speaker is saying. This visual style of learning will enhance the primarily auditory and verbal style of most lectures. Visualize the whole of this subject and associate the image with key words. Draw pictures or diagrams of these key words to help you remember and recall the material. Use your map, diagrams, pictures, drawings, dates, and samples to form a picture in your mind. Use colored pencils, cartoons, and any illustration that adds humor and makes the material come alive.

5. Use Creative Shorthand

Devise your own symbols for note taking. Use whatever is easy for you to remember. Notes are like blueprints, in that they represent a larger subject and they highlight main details. Since it is time consuming to spell out every word, abbreviations and symbols can be effective shortcuts. Examples include:

Symbol	Explanation
>	greater than
<	less than
Q	question
w/	with
w/o	without

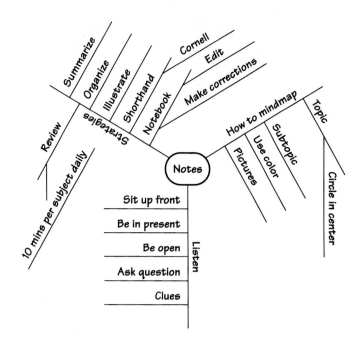

Symbol	Explanation
V or *	important ideas
+	positive
−	negative
×	times
~	lost
>	leads to (motivation > success)

Try using pictures, arrows, symbols, abbreviations, examples, maps, models, and illustrations to help you learn and remember. Have fun putting different examples together. Be outrageous and create eyecatching and unusual elements. Use colored pens, vary the size of your words and the style of your writing, and draw cartoons and illustrations.

6. Write Down All Material from the Board

If your instructor takes the time to put material on the board or on an overhead, write it all down. Copy graphs, diagrams, formulas, and dates. When material is on the board, it is important. If definitions, sentences, phrases, or key words are repeated, write them down in the exact manner in which the instructor has rendered them.

7. Leave Lots of Space for Revisions and Additions

You will want to leave wide margins and plenty of space to make corrections, add notes, clarify, and summarize. Don't crowd your words or the notes will be difficult to understand. Keep all handouts from class. Use a question mark if you do not understand something—you can find the answer later.

8. Review and Revise Your Notes after Class

Set aside a few minutes as soon as possible after the lecture to review, edit, revise, fill in, or copy your notes. Ask yourself what questions could be on tests. Underline what the instructor has indicated is important. Fill in blanks with new material. Clean up, expand, and rewrite sections that are messy or incomplete.

Even if you have only 10 minutes, review your notes for the main ideas and write down any questions you have. Research indicates that your memory is at its most receptive within 24 hours after hearing new information.

9. Edit and Summarize Your Notes

As you review your notes, clean up, expand, and rewrite sections that are messy or incomplete. Summarize the notes. Can you explain the main concepts in your owns words? You might want to write summaries on 3 × 5 cards.

10. Link New Material with What You Already Know

Develop associations between what you are hearing for the first time and what you already know. Compare and contrast, and find similarities and differences. Use key words to link new concepts. Let's say you are learning about groups and group dynamics. Your instructor may declare, "The essential ingredient for groupthink to occur is high group cohesiveness." *Group cohesiveness* is a key phrase that will link the concept of groupthink.

Ask yourself, How does all this new information relate to what I already know? In the above example of groupthink, you might list fraternities/sororities, political groups, sporting teams, and clubs as having high group cohesiveness. You already know a lot of information about a lot of different subjects. When you link new knowledge to what you already know, you create lasting impressions, better recall, and higher retention.

The following selection from a textbook shows how you might take notes on written material. Note how the student uses underlining, outlining, summarizing, and mindmapping as ways to organize and understand information on the page.

The Critical Thinking Connection

Determining what information to record, processing information, integrating various learning styles, linking new material with known information, determining desired results, questioning assumptions, staying focused, reasoning logically, creating an action plan, and evaluating your progress are all critical thinking skills involved in listening and note taking. Use critical thinking to answer the following questions. Be prepared to discuss your answers in your teams.

1. How do you prepare for class? What problems do you have with note taking and listening?

2. What suggestions from this chapter could you use that you think will help solve these problems and overcome your resistance?

What is **Selective Perception ?**

1. Selective Perception
   A. External
      1. Larger, brighter
      2. Different
      3. Repetitive
      4. Contrast
   B. Internal
      1. Needs
         a. hunger
         b. fatigue
      2. Motives
         a. entertain

Selective Perception is the process by which certain events, objects, or information is selected for our attention. Because of selection, we do not process the information required to make decisions or initiate behavior. Perception is selective. We all have the ability to tune out certain stimuli and focus on others or to shift our attention at will. We tend to hear and see what meets our needs, interests, and motivation. We fill in what is missing. We choose what we want to perceive and organize information into meaningful pictures. We block out some information and add to others. What are the factors that cause us to focus on and select certain events and ignore others? These factors tend to fall into (two) categories: external and internal.

   1.   2.

What **External Factors ?**

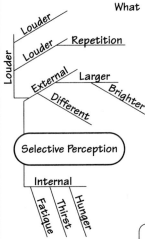

Eat Here   Example:

External factors refer to certain events around us that determine whether we notice something or not.

Many factors affect which objects will receive our attention and focus. Stimuli that activate our senses are noticed more (larger, brighter, louder). Anything that is different and out of the ordinary, colorful, unfamiliar, or that contrasts a background receives more attention. We notice what is different and incongruent (wearing shorts in church), or what is more intense. Besides physical factors, we also notice objects that are in motion or messages that are repetitive. The more information presented (the frequency), the greater the chances that the information will be selected.

Marketing experts study these external factors and use them in advertisements. If a message is loud or bright it increases the chances that it will be selected. We even use external factors in our daily life. John is a public relations executive and wants to stand out and be noticed in a large company. He wears expensive suits and unusual, interesting ties. Even his office is decorated in a unique, colorful, yet professional style.

What **Internal Factors ?**

1. needs
2. motives

There are several internal factors that affect perception:
Motivation: What we focus on is affected by our current motives or needs. If you've ever attended a meeting close to lunch time you may find yourself concentrating on the aroma of the coffee or the smells coming from a nearby restaurant. You tend to respond to stimuli that relate to your immediate needs (hunger, fatigue). If you are driving down the highway and see a host of signs and billboards, you will notice the ones that are directed to your current motivational state, such as those for food, lodging, or entertainment. Related to your motivational state is your attitude.

Summary: Selective perception is the process by which information is selected for our attention. Both external and internal factors affect perception. External factors include stimuli that is larger, brighter, louder, unusual, unfamiliar, colorful, or intense. Internal factors include our motives and needs, such as hunger, fatigue, anger, or our attitude.

Combining different note taking styles.

3. Describe how you could make your least-interesting class more interesting and productive. What kind of choices could you make that would help you get more out of the course?

4. Review a few of your textbook notes. What are some of the problems with them? Write down specific ways that you could improve them. Also, when you take notes, what are you doing that works?

5. Look at the common reasons and excuses that some students use for not listening or taking effective notes. Add to this list and use creative problem solving to list strategies for overcoming these barriers.

Reasons   **Strategies**

My instructor is boring.

I can't concentrate.

I'm easily distracted.

People talk to me during class.

I can't follow my instructor's lectures.

There is too much information, and I don't know what is important.

I listen, but I don't understand the lectures.

_____

_____

_____

_____

CAREER FOCUS

FOCUS ON THE PRESENT

Learning to listen actively and take effective notes greatly increases your chances of success on the job. Being aware, alert, and in the present are key factors in active listening and are critical for career success. Being alert and able to concentrate at presentations and meetings is a key job skill.

Let's look at Mary Dover, who has just been promoted to conference planner in a large hotel. Her job involves taking accurate notes at meetings and conferences, jotting down directions, and predicting questions, concerns, and potential problems. To be an active listener at work, Mary:

1. Observes verbal and nonverbal messages.

2. Concentrates on main points.

3. Takes detailed notes to improve her memory.

4. Makes certain that all details of an event are covered.

5. Asks who, where, when, and why questions.

6. Is totally alert when others are talking and clarifies expectations.

▲ NOTE TAKING FROM BOOKS

1. Survey the chapter. Take notes prior to class. This first read should be done quickly. Drawing a mind map of the chapter is especially helpful. Use 3 × 5 notecards to jot down key words, formulas, definitions, and important data. Write a brief summary of the chapter on the back of your 3 × 5 cards.

2. Compare class notes with lecture notes. Try taking notes on one page of your notebook while studying, and take your class notes on the opposite page. Another way is to divide class notes from lecture notes in sections in your notebook. You might also try the Cornell method: divide the page in half and write your text notes on the left half and the class notes on the right half.

3. Organize information. Note taking is really sorting or organizing information while you read. Make bold headlines and titles to sort information and color code key ideas. This way you can list supporting data, facts, and key points and compare them to lecture notes. Use the largest headline for the main idea. Phrases such as *the main point, it is important to remember,* or any phrase that the author repeats is important. Use large print for most important ideas, facts, places, proper names, numbers, and other supporting data. Fill in under headings with paragraphs, short sentences, direct quotes, personal experiences, and opinions. Key words are very useful in organizing or sorting through material and can help you greatly during exams. Write these down on note cards as well as on notebook paper so you can review often. Key words should be in bold print and followed by association with other facts, ideas, supporting data, and examples.

4. Leave plenty of space. Separate the facts and main points from the filler. Leave space for examples, additional material, information from the lectures, certain points for emphasis, or examples. You will also want to add examples from your text that are not covered in class. Varying the size of your headings helps you to remember key points. Some students find using different-colored pens to emphasize main points helpful.

5. Summarize in your own words. When you finish the chapter, close the book and write a summary in your own words. This can be done quickly and need only cover main concepts and impressions you have of the chapter. You might want to list questions you have. When you are taking notes from your textbook or research notes from a library book, summarize in your own words. Put direct quotes in quotation marks and double check for accuracy. We will cover research notes in Chapter Nine.

6. Evaluate your notes. If they're not effective, try something different. You might try drawing pictures or illustrations. Summarize each main section as well as the chapter and compare your book notes with other students' notes.

Here's an example of accurate note taking on the job.

Initial Meeting for Conference Planning—April 20, 1993

Name of group: National Dental Conference
Dates of Conference: November 28, 29, and 30, 1993

Confirm with master calendar _____

Follow up with _____

Secure budget by _____

Conference facility needs

Hotel accommodations

Number of meeting rooms

Hospitality suites

Reception rooms

Size of groups

Equipment needs

Podium

Head table

Refreshments

Seating

Blackboard

Overhead

Audiovisual equipment

Copy machine

Staffing needs

Secretary

Registration workers

Extra waiters

Dining and reception needs

Coffee and refreshments

Breakfasts, lunches, dinners

Cocktail hour

GRID 5.1
Listening for Transition Phrases and Signal Words

Use this grid for important lectures and classroom presentation. Listen for key words and phrases.

To show importance

The main point

This is important

Truly significant

Without a question

To indicate contrast

In contrast

On the other hand

Although

Yet

To indicate matching or addition

Similar

In addition

Moreover

Then too

To summarize

Finally

In closing

To conclude

In essence

Lecture _____   **Date** _____

During lectures be aware of and record:

Information that is similar to what you already know.

Information that is new.

Examples.

Important ideas.

Terms.

Summary of lecture.

GRID 5.2
Taking Notes

Use this grid to focus on creating an outline of the important ideas presented in a lecture.

COURSE   **Instructor**   **Date**

Lecture topic.

Chapters covered.

Main ideas.

Supporting ideas.

Examples.

Key words.

Important concepts and theories.

Applications.

How this information is similar to known information.

How this information is different.

Summary of lecture.

▲ CASE STUDY 5.1

A. Joe hates his personal finance class and thinks his instructor is boring. It also meets at 9:00 A.M. and since Joe is a night owl, he misses a lot of the classes. When he does go, he is usually late and sits in the back row so he can nap or catch up on his accounting. He never asks questions, volunteers for class exercises, or gets involved with class discussion. Joe is confident that he can cram for the exams and besides, he plans to be an accountant. He already knows how to balance his checkbook and do a budget. Besides, he can learn everything he needs from the textbook, so he feels it's no big deal if he misses a few classes. List Joe's negative behaviors and excuses. What would you suggest to help Joe change his behavior and attitude? What strategies in this chapter would help him most? What is one habit that Joe could adapt that could make a real difference?

_____

_____

_____

_____

_____

_____

_____

_____

_____

_____

B. Joe is an accountant with a large firm, and was recently promoted to a supervisory position. He has learned to manage his time, puts a lot of effort into his job, and gets along well with others. Joe has to attend a number of meetings, which requires him to listen actively and take accurate notes. It is becoming difficult for him to stay aware and alert during long meetings, and Joe often has trouble relating the main content of the meetings to his staff. What would you suggest to help Joe listen more effectively and take better notes? What strategies in this chapter do you think would help Joe most?

_____

_____

_____

_____

_____

_____

_____

_____

_____

_____

A. Lindsay is a fashion design student and works part time in a retail clothing store. She has two roommates, who are also students. Lindsay is an extremely social person. She loves to talk, tells interesting stories, and always cracks great jokes. She is the life of the party! Unfortunately, Lindsay isn't a very good listener. In class she is too busy chatting with the person next to her to hear the correct assignments. She always starts off as a popular study team member, but it soon becomes clear that her share of the assignments is always late and misunderstood.

Her roommates have finally sat Lindsay down and leveled with her. Tension has built up among the roommates, because they feel that Lindsay isn't pulling her weight on household chores. One major bone of contention is Lindsay's difficulty in taking accurate phone messages—she never seems to get the information down correctly.

What strategies in this chapter would help Lindsay be a more effective listener? What would you suggest to her to improve her relationships with others and help her become better at taking down information?

_____

_____

_____

_____

_____

_____

_____

_____

_____

B. Lindsay is a fashion designer in a large department store. She loves working with people and is a talented, responsible employee when she is actively aware and tuned into others. People respond to her favorably and enjoy being around her. The problem is that Lindsay sometimes is too busy or preoccupied to actively listen or write down accurate notes. She forgets directions, misunderstands conversations, and interrupts others in her haste and enthusiasm.

What would you suggest to help Lindsay become a better listener? What strategies in this chapter would help her become more aware, sensitive to others, and able to record information more effectively?

_____

_____

_____

_____

_____

_____

_____

_____

_____

▲ Exercise 5.1 Active Listening

See if you can apply these active listening skills to out-of-class situations. Not only will improved listening heighten your learning at school, you'll probably notice that you'll also learn more from your friends and family. Write a list of daily situations where active listening is a must. Some situations could include talking to your child about his or her day at school, listening to your spouse's views on politics, or meeting with a community group to plan a fundraising event. Hold this list against our active listening tips. Would some of these tips and hints increase your attention and responsiveness in the situations you've listed?

Think of someone you consider thoughtful and receptive. Does he or she appear to be an active and open listener?

▲ Exercise 5.2 Mapping Practice

Make a map of this chapter in the space below. Begin by putting the title in the middle and branching out with subtopics, supporting ideas, examples, etc.

▲ ACTIVE LISTENING STRATEGIES ▲

1. *Keep an open and positive mind.*

2. *Be alert and in the present.*

3. *Observe and pay attention to details.*

4. *Listen for the intent of the speaker.*

5. *Sit in front row.*

6. *Listen, don't talk.*

▲ NOTE-TAKING STRATEGIES ▲

1. *Summarize—don't duplicate.*

2. *Organize notes according to learning style preference.*

3. *Visualize and illustrate.*

4. *Use creative shorthand.*

5. *Write down all material from the board.*

6. *Review, revise, and edit notes after class.*

ACTIVE READING

"To read a writer is for me not merely to get an idea of what he says, but to go off with him, and travel in his company."

André Gide, author

"There are no doors we cannot unlock. We will place no limits on achievement."

Geraldine Ferraro, first female vice-presidential candidate

Learning Objectives

In Chapter Six you will learn:

1. The different types of reading.
2. The importance of knowing the purpose of reading.
3. How to interact with a textbook.
4. The importance of a positive attitude.
5. Active listening strategies.

Knowing the purpose of your reading and interacting with the text makes the process much more enjoyable and effective. In this chapter you will discover how to be an active reader, how to read difficult material, and still keep your attention and concentration. Since reading is a large part of school, you'll be able to apply these strategies and see results right away. Using your preferred learning style makes the process much more enjoyable and increases your comprehension. You will discover how to be an active reader and how to best use your learning style to keep your attention and concentration.

Let's approach reading as a climber approaches a challenging mountain. (In fact, some students have expressed dismay at the "mountain" of reading that they have to complete each week.) Experienced climbers are alert and aware of the terrain and weather. They are certain of their objectives, inspired by the challenge, and confident with their skills. They communicate, in a sense, with the mountain, getting to know the various ridges and feeling the unique energy and rhythm of each mountain. They know the importance of concentration. They maintain a relaxed, calm, and centered focus, but never allow themselves to get too comfortable or inattentive to even minute details. This same sense of adventure and purpose, concentration, and attentiveness are necessary if you are going to make reading more enjoyable and increase your comprehension. This kind of reading is called *active reading*. For the purpose of this book, the strategies will be targeted to reading textbooks. Our goal is to provide a guide to help you really learn material and do well on exams.

Reading is the foundation for learning; all other skills build upon it. In school and in life, developing good reading skills is one of the most valuable tools for being a peak performer. Take some time to read and invest in better reading skills and habits. They will stay with you and serve you for life. Even in this electronic age, reading is still critical. It is vital to almost any job to keep up to date with job-related reading. Many top executives say that they spend a great deal of their time in complex, professional reading.

BEFORE YOU BEGIN

1. Know Your Purpose. One of the biggest barriers to effective reading is not knowing your purpose. There are different kinds of reading that depend on the goals you have. You do not need to read all your textbooks from cover to cover. To be an effective reader, you will want to adjust your reading to the *type* of reading material and the *purpose* of it. Ask yourself your purpose for reading this material, and the author's purpose in writing the book.

Determine whether the reading is for pleasure, for studying, for enhancing classroom lectures, for background information, for understanding ideas, to find facts, for memorizing formulas and data, for research questions, or for analyzing and comprehending difficult or complex subject matter.

2. Have a Positive Attitude. Reading requires not only skill, but also a positive attitude. Many students have ambivalent feelings about their textbooks. They know they're important, but consider most as boring, and too often read only what is required. Does your self-talk include any of these phrases: "too complicated," "too hard," or "too boring"? The amount of reading required in school is enormous and demanding, and it is easy to get discouraged and put off reading until it piles up. Too many people associate reading with school and work. They haven't discovered the pure joy of reading a variety of good books. Like any other skill, you must want to be a better and faster reader. You have to believe that you can learn the skills and have the motivation to practice them. Before you begin a reading assignment, check your attitude and program yourself to become a better reader. Bring back your wandering mind and stay in the present. Retention is the process by which we store information. If you think something is important, you will retain it.

3. Set Clear Reading Goals. A common barrier in effective reading is not setting clear goals. Determine what you want to get from this assignment, plan the amount of material you intend to read, and set a goal for the time it will take. Ask yourself, What is my intention? Why am I reading this? How much time should I devote to this? What amount of reading can I finish in this time? You will be more motivated when there is a set goal and time for completion.

4. Create a Comfortable and Supportive Climate. Your physical posture affects your reading comprehension. Reading in bed or in a comfortable easy chair results in a casual attitude that produces sleepiness, poor concentration, and daydreaming. Don't read in bed unless it's for pleasure. Read at your study area—which by now should be organized and supplied with necessary study material. Your brain will begin to associate this spot with being alert and producing results. Try sitting at a desk with only your desk lamp on, and not the overhead light. This takes away many distractions and is easier on the eyes. Most students cannot study with music on. However, if you love to listen to music, vary its mood depending on the degree of concentration required.

BE AN ACTIVE READER

In order to increase our concentration and comprehension, we need to redefine what we mean by *reading*. Reading is often viewed as a passive activity. When you were a child you may have been told, "This is quiet time, go read a book," or "Curl up with a book and just relax." To be effective, however, you must get actively involved with your material—take notes, outline main points and ideas, jot down key words and definitions, ask and answer questions, underline important points, summarize in your own words, and carry on a conversation with the author. This is active reading and can greatly improve your comprehension of the material.

Often students find themselves bogged down if they open a textbook and start reading chapters one after another. This is passive reading, and it is not effective for studying. Don't read a textbook as if it were a novel, or you may find yourself dozing off. Picture yourself at your desk. You've had a busy day of classes or work, and you've just got your children to bed. Now it's 8:30, and you sit down to read your business law textbook. Your mind wanders, and before you know it, it's 10:30 and you can't remember a thing you've read. You can spend hours on one chapter unless you learn to be an active reader. The strategies that follow are based upon active reading. Active reading is a process that involves previewing, asking questions, reading and summarizing, reciting, and reviewing.

1. Previewing is surveying the material to gain an overview of the information.

2. Asking questions can help you find main points, details, and facts. Turn every heading into a question.

3. Read again, and summarize each major section and then the chapter in your own words. This helps you gain understanding of the material.

4. Reciting each section and chapter summary helps you really understand the material. Recite out loud to reinforce learning.

5. Do a quick review of the material right after you read it, a second review within 24 hours, a longer review session in one week, and a thorough review before a test.

ACTIVE READING STRATEGIES

1. Be Alert and Awake

Your energy level, physical posture, and state of mind affect your reading comprehension. Active reading requires energy and alertness. You wouldn't climb a challenging mountain if you were sleepy, nor could you safely drive a car, fly an airplane, or work with power tools. Get enough sleep and read when you are most rested. Generally, the daytime hours, especially the mornings, are when people are most alert. Sit up in your chair, keep your spine straight, and take deep breaths frequently.

Take breaks regularly. Everyone daydreams at times. In fact, many people complain that a lack of concentration is their biggest reading problem. We have learned how important it is to give the left brain a break periodically. Daydreaming provides the rest that your active left brain requires while your right brain takes over with images and creativity. When you do daydream, don't become judgmental and think that you are lazy or have an unusually short attention span. Change your activity cycle and let your brain renew itself, then bring back your wandering mind by focusing on the present. If you are tired, take a quick break, drink a glass of water, or stretch, but don't get discouraged. This is just your brain telling you that it needs a change of activity. Become aware of your posture, your thoughts, and your surroundings, and then gently bring your thoughts back to the task at hand. Do this consistently. You can train your mind to concentrate and be fully in the present by respecting your brain's need to integrate and refresh itself.

2. Preview Your Reading

Previewing the entire assignment is a key reading tip. When you first buy your textbooks, give each a preliminary survey to find out what you're reading, why you are reading it, and how it connects with what you already know. Predict what the reading assignment will cover. Preview the following sections:

Table of contents.

Preface and introduction.

Footnotes.

Glossary.

Bibliography.

Appendixes.

Index.

Summaries.

The first step in reading an assignment is to browse through it. Get a feel for the chapter, look at how it is laid out, how it is organized, the level of difficulty, and the illustrations, diagrams, pictures, summaries, graphs, and structure.

Look for familiar concepts, definitions, summary statements, or facts. Ask yourself, "What do I already know about this subject? What could I be tested on? How much time will this assignment take?"

Keep the preview short. Remember, previewing is skimming material and warming yourself up for incoming information. Your goal at this stage is to become familiar with the information. Therefore, read to understand, not to memorize facts. Don't worry if you don't know words. At this point you want to grasp overall concepts rather than details. You are setting your mind in the proper state to receive information. Always preview a chapter before you go to class!

The Critical Thinking Connection

Determining what information is important, processing information, integrating various learning styles, linking new material with known information, determining desired results, questioning assumptions, staying focused, reasoning logically, creating an action plan, reviewing, and evaluating your progress are all critical thinking skills involved in active reading. Use critical thinking to answer the following questions. Be prepared to discuss your answers in your teams.

1. Stop reading this chapter! Go back to the beginning of the chapter and jot down the types of information you might look for when previewing this material. List the heads that might help you figure out what's in the chapter. List the ideas you guess might be presented in this chapter. Write down the questions you hope this chapter will answer. Predict test questions.

2. How do you feel about reading textbooks? What is your biggest obstacle to reading more and remembering what you read?

3. What are you willing to risk and practice to overcome your barriers? What strategies do you commit yourself to doing this week?

4. Look at the common reasons and excuses that some students use for not reading effectively. Add to this list and use creative problem solving to list strategies for overcoming these barriers.

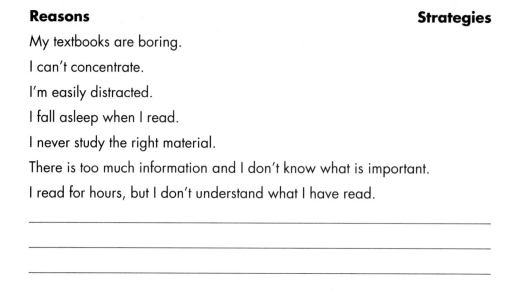

Reasons   **Strategies**

My textbooks are boring.

I can't concentrate.

I'm easily distracted.

I fall asleep when I read.

I never study the right material.

There is too much information and I don't know what is important.

I read for hours, but I don't understand what I have read.

_____

_____

_____

_____

3. Outline Main Points

Organizing information in an outline creates order and understanding. You may prefer a traditional outline, or you may want to use mapping as a creative tool to organize material and increase understanding. Many students find that mapping integrates and connects information and serves as a visual map. The purpose of a brief outline is to add meaning and structure to material, simplify, and organize complex information.

In addition, the physical process of writing and organizing material creates a foundation that is most useful in committing it to memory. Either write the outline in your book or on note cards. (See Chapter 5 for more note-taking strategies.) Your textbook may provide an outline. If not, use section titles and paragraph headlines as a guide.

4. Predict Questions

"Talk" with the author and jot down notes on points with which you agree or disagree. Make a list of all the questions you have on this subject. Look up words you don't understand. What isn't clear? You don't have to find the answers—just dig up the questions, take them to class, review them with other students, and use them when you begin to read seriously. Some answers will come up when you read later. Asking questions gets you absorbed and involved, keeps you interested, and helps you prepare for tests.

Go through the chapter and ask questions about chapter headings, sections, titles, and definitions. Make a question out of each chapter and section heading. Write down the main questions you have about each chapter. What do you want to get out of this chapter, what questions clarify the topic, what definitions help in understanding? What are possible test questions? Look up words you don't understand. If there are sample questions at the end of the chapter, answer them and tie them in with the main concepts.

This is a serious stage of reading, but you can make it fun. Be creative with your questions and compare them with others in your study team. Turn over questions as you walk to class and reflect upon what you have read. Recite important material out loud to increase recognition and recall.

5. Read Actively and Quickly

Active reading requires energy and alertness. Sit up in your chair, keep your spine straight, and take deep breaths frequently.

With your goal firmly in mind, read quickly. Use your finger and go quickly down the page reading sentences, not individual words. Going back over words, rereading sentences, stopping and staring at words, losing your place—all are examples of poor reading habits that can lead to boredom and fatigue. (Boredom and fatigue can also lead to poor reading habits.) You retain information by practicing, reviewing, and maintaining an alert mind. Reading slower does not help you retain information, but instead causes your mind to wander and daydream.

Your reading rate and attention will improve if you read with your finger and adjust your rate to the purpose of your assignment. Most paragraphs contain a unit of thought with a summary sentence. Reading phrases and uniting ideas can help you understand the main points. For technical texts, you will want to read in shorter sessions to improve comprehension and recall. Generally, reading quickly keeps concentration and energy high. If your mind does wander take a short break.

USE THE MARGINS!

6. Pick out Key Words

Actively pick out key words. Write, draw, underline, sketch, take notes, and become actively involved. Active reading means using your body. The physical process of writing activates the kinesthetic learning style and is most useful in committing information to memory. Write in the margins, sketch pictures, draw illustrations and cartoons, ask and answer questions, and circle words that you need to look up.

Underline and highlight important material. Almost all students use highlighters to underline main points, emphasize areas, and mark sections that are important to review later. Use a graphic device such as wavy lines (~ ~) to indicate difficult material that you need to review later.

Underline just the key points and words and think about the ideas expressed. The only problem with highlighting is that some students highlight in the first read and highlight so much that their book becomes cluttered. They have not taken the time to really identify what is most important. Highlighting is not a substitute for learning. Use a colored highlighter for underlining only important material. Don't underline until after you have previewed information.

7. Paraphrase and Summarize in Writing and Out Loud

Write a brief summary in your own words of each section. Then close your book and write down everything you can recall about the chapter and the main topics. In just four or five minutes brainstorm main ideas and key points and summarize the material in your own words. You can use a mind map if you want and simply do a rough outline. Don't get caught up in detail—spelling, sequence, organization, etc. Write quickly and test yourself by asking questions. What are the major themes in this chapter? What are the main points? How does this material relate to your experiences? How does it relate to what you already know? Use a mind map to link and associate ideas. Restructure and organize both by writing and by mentally grouping material into an order that helps you make sense out of a large amount of material. Writing produces an active process that produces involvement and comprehension. Summarizing helps you in recognition, retention, and recall.

	Math	English	Basic Finance
Symbols			

Another way to summarize is to do it out loud. Go to the front of an empty room and pretend you are giving a lecture. Summarize in front of a mirror or with a friend. Even better, explain the material to someone else in your own words. Recite the main ideas to your study team. (By now you know the value of studying with others.) You can take turns summarizing, and the benefits are enormous. Not only are you reciting the material in your own words, but you are hearing other viewpoints. Summarize in your own words and recite. This strategy really works!

8. Review

Be aware of your purpose, and be able to adjust to different types of material. More difficult material may require several readings at different paces to really understand and comprehend it. Pay closer attention to headings, main topics, key ideas, first and last sentences in paragraphs, summaries, and questions. Don't struggle with material that is not clear at this time. Take frequent breaks (about

▲ Set up a chart of the notations you plan to use in each of your courses this term. (Use the grid on page 154 as a model). Be methodical about using the symbols, but adapt them to your needs.

You may need to use different symbols in each course, although some can be shared.

Take the chart of symbols to your next series of classes and see if the system works. If not, how can you make it more efficient?

Effective reading is active reading. Take notes as you read. Write in the margin, create mind maps, jot key ideas on notecards, write down questions, underline points, check the margins, and group ideas into logical categories. Circle words that you need to look up. Write notes to yourself in the margins, answer questions, etc. This is the time to look up words and gain an understanding of the vocabulary used in the chapter. This increases your vocabulary and helps relate unfamiliar words to key concepts. Jot down key ideas in every paragraph and then connect them to create continuity and understanding.

Use notecards and carry them with you. Transfer onto 3 × 5 notecards any formulas, diagrams, key words, dates, answers to questions, and major concepts that you need to learn, and carry them with you to review and recite out loud. Writing and reciting reading material use different senses, which enhance the learning process. You are using the kinesthetic, visual, and auditory senses, and you are making learning physical. Dig out the answers to the questions you asked and record them on your notecards.

every 40 minutes or so). Remember, the brain retains information best in short study segments. Go back to the difficult areas later when you are refreshed and when the creative process is not blocked.

Get some exercise to get the blood flowing, and even read aloud while standing up or walking around. If you are still having trouble with a concept, try another textbook to get a different view.

You have previewed your material to get an overall view, summarized main concepts, and recited out loud. Now it is important to review again for understanding of main ideas. Continue to read quickly, paying attention to headings, main topics, key ideas, first and last sentences in paragraphs, and summaries. Your brain remembers much better when you review material right after you read it and again within 24 hours. This tip will save you hours of study time later and will tremendously help your comprehension and recall. The review moves the information into long-term memory. Fill in the areas and gaps that you understand, and don't struggle with material still not clear at this time. Go back to the difficult areas later when you are refreshed and have more information and when the creative process is not blocked. Review often!

As stated earlier it's a good idea to carry your notecards with you and review when you have a few minutes before class, waiting for the bus, waiting in a line, waiting for an appointment, or during lunch. Reviewing often and in short sessions kicks the material into long-term memory. Your 3 × 5 notecards are the most effective tool for reviewing information.

9. Evaluate Your Notes

If your notes are not effective, try something different. You might want to try drawing pictures, diagrams, or illustrations. Summarize each main section as well as the chapter and compare your book notes with those of other students in the class.

You can also review chapter summaries, your classroom notes, and notes you have written in your book. Ask your study group to review chapter questions. Review weekly, and conduct a thorough review a week or so before a test.

Finally, relax and enjoy reading. When your anxiety level is reduced, you will read more and become a better reader. If you want to read better, just read more and read for fun. Even when you are very busy, keep a book to read for pleasure and sheer escape.

DEVELOP A READING SYSTEM

Developing a system will help you actively read, retain, and recall material. You can follow a tried-and-true system, such as the 4 Part System or the SQ3R Method, or develop a working system that fits your needs. Whatever method you use, make certain that you enhance and integrate it with your learning styles. For example, if you are a visual learner, you can draw pictures, make charts, diagrams, and highlight illustrations. If you are primarily an auditory learner, listen to tapes and write out your vocabulary, formulas, and key words on notecards and read them to yourself. if you are a kinesthetic learner, collect samples and recite and summarize your material with your study team. Create a system that is easy to remember and that reinforces positive reading habits.

The 4 Part Reading System

Preview. Preview the entire chapter to get an overview. This quick survey takes just a few minutes. Look for main ideas, connections between concepts, terms, and formulas.

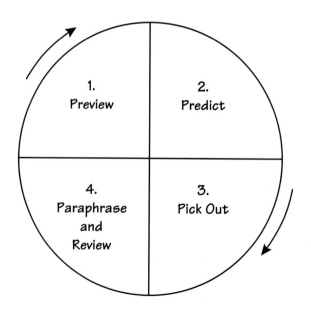

Predict Questions. Next, change every heading into a question. Predict test questions and search for answers as you read. Ask what, who, when, where, why, and how.

Pick Out Key Words. Read for meaning and understanding. Underline and highlight key words, main ideas, definitions, facts, and important concepts.

Paraphrase. Paraphrase and summarize. Write a short summary and then recite it out loud. Practice reciting this summary right after class and again within 24 hours of previewing the chapter. Review several times until you understand the material and can explain it to someone else.

The SQ3R Reading Method

In 1941 Professor Francis Robinson developed a method of reading called SQ3R. It is a reading method that has helped many students improve their reading comprehension.

Survey your textbook before you start reading it.

Question yourself on the main points and ask questions.

Read the material.

Recite the main ideas and key points in your own words.

Review the material carefully.

MAKING A CONNECTION BETWEEN WHAT YOU READ AND WHAT YOU KNOW

Link new information with what you already know. Ask yourself a series of questions that will help you make associations and jog your memory. What conclusions can you make as you survey the material? How can you apply this new material with other situations, other material, and lectures? What has been your past experience reading similar subjects or with reading in general? What do you know about the topic that may influence how you approach the reading? What images do you have of past readings that would help you make connections to this information? Remember, when your brain has been exposed to a subject, it is far more receptive to taking in more information. So jot down in the margins everything you can think of that you already know about this topic—even if it is just a word or image.

FOCUS ON THE MEANING

CAREER FOCUS

Increasing your comprehension and getting more out of your reading is an essential job skill. The amount of your on-the-job reading increases throughout your career. Besides a mountain of memos, professional journals, letters, forms, manuals, annual reports, legal documents, government requirements, and codes, you will be reading community items, newspapers, and magazines. The employee who reads quickly, has the ability to concentrate, and comprehends accurately has a huge advantage over an employee who dislikes reading or has difficulty concentrating. Consider Mark Layos, a paralegal in a large law firm. To practice active reading on the job, he routinely scans the table of contents to get the big picture and determine how much time to devote to an article, law brief, specific case, or book. He uses fast reading, previewing, reading summaries, and asking questions as techniques to improve his reading comprehension. He reads hundreds of memos each week, and has developed the ability to quickly dig out essential information, deadlines, main points, and action items. Take a look at the memo below and highlight important information using the active reading techniques in this chapter.

VOCABULARY BUILDING

You will need a fundamental vocabulary to master any subject. To be effective in a career, it is necessary to know and understand the meaning of words that you encounter in conversations, reports, meetings, and professional reading. People often judge the intelligence of another person by the ability to communicate through words. Words are the tools of thinking and communicating. The following are techniques for building your vocabulary.

1. Realize the Power of Words. Understand the value of effective communication. You must make a conscious decision to learn new words and see the value of building a larger vocabulary. Like any other skill, your attitude toward it is the key to learning. Associate with people who have effective and extensive vocabularies. If you spend your time with people who constantly use limited words, profanity, or slang, such as "you know" and "like, well ah," you will talk the

---

MEMORANDUM

October 2, 1996

To: Faculty, School of Business Administration

From: Robert E. Henderson
             Chair, School of Business Administration

Subject: Promotional material for Junior Colleges

Our enrollments in Acct. 210 are down substantially. Investigation by Bob Iannetta indicates that our number of incoming students selecting Business as an area of study has also declined over the past few years. This is consistent with the national trend.

In an effort to get our share of the pot, Jan Muller and I are preparing a letter with other material to send to the Department Chairs at the Junior Colleges. I am including this material with this memo and ask that you review the material and get back to me as soon as possible with any suggestions.

Thanks!

---

same way. Associate with people who are creative, expressive, articulate, and have effective communication skills. Model the behavior you want. An effective speaker who has a command of language can influence others.

2. Be Aware and Alert. You must be aware of words you do not know. Examine words that you see every day and ask yourself if you know what they mean. Most of us come across new words daily. Look them up and become familiar with them. Develop an interest in new or unfamiliar words and use them as often as possible until you feel comfortable with them. Write them in a vocabulary notebook. Draw a line down the middle of the paper and write the word on one side and the definition on the other side, or use note cards.

3. List New Words on a 3 × 5 Card. Put the new word on one side of the card and the definition on the other side. You may want to use it in a sentence or use a memory cue, a drawing, or an explanation. You can use different-colored cards or ink for different courses. Carry the cards with you and review between classes, while you wait for appointments, while commuting, etc. Keep your vocabulary stack in a folder and periodically take out the words you know well and replace them with new words. Keep your vocabulary stack handy to review often.

4. Use New Words in Conversations. Make a commitment to use new words until they are a working part of your vocabulary. Use creative, interesting, and colorful words that precisely describe what you want to say.

5. Study the Word. You will remember the word better if you learn it in an understandable context and use it in similar settings. Say it over and over again in your mind as you read and think of appropriate settings where you could use this word. Would this be an appropriate word for a speech that is coming up or for a paper? Does your instructor use this word in lectures?

6. Learn Common Word Parts. Knowing root words, prefixes, and suffixes makes it easier to understand the meaning of many new words. Also learn to recognize syllables. When you divide words into syllables you learn them faster, and doing so helps with pronunciation, spelling, and memory recall.

Root	Meaning	Example
auto	self	autograph, autobiography
sub	under	submarine, submerge
circum	around	circumference, circumspect
manus	hand	manuscript, manual, manufacture

7. Keep a Dictionary at Your Desk. You will find that it is an easy and quick habit to look words up if the dictionary is always at your fingertips. If you have to look for it, you won't make it a part of your life. If you don't have a dictionary with you, write down unfamiliar words and look them up as soon as you can. The unabridged dictionary is larger and provides more complete information on words and definitions than your desk dictionary. It is available in the library.

8. Be Aware of How Often a New Word Is Used. Do you remember a time when you first came across a new word? After you looked it up, you may have seen it several times during the next week. Look for new meanings to the words you have just learned. When reading a new chapter, pay attention to how key words are used, check the spelling, and write the words on your note cards.

1. Dig out
2. Underline
3. Uncover facts, ideas, concept

Skim

General to specific

Map and use 3 x 5 cards

Recite summaries

Break every 40 minutes

Summary
Difficult reading requires previewing, reading it again, writing a summary and studying in short sessions. Take more breaks and use mind maps and 3 x 5 cards.

9. Read. The best way to read better and improve your vocabulary is to read more. Read for fun and pleasure. Read newspaper columns, novels, nonfiction, and famous speeches. Go to the library and browse; read magazines, periodicals, and autobiographies. Look at how Abraham Lincoln, Benjamin Franklin, Winston Churchill, Jesse Jackson, Adlai Stevenson, Thomas Jefferson, and other effective speakers chose words and used meanings of words to make a point or comparison. Jot down words you don't know, words you've just learned, words you like, and themes, speeches, and poems that you feel are especially good. What words are really effective? Read letters written during the Revolutionary and Civil War times. You may find that the common person at that time was more articulate and expressive than many educated people today.

Further discussion of vocabulary building is beyond the scope of this book. To learn more, consult *Word Power Made Easy* by Norman Lewis. Building your vocabulary is a lifelong process. Be curious and open, and have fun using new words.

GRID 6-1
Creating a Reading Outline

Get into the habit of outlining your reading; use the format below to start.

COURSE   Chapter   Date

I. _____

   A. _____

      1. _____

      2. _____

      3. _____

      4. _____

   B. _____

      1. _____

      2. _____

      3. _____

      4. _____

II. _____

   A. _____

      1. _____

      2. _____

      3. _____

      4. _____

   B. _____

      1. _____

      2. _____

      3. _____

      4. _____

III. _____

   A. _____

      1. _____

      2. _____

      3. _____

      4. _____

GRID 6.2
Analyzing Textbook Chapters

As you start to read a new chapter in your textbooks, use this grid to prepare for reading. Phrase each heading as a question.

COURSE _____   **Textbook** _____

Chapter _____

Heading 1

Question 1

Heading 2

Question 2

Heading 3

Question 3

Heading 4

Question 4

Summary of section

Summary of chapter

A. Kent has problems keeping up on his reading. He is overwhelmed by the amount of reading and the difficult nature of his textbooks. He has never been much of a reader, preferring TV instead. He explains this as "just my nature." He has always read in bed or in a nice, comfortable chair, but often falls asleep. He knows this is not the best way to study, but it has become a habit, and it's so cozy and warm. Several times he has noticed that after reading for an hour or so, he can recall almost nothing. This has caused him frustration, doubt about his ability to make it in college, and anger at himself for not being able to concentrate better. What can you suggest to Kent that would help him improve his reading skills? What strategies in this chapter would be most helpful? Suggest one or two habits you think would help him most.

_____

_____

_____

_____

_____

_____

_____

_____

_____

_____

_____

B. Kent is a stockbroker. He never thought that he would end up in this business, but a part-time summer job led him into the finance world and he found that he really likes the challenge. He is surprised, however, at the vast amount of reading involved in his job. He must read piles of reports, letters, magazines, and articles. He also reads several books on money management each month. Additionally, he is involved in several community organizations that require a great deal of reading. What strategies in this chapter would help Kent become a better reader?

_____

_____

_____

_____

_____

_____

_____

_____

_____

_____

A. Sabrina is majoring in library services. She has always enjoyed reading books, newspapers, and weekly magazines each week. Sabrina's problem is completing her *required* reading for class. She is a fast reader, but has never learned to read textbooks in an active and critical manner. Instead, she treats all books the same and becomes bored or frustrated with textbooks. Sabrina reads the material quickly and feels that she has a fairly good grasp of the material. However, she doesn't do well on tests. She knows she is a good reader and is resentful of friends or instructors who offer advice. What suggestions could you offer that would help Sabrina pick out important information and data? What strategies in this chapter could help her read actively and remember the material she has read?

_____

_____

_____

_____

_____

_____

_____

_____

_____

_____

B. Sabrina is a library technician who has recently been promoted to supervisor. Because of budget concerns, Sabrina continues to perform many of her old duties as well as a heavy administrative load and is amazed at the amount of reading that is required in her new job. In addition to memos, reports, and letters, she is on the editorial board for her professional organization and also likes to review new books that the library has ordered. She feels overwhelmed. What suggestions could you offer Sabrina that would help her skim the pile of daily mail and pick out important information? What strategies from this chapter would help her become a more effective reader?

_____

_____

_____

_____

_____

_____

_____

_____

_____

_____

Read the following section on conflict. Mark it and write a short summary in your own words. Use the left margin to ask questions and make notes.

*C*onflict is everywhere. Wherever there are people, there is **conflict.** Frank's frustration with the people in his own company is **quite** typical. The results of conflict can range from minor inconveniences to major losses, even company failures. In American business, the **work**-place contains a greater amount of conflict today than in the past, **mainly** because of the movement of America from an industrial to a service-dominated economy. The service sector of the U.S. economy accounts **for** approximately 73 percent of all jobs. Most of the jobs created between **now** and 2005 will be in the service areas.[1] Services rely on human relations skills even more than does industry. Because of this increased conflict problem, we are badly in need of both managers and employees who can handle conflict realistically and deal with it in a helpful manner.[2]

Conflict has been defined in many ways. However the word is defined, several common aspects are involved.

- Conflict must be *perceived* by all people involved in it, because whether or not there is a conflict is a matter of perception.
- Nearly all definitions of conflict involve *opposition* or *incompatibility*.
- Some type of *interaction* is going on (or all parties would be avoiding conflict).[3]

Conflict

For our purposes here, we will define **conflict** as a process **that begins** when one person sees that another has damaged something the first **person** cares about—or is about to damage it.[4] Someone might simply **perceive** that damage is a possible outcome, and that perception itself **can begin a** conflict. The damage or perception of attempted damage does **not have to** involve a physical object; it can mean damage or a threat to ideas, **values,** or goals.

TYPES OF CONFLICT

Functional/
dysfunctional

Conflict is usually seen as a negative factor in the workplace. However, it can be both beneficial and constructive when approached correctly. One way to classify conflicts is to see them as either **functional** or **dysfunctional,** that is, either constructive or destructive. For example, when a group of workers meets to make a decision that affects all of them, some conflict can be good; too much harmony and agreement can result in a poor decision. However, if the same group generates so much conflict that fighting and polarization result, that decision too may be negative. A manager should try whenever possible to change a dysfunctional conflict into a functional (constructive) one.

Another way to classify conflict is by the actors in the conflict.

Inner Conflict.   This is conflict within an individual, which might involve values, loyalties, or priorities. Suppose that your manager wants you to do something, but your co-workers will call you a fink if you do. Or suppose that you have two job offers, both with attractive qualities that pull you in opposite directions.

Inner conflict

Person against Person.   This type of conflict involves two people who are at odds over personality differences, values conflicts, loyalties, or any number of issues. When only two people are involved in a conflict, the focus tends to be personal on both sides. Imagine an employee in a service organization, whose purpose for working is to help people. But in the desk next to him is someone whom he perceives to be "just putting in time." Values, personalities, and loyalties could all be involved in a conflict between them.

Intragroup Conflict.   When two groups form and take sides, this type of conflict results. Sometimes intragroup conflict evolves from person against person conflict, as people take sides with the two opposing individuals. An example of this occurred in a government agency, when factions formed behind two leaders who were both perceived as powerful. The conflict continued until members of the "winning" side were running the agency, and the opposing members gradually quit and found other jobs.

Person versus Group.   This type of conflict occurs most often when a member of a group breaks its rules or norms. It can also involve someone who never was a member of the group, but who opposes it. A group of six men from an auto body shop had a tradition of shooting pool together at a local bar every Friday evening. One of the six quit and was replaced by a non–pool player. Many conflicts resulted from the new man's breaking of this group norm.

   Figure 11–1 shows these four types of conflict. In this chapter, we will focus especially on the last three types. In Chapter 12, we will discuss inner conflict in greater detail.

SOURCES OF CONFLICT

The four types of conflict listed above describe in general terms who is involved in each type, but not how a conflict starts. All disagreements are not alike; they start at different points over different issues. If you know

FIGURE 11–1

Conflict Actors
and Factors

Inner	Person vs. Person	Intragroup	Person vs. Group
Values	Personalities	Choosing sides	Rule-breaking
Loyalties	Values		Anti-norm
Priorities	Loyalties		

FIGURE 11–2

Sources of
Conflict

	Source	Potential Solution
Content Conflict	Disagreement on items of content, or "rightness" of ideas	Check another source to verify who is right
Values Conflict	Disagreement on basic values and beliefs	Tolerate value differences, listen, communicate
Negotiation-of-Selves Conflict	Difficulties with self-definition	Build positive and stable self-concept
Institutionalized Conflict	Competition over resources or power within a company	Address/revise organizational policies or structure

what type of conflict you are involved in, that knowledge can help you discover how best to resolve it.[5] Figure 11–2 shows the sources of conflict and their potential solutions.

Content Conflict

Content conflict

When disagreements stem from **content,** they tend to focus on disagreements over what a statement or concept means. An old story tells about several Medieval monks holding a heated discussion about how many teeth are in a horse's mouth. After the discussion had gone on for nearly an hour, a young monk offered to go out to the post where his horse was tied and count the horse's teeth. As the story goes, the young monk was scolded and called a troublemaker. He had reminded the others that their arguing was pointless, and they were angry. When we disagree about content, the issue is whether or not an idea is right.

The rightness of an idea usually focuses on one of two factors: existence or meaning. If we are arguing about whether or not there really is a Loch Ness monster, for example, the disagreement is over existence. If we are arguing about whether or not the job I was just assigned is included in the vague wording of my job description, we have probably moved into disagreement over meaning.

If the conflict is over existence, it helps to have some way of verifying whether or not something is real. The Loch Ness monster is real to a few people, and to prove conclusively that it *doesn't* exist would be difficult. Thus, conflict over its existence still abounds—as it does over the conspiracy theories of President Kennedy's death, the existence of UFOs, and many other issues that are difficult to prove or disprove to everyone's satisfaction. However, most existence issues are more like the number of a horse's teeth. When a book or a document will settle the dispute, arguing is pointless. Both sides should wait until proof is available.

More commonly, content conflicts are over meaning, that is, interpretation. For example, I might find a copy of my job description and discover that it contains wording so ambiguous that my present task may or may not be appropriate to it, according to different interpretations.

Values Conflict

Conflicts over basic values usually go very deep. For example, a dedicated communist and a Christian fundamentalist would most likely disagree on many issues related to political and religious viewpoints. In the workplace, managers may have deep disagreements with each other over management practices. These disagreements may be rooted in their values and the basic beliefs they hold about people and how they should be treated. Many people exaggerate the number of values conflicts they have. Often, a conflict may seem to be over values, but is actually over the other's perception of you and your perception of yourself, and neither side is identifying the real issue.

Values conflicts can be solved, rather than avoided. Many of us need to have a greater tolerance of values differences. By listening carefully and communicating your values cautiously, you can often create a sense of trust and mutual respect for differences. You will find that if you reflect on your own values and examine them regularly, you will feel less threatened by someone with values unlike your own. Often that security becomes contagious.

Negotiation-of-Selves Conflicts

This type of conflict erupts over differences in self-definition. We generally define who we are based on our own self-concept. In Chapter 2, we learned how distorted the self-concept can be. Many people see themselves as less than they really are. Employees are likely to see themselves differently than the manager sees them. Children see themselves differently than their parents see them, and so on.

Consider these examples involving negotiation of selves:

Employee: Why is it always my job to take messages? I'm not good at things like that. I get messages wrong, and mess up a lot.

Boss: I ask you to take messages because you are, in fact, very good at it.

Mother: What on earth are you thinking, coming home at this ungodly hour? You're not old enough to be trusted out this late.

Daughter: I'm only two years younger than you were when you met Dad. Lighten up. I can take care of myself.

Employee #1:   What do you think of this report? I'd really like some input on it.

Employee #2:   Don't look to me for approval. I'm not your boss.

All three of these mini-dialogues have something in common. They express conflicts that originate from the speakers' self-concept and self-definition. Conflicts such as these can focus on power or authority (as the first two do), on personality traits (as all of them do), or on questions of duty and obligation.

Negotiation of selves

Many of our interpersonal conflicts are based on **negotiation of selves.** We are all continually involved in a process of defining ourselves to others and responding to their implied definitions of themselves. Most of this activity goes on unnoticed. A rude bank loan officer will hardly say, "Well, I'm responding this way to you because I feel that I'm superior to you." Even the nonverbal cues in such a case might not deliver the correct message, because we try so hard to play the roles that society has constructed for us. The loan officer is playing the role dictated by the bank, while a loan applicant will likely play the role which will be most likely to get the money. Both are involved in negotiation of selves.

Institutionalized Conflict

Sometimes a conflict factor is built into the structure of the organization. A common example is a company with five departments, all bidding for a portion of a limited company budget. Whatever one department gains, the other four will see as a potential loss. In the end, it's very possible that none of the five will be completely content with the outcome. Another example is an unclear or arbitrary duty assignment in a department, which causes workers to quarrel over who should be doing what. When you see a conflict developing in your workplace, take a minute to notice whether the conflict is being encouraged by the structure or policies of the organization.

CONFLICT ANALYSIS

Anyone wishing to arbitrate a conflict should begin by looking closely at what is really happening. When strong emotions are involved, we are tempted to jump to conclusions before we have examined the interests of both sides, and our own interests as well.[6]

Who is involved? How many people are taking part in this conflict? How well do they understand the basic issues? Are any of them repeatedly involved in conflict, or is this a unique situation? By knowing these details, a leader can do a better job of designing a conflict management process that addresses everyone's interests.

What is at stake? Do all or both sides in the dispute agree about what is really at stake? If duties and responsibilities are at stake, does everyone agree on exactly what those issues are? If money is involved, is everyone talking about the same amount? Does the issue center on assigning blame for misconduct, or could the issue be expressed as a desire to define what is proper conduct in the future? Without this step, the entire issue can become blurred.

How important is time? Does this dispute have to be settled right away in the best interests of everyone? Does one side benefit from stalling? A conflict manager should consider the time factor for tempers cooling on both sides, if that is likely. Or will the passage of time simply aggravate the issue?

What are the tie-ins with other issues? What relationship does this dispute have with other disputes between the individuals or groups involved? What working relationships will likely be affected by the outcome of the conflict?

After these questions are answered, and assuming you decide that the issue is worth resolving, the conflict can be resolved.

POTENTIAL SOLUTIONS

Generally speaking, there are three possible solutions to conflict: win–lose, lose–lose, and win–win. The first two tend to produce a negative side-taking mentality, and are not likely to solve the problem. They serve as a

▲ Reading Strategies ▲

1. *Be alert and awake.*

2. *Survey your reading.*

3. *Outline main points.*

4. *Interact with the author.*

5. *Read actively and quickly.*

6. *Underline and take notes.*

7. *Summarize in writing and out loud.*

8. *Review.*

9. *Evaluate your notes.*

CHAPTER SEVEN

LEARNING STYLES AND MEMORY

"The true art of memory is the art of attention."

    Samuel Johnson, essayist and poet

"Remember people and learn their names . . . The three Cs of management: communication, consideration, and cooperation."

    Yuki Togo, former president, Toyota Motor Sales

Learning Objectives

In Chapter Seven you will learn:

1. That you are in control of your memory.

2. How to use learning styles to enhance memory.

3. How to use your senses to increase your memory and recall.

4. How to integrate various learning styles.

5. Memory techniques and strategies.

Peak performers have the ability to recall information when it is needed. They can remember people's names, important dates, deadlines, appointments, formulas, equations, and what they read. It's not only important in helping you on tests; it can be essential for your career. This chapter will help you to discover how powerful your memory is—you actually never forget information.

You will learn memory techniques that can help you find relationships between new information and what you already know. Memory strategies will help you remember names, course material, and recall information on tests.

In this chapter you will learn the tools and strategies for recalling information. Your brain is like a computer, in that it never loses anything. You never forget. Once information has been put into the memory, it stays there forever. Tapping your preferred learning style and using all your senses are powerful memory-enhancing skills.

The memory process involves three steps: (1) observation, (2) retention, and (3) recall. *Observation* means becoming aware of the information and recording it in the brain. *Retention* means storing the information in the brain. *Recall* means actually remembering the information.

Most people can remember a telephone number for the time it takes to dial it. This is called *short-term memory.* Unless they use a number several times, it disappears. *Long-term memory* requires that you use the information from day to day. After you learn to drive a car, you don't even think about all the steps that are required to start it and back out of the driveway. The information is in long-term memory. The more often you use information, the easier it is to recall. Practice, rehearse, and review to improve your memory.

Are some people just born good at remembering? Memory is a process, not an organ. You are not doomed to a poor memory. Most people who are known for having good memories say it is a skill to which they have devoted time, effort, and discipline in order to learn the strategies that help them store and recall information.

YOU ARE IN CONTROL OF YOUR MEMORY

The first step in using your memory effectively is to realize that you are in control of it. I wish I could remember names, I'm just not good at taking tests, or I try to remember numbers, but I just can't—have you ever said such things to yourself? When you make excuses for your failure, your mind refuses to learn new information. As Chapter Two pointed out, a positive attitude and motivation are key to learning any skill. If you think a subject is boring, you will have difficulty remembering it. Some people have problems with math or science because of their negative attitude toward those subjects. If you are judgmental or have your mind already made up, you will distort facts, ignore information, and discount ideas that don't support your belief. So take full responsibility for your attitude. *You* control your memory process. Use affirmations—say "I am able to remember this list of management strategies" or "I can retain this information because I will use it in my career." Avoid using words such as *try, wish,* or *hope.* Those words imply that failure is possible. Trying is not doing.

Part of being in control of your memory is to eliminate anxiety and fear. Anxiety and fear are big blocks to memory. They keep you from concentrating. When you are nervous, you forget information that you actually know very well. For example, suppose you are with a good friend and meet your spouse's boss. You may

be so anxious to make a good impression that your friend's name is lost for a moment. Learn to relax by being totally in the moment instead of worrying about forgetting, how you look, what others may think, or being nervous.

The memory process is enhanced by understanding how you learn best and what senses enhance your memory. You should respect your natural preference rather than "trying" to remember. Let's look at learning styles.

Using Learning Styles to Enhance Memory

We've all had the experience of smelling a lilac bush or homemade bread and being flooded by old, rarely recalled memories. Sometimes seeing a Christmas tree or watching children play in the sand will bring back childhood memories. Hearing a particular campfire song or frogs croaking will remind some people of camping trips. For other people, a particular emotional state of great sadness or joy will trigger memories of similar feelings from their past. Most of us can relate to these familiar examples. People tend to remember events in a preferred way. Our senses are enormously important tools for summoning up past memories.

Consider three students who are preparing for a test in a computer class. The first student may feel most comfortable reading the manual, her textbook, and reviewing her notes. The second student prefers listening to lectures and reading his notes out loud in a private place. The third student likes to move around, watch demonstrations, and actually work on the computer. All three students are capable of doing well in the class and will have more success if they choose a study method that matches their individual learning styles.

The Senses and Memory

There is a tendency to think of learning as a passive activity that quietly goes on in the brain. In fact, everybody has a different learning style—that is, a preferred way to process, recall, and remember information. That style may be as unique as your fingerprints. Although there are several different ways to activate memory, one of the most common ways to recall information is to categorize it by sense: visual, auditory, or kinesthetic (tactile). Some people's memories are activated and inspired by pictures, some respond more to spoken words, and some need to actually perform a task in order to learn and remember it. Interestingly, people with the same sensory learning style tend to share favorite turns of phrase. For example, a visual learner may say, "I see the big picture"; an auditory learner may say, "I hear you"; and a kinesthetic person may say, "I think I have a grip on this problem."

Vision and Memory. In the examples of the three computer students mentioned above, the first student is primarily a visual learner. Visual learners recall information best when they see it, such as reading, watching a video, or writing notes. Videos, movies, word processors, typewriters, newsletters, and books are tools that create opportunities for learning and remembering. If you are a primarily visual person, your desk is probably stacked with a lot of your work. You feel comfortable seeing it around you. You like sitting up in front and want to see the board and the instructor's face. You may want to draw pictures to represent words or concepts. To prepare for a test, you may want to review your notes and rewrite them several times.

Hearing and Memory. The second student in the computer class mentioned above is an auditory learner. He remembers best when he hears instructions and responds more to spoken words. Auditory learners need to hear the message. People whose memory is activated by hearing learn best through records, tapes, writing, reading, and being read to. If you think you are a primarily auditory person, you may want to tape lectures and talk out loud when you study. When studying for a test try a quiet environment, since noise may disturb your concentration. Reciting information and teaching others work well for you. You will find that a word processor, tape recorder, typewriter, and tapes are effective learning tools. Auditory learners are good with clues and use associations and comparisons to understand information.

Touch and Memory. The third computer student is most likely a kinesthetic or tactile learner and would rather sit down and start typing at the computer than read the manual. Kinesthetic, or tactile, learners prefer hands-on experience. They need to *do* a task, touch or manipulate subject matter, or become emotionally involved in the learning process. The kinesthetic person learns and recalls best through dramatic improvisation, creative movement, dance, role-playing, workshops, working with clay, building models, sports, camping, games, and all kinds of physical activities. If you are a primarily kinesthetic person, you like to work with things, touch them, and discuss ideas. Try forming study teams to share ideas, speeches, reports, notes, and summaries. Listen to experiences related to the information. Don't try to memorize information from a list. Put material or answers on one set of 3×5 index cards and questions or definitions on another, and match them. When studying for a test, you may like to move around and need more frequent breaks. When learning is triggered through touch, the information tends to remain in long-term memory longer. Kinesthetic memory can enhance both verbal and auditory memory.

Learning Styles for Reinforcing Recall

Of course, it would help if all instructors taught their classes with different student learning styles in mind. Unfortunately, many rely on the lecture method, which makes it more difficult if you're a visual or kinesthetic learner. That means that if you have a learning style that doesn't mesh with an instructor's lecture method, you'll have to adapt your out-of-class study methods accordingly.

Experiment with the learning style that seems to fit you best, but at the same time try integrating other learning styles into your studying. Most experts agree that you retain information better if you use all your senses. This reinforces absorption and recall of material. Class discussions, lectures, activities, tapes, videos, writing, speaking, overheads, films, and physical activities are all modes that engage different learning styles. If possible, try to vary the way you take in information.

Start to study for a test from the first day of class. Your brain needs time to absorb the information in different ways. Try enhancing your own style:

Take notes in several colors and styles.

Practice visualizing the material.

Use models.

Recite material out loud.

Listen to how it sounds.

Practice while you are jogging.

Act out a scene using role-playing.

Get samples.

Draw maps.

Rewrite the syllabus using a computer or typewriter.

Pretend you are the instructor. Go to the classroom where the exam will be given, and write a summary of the material on the board. What questions are most important for each chapter? How would you conduct each class to integrate learning styles? Use different styles as you explain material out loud.

Now sit down and take a sample exam. During the actual exam, sit in the same desk, use the same pencil, and note pad, and sit in the same position. Help kinesthetic memory work for you by making the classroom setting realistic during your sample exam. Physically recreating a sequence of motions helps jog your memory and integrate the verbal and visual parts of memory.

MEMORY STRATEGIES

Few of us have had training in or taken a memory class. Fewer than 1 percent of all schools in this country offer a class in memory. You may not know how to organize information in a way that makes sense, is interesting, and is easy to understand. There has been a great deal of research and writing on memory and on how the brain stores information. There are proven strategies that can help you remember—in this section you'll learn what they are.

1. Pay Attention and Observe

The first step in developing a better memory system is to pay attention. Pay attention to details and become part of the process. Like everything else in life, to be successful you must be fully alive, attentive, and involved. Most memory problems are attention problems, not retention problems. Make a conscious, active decision to remember, and state this intention in a positive way. How many times have you physically been at one place but mentally and emotionally been thousands of miles away? Use affirmations to create an attentive state of mind.

Observe what is going on around you; be aware of information, your surroundings, the material, and your own attitude toward the information. Be aware of details.

2. Avoid Distractions

Distractions can keep you from paying attention, and, thus, from remembering what you're trying to learn. One way to avoid distractions is to study in an appropriate learning climate. For example, if you're serious about remembering what you read, don't read in bed. Study in a place that is designed for serious intent.

Reduce distractions and don't be someone else's memory support. If someone asks you to call her with the notes from class, ask her to call you instead, or if your roommate asks you to wake him or her up in an hour, suggest setting an alarm instead, because you want to get totally involved in a project. You have enough to remember without taking responsibility for someone else's memory. Keep your mind active and in a receptive state for learning.

3. Stay Alert

Don't eat a big meal just before you sit down for serious studying. This sends the blood to the stomach and away from your brain, where you need it. As a result, you'll end up taking a nap. Eat a light meal, take a walk, or do a few jumping jacks before you study. You cannot learn or remember if you are tired, hungry, worried, or upset. Realize that if you are well rested, nourished, and alert, you will remember much more easily. Eating protein and a well-balanced diet has been linked with remembering more effectively. Sit up straight in your chair. Support your body and your emotional state of mind so it can retain information.

Study in the daytime. Most people are more alert during the day. Study your hardest subjects when you are most alert and awake. The morning hours are most productive for learning. Waiting until 9:00 P.M. to study is usually not effective. You may spend hours studying, but your recall is often poor. Think of school as your job. Study during the day when you can concentrate better.

4. Alternate Activity with Rest

Physical activity increases academic performance by getting the blood flowing. Take a walk, jump rope, or jog when you feel your energy dip. Be an active part of the learning process by making the subject come to life. Keep a note pad, and write it down. Understand when your internal time clock is most alert. For most of us, that is in the morning.

Tune in to activity and your body. Practice reciting information while doing physical activity. Recite while in the shower, while you walk, jog, sing, or do exercises. Write out what you want to remember. Look at it, say it out loud, or draw it.

Learning occurs when you are relaxed, focused, and your mind is receptive. Trying to memorize information when you're tired is a waste of time. Relax, close your eyes, breathe deeply, create a quiet climate, and let your mind flow. Become absorbed in the process and subject. Focus your attention by concentrating on one thing at a time. Anxiety and stress are the biggest blocks to memory, since they prevent you from concentrating. Learn deep-breathing techniques for relaxing or try doing yoga or stretching exercises.

Simplify your life so your brain isn't overloaded with too many details, commitments, and demands.

5. Spark Your Interest in a Subject

When you get really interested in a subject, it is easy to remember. Too often students study just enough to get by on a quiz and forget the information immediately thereafter. This is short-term memory. It is much better to learn a subject so that it becomes interesting and part of your long-term memory. Uncover the facts, interesting points, related material, details, and fascinating aspects of the subject. Ask your instructor for interesting stories to enhance a point. Read a novel on the subject or look for another textbook at the library that explains the subject from a different view.

6. Study in Short Sessions

The brain retains information better in short study sessions. After about an hour, the brain needs a break in order to effectively process information. Break large goals into specific objectives, and study in short sessions. For example, "I am going to preview my marketing chapter for 20 minutes and mindmap the chapter on sales for 30 minutes. Then I'll take a break." Set a goal to study a certain amount of time each day rather than cram all night before a test. When you have a goal in mind, study in short sessions, and take frequent breaks, you make learning and remembering much easier. Tips for this type of studying include:

— Take regular breaks.

— Reward yourself with a small treat.

— Return to completing your goal.

Even when you are working on something complex, like completing a term paper or a major project, you are more effective when you take frequent breaks.

7. Integrate Your Left Brain and Your Right Brain

Chapter One discussed the left and right sides of the brain and what each side specializes in. You learned to discover your natural brain preference and to understand how this preference affects your work and study habits.

The next step is to strike a balance between the two sides of the brain. Let's begin by acknowledging the positive aspects of both sides of the brain. The eager, playful, enthusiastic, and creative right side can balance the firm, structured, practical, organized, and strategic left side of the brain. Clearly, the most productive and creative way to study and work is to integrate both sides of the brain. Think of the sides of your brain as a team that can cooperate, appreciate, and support each side. You can enhance your memory and learning power and become a more rounded person, able to adapt to different challenges and opportunities.

Imagine that you are rock climbing. At first you rely only on your bare hands to climb the rugged peaks, and with much frustration, you make little progress. Later you realize that if you use a pick, a rope, and the right shoes, you can climb with more agility, satisfaction, and speed. Using this metaphor can help you understand how much more potential you will have to be effective and powerful when you integrate the whole brain.

Let's look at a few practical suggestions for integrating both sides of the brain. You must turn in a neat and correct typed paper. The left side of your brain is insistent that it be error free. Your preferred style leans toward the right side, so your reaction to this assignment is frustration, fear, and resistance. Using the word processor can support both sides of the brain. You satisfy the structured side that wants a flawless paper while allowing your creative side to correct mistakes easily, using the spell check.

You can also form a study team that can help you accomplish your assignments, test each other, review questions, and still satisfy your need to socialize. Use 3 × 5 note cards for writing and organizing materials (left side) and color code them, draw mind maps on them, recite out loud, and have team members quiz each other (right side of brain).

8. Organize the Information

Organization brings material together and makes sense out of it. Nothing is harder to remember than isolated or unconnected facts, dates, or theories. Use whatever form of an outline that works for you; just make certain that information is in sections and units and you can demonstrate the interconnections and re-

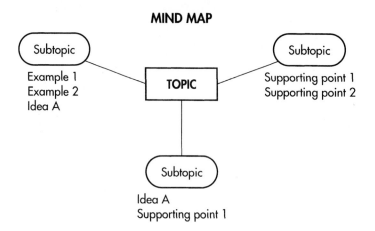

MIND MAP

Subtopic

Example 1
Example 2
Idea A

TOPIC

Subtopic

Supporting point 1
Supporting point 2

Subtopic

Idea A
Supporting point 1

lations between separate units. Ask yourself, How can I bring order to this material? You cannot recall information unless you understand it. Understanding means that you see connections—an indispensable part of long-term memory.

To help organize information to be memorized, create a map. To do so, take a blank sheet of paper (any size, even a notecard, will do). Write the main topic in the middle and draw a circle or a box around it. Then, surrounding the main topic, write down the subtopics. Draw lines from subtopics to the main topics. Under the subtopics, jot down supporting points, ideas, and illustrations. Be creative. For example, use different colors of ink, write main topics in block letters, and draw pictures for supporting points. The point is to draw a diagram that will organize all the information about a particular topic in one place. The mapping style of outlining organizes in a visual and creative form. Not only will the map organize the information, but the physical act of writing will help you commit the material to memory.

Use 3 × 5 index cards for recording information you want to memorize and organize them according to category, color, size, order, weight, and other areas. Make a map of each chapter. In your own words, write brief summaries and the main points of your chapters on the backs of the notecards. Carry these cards with you to review when you wait in lines, sit before class, ride on the bus, eat, before you go to sleep at night, or any time you have a few minutes. You can also write a map on a sheet of notebook paper and put it in your three-ring binder. Write a large one on a giant piece of paper and post it on the wall or bulletin board. These are powerful tools.

A good map also starts with the general (main topic) and goes to the specific (subtopics). Learning from the general to the specific gives an overview and makes the topic more meaningful. This is one reason why it is so effective to preview chapters before the lecture. Your brain is more receptive to specific details when it has a general idea of the main topic. Mapping was discussed as a note-taking strategy in Chapter Five.

9. Use Imagery to Create Associations

Use your imagination to make images exaggerated, absurd, animated, colorful, or oversized. Memory is primarily a process of imagining key words and associating them with others. Students have reported that they can create a mental image of the page just by visualization. They see headings, main titles, graphs, and lists of items that stand out for them.

Some people find that exaggerated, humorous, or unusual images help them re-

▲ LET'S TAKE A WALK DOWN MEMORY LANE

▲ Let's think of your memory as a beautiful garden and apply the method of place technique. This garden is rich in detail and full of lovely flowers representing thoughts, images, and ideas. You always enter the garden through a beautiful white garden gate. But you are not just standing at the white garden gate looking—you are actively involved and *attentive* to all the details and are *in control of your memory.* You can vividly see each distinct point in the garden: the garden gate, the birdbath, the gazebo, the fountain, a garden swing, and a flower bed. The key is to set the items clearly in your memory and visualize them. Draw a picture of your garden in detail.

Now let's say that you want to memorize four stories that emphasize four key points for a speech you are giving in your Speech 100 class. The first story in your speech is about a monk, so you draw a monk and place him at the garden gate. You want to tell a joke about a robin, so you place the robin in the bird-

bath. Your third point involves people of a bygone era, and you have chosen a Victorian woman as the image to represent this key point—you place her in the gazebo. Your fourth point involves the younger generation, so you choose a little girl and place her playing in the fountain. The key steps to the method of place technique are:

1. Imagine your beautiful memory garden. You know this illustration so well that you can visualize it with your eyes closed.

2. Imagine each distinctive detail of the locations: the white garden gate, bird-bath, gazebo, fountain, garden gate, flower bed, and the flowers arranged by colors.

3. Create a vivid image for each item you want to remember and place it at a specific location.

4. Associate each of the images representing the stories with its distinctive location. Repeat this association over and over again.

5. Mentally walk through the garden and see the images at each location.

As you mentally stroll down the lane, you see a monk standing by the garden gate. As you go further, you see a bird drinking at the birdbath. Next you see a beautiful Victorian woman having tea in the gazebo, and finally a pretty little girl playing in the fountain. You create pictures in your mind of each of your four stories through association.

If you have additional points you want to remember, place one at the garden swing, and one at the flower bed. If you have more than six items to remember, you can illustrate a rainbow over your flower bed. Each item you wish to remember can be represented by flowers in the various colors of the rainbow. Learning experts say it is easier to remember information that is *grouped together* and *associated by categories*. The colorful flowers in the flower bed could be arranged in groupings according to the colors of the rainbow—red, orange, yellow, green, blue, indigo, and violet. As children, many of us remembered the colors of the rainbow by the name, ROY G. BIV. You can apply this method of place by always remembering the flowers grouped according to the rainbow colors. First red roses, next orange poppies, then yellow daisies, further down a clump of green ferns, then blue-indigo irises, and finally a grove of violets.

You can use your memory garden every time you have information to remember. Say you are going to the store and need to buy bread, milk, cheese, and eggs. Always start by remembering your first item (bread) on the garden gate, your next item on the birdbath, and so on.

Be creative and flexible with the method of place technique. If a garden doesn't work for you, use a car, a bike, or your home and apply the same concept. Start with the bell on your bike, go to the handlebars, and so on. Just make certain that your illustration is clear and you always start out in the same place. Draw it out in detail and color it.

Use a Checklist in Your Memory Garden

A checklist is an effective technique to remember items. Just as a pilot uses a checklist to make certain that all preflight points have been covered, you will find that a checklist provides a way of reviewing and checking off each item you want to remember. You can use it with the method of place technique. For example:

Memory Checklist

1. Garden gate
2. Birdbath
3. Gazebo
4. Fountain
5. Garden swing

6. Flower bed
7. Monk
8. Bird
9. Victorian woman
10. Little girl

Check off each memory point and the item that you want to remember. By using imagery, association, color, and repetition, you become part of the learning process and take control of your memory. The method of place technique is an effective way of remembering a series of stories, items, or information.

Using Your Memory Garden on the Job

You can also use your memory garden to memorize any list of items that you need to know in your job. For example, you may have a large inventory of items to monitor or sell. You don't want to keep customers waiting while you look through a catalog to locate items. Try grouping items in a certain area of your memory garden. Remember the location of each item: the garden gate, the birdbath, the gazebo, the fountain, the garden swing, and the flower bed. If you have more than six items, recall the name ROY G. BIV, which represents the colors of the rainbow, and group your items in these areas. Let's say that you are an interior designer and have a large book of samples. The first section may be devoted to basic fabrics—you can visualize bolts of fabric sitting on top of the garden gate. The next items are specialized living room furniture—you visualize a couch sitting on the birdbath. The bath items are organized together and sitting in the gazebo, the bedroom furniture is grouped and visualized on top of the fountain, and so on.

You can also use color and graphics to activate your memory. Use appropriate-colored tabs to mark and separate categories in your catalog. Draw a large map and, using colored pens, group various sections and associate them with sections in the catalog. Put this colorful map in the inside cover of your catalog to jog your memory. Using imagery, color, association, and repetition, the map can be an effective memory-enhancing tool on the job. You can also use your memory garden to recall products, people's names, and agenda items for meetings and presentations.

member. Suppose you want to remember Ms. Brown's name. Visualize brown gravy all over Ms. Brown. When you see Ms. Brown, you will associate her with brown gravy and remember her name.

In a geography class you can draw a map, color different sections, and visualize this map during a test. You can form an image of almost any drawing, mind map, illustration, or structure.

The Method of Place Technique. As far back as 500 B.C., the Greeks were using a method of imagery called *loci,* or the *method of place* technique. The method of place technique is still effective today, because it uses imagery and association to help you remember. Here's how it works. You memorize a setting in detail, and then place the item or information that you want to remember at certain places on your "memory map." Some people like to use a familiar street, their home, or a car as an illustration for placing their information. The concept is the same. You always start at the same place and memorize certain places on your street, in your home, or on your car. Once you have this method of place illustrated you can position various items at different points. We've illustrated a garden in the accompanying sidebar, since it is so vivid and colorful. You can clearly see each item that you want to remember as you stroll down memory lane.

10. Associate and Connect

Connecting new information to what you already know helps in reading, listening, note taking, and recall. This is also a key memory technique. Connect the familiar with the unfamiliar. This makes the new information meaningful. Connect, compare, contrast, organize material, and look for interconnections. You learn to associate and link new material with old material. Say you want to remember a girl you've just been introduced to. Her name is Sarah, and so is your sister's. You visualize your sister while you are talking to this new person. Look for associations between the new Sarah and your sister. Say her name silently and also out loud. Whenever you see this new Sarah, you will associate her with your sister.

Here's another example. You are learning about the three ships that Columbus sailed. Think of three friends whose names start with the first letter of the ships' names (*Pinta, Santa Maria,* and *Nina*). (Example: Paul, Sandy, and Nancy. Associate these names when you think of the three ships.)

The Critical Thinking Connection

Preparing yourself both mentally and physically, determining what information is important, processing information, integrating various learning styles, linking new material with known information, creating associations, creating a willingness to remember, staying focused, reasoning logically, creating an action plan, and evaluating your progress are all critical thinking skills involved in memory. Use critical thinking to answer the following questions. Be prepared to discuss your answers in your teams.

1. How can you use imagery and association to help you remember something you forget often, like your keys?
Try your techniques for a few days and record the results.

2. Look at the common reasons and excuses that some students use for not remembering. Add to this list and use creative problem solving to list strategies for overcoming these barriers.

Reasons   **Strategies**

I don't have a good memory.

I can't concentrate and I am easily distracted.

This class or book is boring.

I never study the right material.

There is too much information and I don't know what is important.

My mind goes blank when I take tests.

I don't know why I have to remember all this stuff.

_____

_____

_____

_____

11. Trigger Your Preferred Learning Style

We have seen that all memory is sensory. So when you use all your senses (touch, sight, hearing, taste, and smell) to review, information has a better chance of being retained by your brain. Many students say they learn best by doing, then by seeing, and then by hearing. Learning experts say that most people learn best by combining all the senses. If you are studying plants, you may know the definitions in a general way, but the specific uses and details will not stay with you unless they appeal to your senses. Touch the plants, look at all the details carefully, hear yourself repeat definitions and uses as you come across them in their natural setting, smell the plants, and imagine how they might taste. See the plants in relationship to place, time, cause, and effect, and look at the whole and at the parts. The effect of using all your senses is synergistic in that the sum is greater than any part alone.

Make full use of as many senses as possible when you are listening to a lecture and studying. Look at the instructor, actively listen to the words, write down notes, tape the lecture and play it back later, rewrite key words and formulas on note cards and recite them, use the computer or typewriter to write summaries, and draw pictures and mind maps. Say you have just listened to a lecture on designing and marketing fashions. Pictures and drawings are helpful for remembering information. Even better is actually seeing and touching the merchandise and reciting, out loud, the names of fabrics, designs, and marketing techniques. Create action out of the information, and get all your senses and your body involved in learning.

12. Put It on Paper

Writing is physical and enhances learning. When you write information down you are reinforcing learning by using your eyes and your hand, fingers, and arm. Writing uses different parts of the brain than speaking or listening. Writing down a phone number or writing notes to yourself helps you remember them. Taking notes in class prompts you to be logical and concise and fills in memory gaps.

Underlining passages can also be effective as long as you do not delay learning by saying, "This is important, I'll study it later." It's better to take the time to review it, underline it, and then copy the most important passages onto notecards.

Write a summary in your own words. Encoding information into your own words is shown to produce long-term memories. This technique is enhanced when you write out a summary and recite it orally as well. You will not only remember the material, but understand it better and relate it to what you already know. After previewing a chapter and reading it quickly for headings, opening and closing paragraphs, main ideas, summaries, and questions, close the book and write everything you know about the chapter. Recall all information and answer all the questions you can. Next read the chapter again and see what you missed. Answer the questions that you didn't get the first time.

▲ USE MEMORY TRICKS

▲ Memory tricks—sometimes known as *mnemonic devices*—can be helpful in memorizing long lists of items, dates, and numbers. Such tricks fall into several categories:

Rhythm and Rhymes. As an elementary school student, you probably learned the rhyme "In 1492 Columbus sailed the ocean blue," which helped you remember the date of Columbus's voyage. Rhythms can also help. Many children have learned to spell the word *Mississippi* by accenting all the i's and making the word rhythmic.

Acronyms. Acronyms are words formed from the first letters of a series of other words, such as Homes for the Great Lakes (Huron, Ontario, Michigan, Erie, and Superior). Many science students have learned the colors of a prism by remembering the name ROY G. BIV (red, orange, yellow, green, blue, indigo, and violet).

Grouping. Grouping long lists of information or numbers can break up the task and make it easier. Most people can remember up to seven numbers in a row, which is why phone numbers are that long.

Association. Say your ATM identification number is 9072. You might remember it by creating associations with dates: maybe 1990 is the year that you graduated from high school, and 1972 was the year you were born.

There are problems with memory tricks, however. For one thing, it can take time to develop a trick—perhaps more time than it would take to memorize the information without a trick. It also can be hard to remember the trick if you make it too complicated. Further, memory tricks don't help at all in understanding the information—which is why they are best used for sheer rote memorization.

Remember, you never forget anything. Your mind works better than you can imagine. It is capable of complex task and high memory performance. Developing better memory is a skill that takes discipline and practice, but it will pay off throughout your life. If you block, remember something else. If you can't remember one formula, remember another. Recall information that is related. Related information is stored near each other.

13. Summarize Out Loud

Recitation is an excellent memory strategy. It is far more effective if you are attentive, encode the material into your own words, use mental images, link the information to what you have already learned, and say it out loud. When you say information out loud, you are again using a synergistic approach to learning. You use your throat, voice, and lips, and you hear yourself.

Say you want to memorize and give an effective speech. Go to the classroom and recite it several times. Visualize the audience, practice your visual aids, write on the board, use gestures and pauses, and practice over and over again, listening to how you sound. Tape your speech, and play it back.

Be creative with reciting. Make up a song about your test, sing it, make a comedy skit out of it, or recite it using the voice of a well-known personality (e.g., John Wayne's voice reciting electronics formulas). Before a test, go to the class-

▲ USE YOUR NOTECARDS!

▲ You might ask yourself, What can I do right now in just a few minutes to improve my memory skill? You may choose to review your flash cards from history for 10 minutes. Let that be your specific intention. Keep it simple, do it quickly, and do it often. Use flash cards, and review your notes over and over again in short segments. Carry them with you, and review out loud as well.

On the back side of the card, write the material in your own words. Writing a summary in your own words helps you to not only remember, but also to understand the material. Use these cards to review in 10-minute periods throughout the day.

When reviewing with note cards, you are doing many things to help with the memory process:

1. You are learning to be attentive to main ideas and key points.

2. You are identifying how the material is organized.

3. You are physically writing these main points down on a card.

4. You are encoding the information into your own words.

5. You are programming your mind in brief study periods.

6. As you recite out loud you are reinforcing the auditory learning style.

7. You are asking questions, which helps make the material personal and relates it to known material.

room and pretend you are lecturing on this subject or preparing a test for students and you want them to thoroughly understand it.

After you write a chapter summary, recite it to a classmate, and then listen for feedback. Ask the listener to ask questions, correct errors, add information, etc. Take the subject apart, examine it, compare it. Look at the whole and its parts. Add to it, review it, and contrast it to other topics. This really works, and you will be amazed at how well you really know the information.

14. Practice, Recite, and Repeat

Repetition and the importance of the information are what make memory long term. Repetition really works. You could not become a good musician without hours of practice. Sports, public speaking, flying an airplane, and learning to drive all require skills that need to be repeated and practiced many times. All learning requires active repetition. Repetition wears a path in your long-term memory. The more times you use information, the easier it is to recall.

For example, say a person's name out loud several times when you talk with him or her. Say it again mentally after you meet someone. If you forget the name next time you see this person, ask him or her to remind you, and go through the repetition process again.

15. Review Often

As mentioned previously in this text, the more often and the sooner you review information, the easier it is to recall. Ideally, your first review should be within the first hour after hearing a lecture or reading an assignment. Carry note cards with you and review again during that first day. Studies show that within 48 hours you forget 84 percent of what you learned. However, if you review right after you hear it and again within 24 hours, your recall soars to 90 percent. So reviewing within the first day dramatically increases your memory. Discuss, write, summarize, and recite in your own words what you have just read or heard.

CAREER FOCUS

FOCUS ON RESULTS

The career professional who can learn and recall new information and remember names is in demand. Employees are called on to learn new information, continue their training and education, and upgrade their skills. Consider Elizabeth Downing, a sales assistant for a large software company. She has found that increasing her ability to remember and understanding how she learns best has helped her succeed in her job. Since she is primarily a kinesthetic and visual learner, she uses a hands-on approach to learning about the product she sells. Elizabeth routinely tries out various computer products and uses a lot of visual aids when demonstrating a new product. Elizabeth uses memory tips such as visualizing a person's name, repeating the name mentally, or imagining a character to help her remember names of her clients and customers. As she writes down the names of new contacts and colleagues she meets at professional organizations, Elizabeth is developing good rapport and business relationships. To remember products and specific points when giving presentations, Elizabeth uses the memory garden technique discussed earlier in this chapter.

GRID 7.1
Connecting Learning Style with Memory

For each course you are taking, consider your best learning style. How can you accommodate this style in each course?

COURSE	Visual	Auditory	Kinesthetic

GRID 7.2
Keeping Your Memory Sharp

To make sure your memory skills stay sharp, review these questions periodically. Can you answer yes to these questions?

	Yes	No
Do I have a positive attitude about the information I want to remember?		
Have I created interest?		
Have I eliminated distractions?		
Have I organized and grouped material?		
Have I reviewed the information often?		
Have I reviewed right after the lecture?		
Have I reviewed classnotes within 24 hours?		
Have I set up weekly reviews?		
Have I used repetition?		
Have I summarized material in my own words?		
Have I summarized material out loud to my study group?		
Have I compared, contrasted, and associated new material with what I know?		
Have I used memory techniques to help associate key words?		

A. Janet is fun, bright, and popular, but has a reputation of being a bubblehead. She forgets appointments, projects, and due dates. She is continually losing her keys and important papers, is late, and forgets meetings and even social events. She continually tells herself, I'm just not good at remembering names and I really am going to try harder to get more organized and remember my commitments. She blames her "poor memory" for not doing better on tests and wishes that people would just understand that she's doing the best she can. She insists she's tried, but just can't change. What would you suggest to help Janet improve her memory skills? What strategies in this chapter would be most helpful?

_____

_____

_____

_____

_____

_____

_____

_____

_____

_____

_____

B. Janet is in hotel management. She loves the excitement, the diversity of people, and the challenge. She has recently been assigned to plan and coordinate special events, which include catering, parties, meetings, and social affairs. This new job requires remembering lots of names, dates, and endless details. What strategies in this chapter would be most helpful for Janet? Design a program for her that would increase her memory skills.

_____

_____

_____

_____

_____

_____

_____

_____

_____

_____

_____

A. Danton is a business student majoring in marketing and sales at a business college. He has always been outgoing, works well with people, and does well on team projects, presentations, and essay tests. He has trouble remembering data, formulas, and specific information, however. Danton recently took a self-awareness workshop and discovered that he is a visual learner. How can this knowledge about his learning style help Danton remember dates and class information? What other strategies from this chapter could help Danton increase his memory skills?

_____

_____

_____

_____

_____

_____

_____

_____

_____

_____

_____

B. Danton is a sales representative at a medical laboratories company. Every day he meets new clients, deals with a large number of customers, works with administrators and staff at the main and branch offices, and meets with other sales representatives at various medical supply outlets. He is also active in his professional organization and in the community. It is critical for Danton to remember names of clients and the people that he works with. He also must remember new products and his standard equipment and supply inventory. Memory is important to Danton's ability to do his job well. What would you suggest to help him keep track of his products? What strategies in this chapter would help Danton become better at remembering names?

_____

_____

_____

_____

_____

_____

_____

_____

_____

_____

_____

1. Close your eyes and describe what is in the room. Now open your eyes. What did you miss?

   Look at a painting or a poster for one minute. Now turn away and write down the details. What is the overall design, what details stand out, and what did you miss the first time?

2. How can you use your preferred learning style to enhance your memory? What can you do to integrate both sides of the brain and to use all your senses to help recall?

_____

_____

_____

_____

▲ Exercise 7.2 Creating Associations

Keep an ongoing list of words or names you have trouble remembering. Write
down the word and any associations and pictures that will trigger your memory.

Word	Associate With	Visualize
Susan Bickle	pickle	green sweet pickle

▲ MEMORY STRATEGIES ▲

1. Pay attention.

2. Avoid distractions.

3. Stay alert.

4. Alternate activity with rest.

5. Spark your interest in a subject.

6. Study in short sessions.

7. Integrate your left brain and your right brain.

8. Organize the information.

9. Use imagery to create association.

10. Associate and connect.

11. Use your preferred learning style.

12. Put it on paper.

13. Summarize out loud.

14. Practice.

15. Review often.

TEST TAKING, EVALUATION, AND FEEDBACK

"Do what you can, with what you have, where you are."

Theodore Roosevelt,
26th president of the United States

"You must learn to plan effectively if you want to make things happen rather than be a passive bystander. Good planning makes you more promotable."

Norma Carr-Ruffino, Ph.D.,
professor of business
and author of The Promotable Woman

Learning Objectives

In Chapter Eight you will learn:

1. How to overcome test anxiety.

2. The importance of reviewing and rehearsing.

3. How to prepare early.

4. Strategies for test taking.

5. How to take different types of tests.

In Chapter One we learned how important self-assessment is for understanding where you are, what you need to learn, and professional and personal growth. Change requires seeing yourself as you are now. How other people see you is also important. Taking tests is part of school, performance reviews are a part of a job, and tryouts and performing are a large part of the life of an athlete, dancer, actor, or public speaker. In fact, there are few jobs in life that don't require you to assess skills, attitude, and behavior. This chapter will give you specific tools to help you prepare for and do well on examinations.

Everything that you have learned in previous chapters will help you deal with tests. The goal of this chapter is to explore specific strategies that can help you prepare for tests, overcome test anxiety, relax before and during tests, and recall information easily.

OVERCOMING TEST ANXIETY

A mountain climber prepares for climbs and sees the mountain as a test of endurance, skill, and concentration. A climber is constantly monitoring and assessing skill level, mastery of technique, and tools. You, too, can learn to scale even the toughest cliffs by acquiring the necessary skills, strategies, and confidence to overcome your fear of evaluation. Many people see tests and performance assessment as huge mountains. They see tests as devices to trip them up, or performance assessments as competing with other people. Exams, tests, quizzes, tryouts, presentations, interviews, and performance reviews are all evaluations. Someone else—your instructor, coach, trainer, team member, co-worker, or boss—is giving you feedback on how they assess or evaluate your skills, behavior, or attitude. Your job is not to compete with others, but with yourself to become a true peak performer. The first step to doing well on evaluations is to overcome fear.

Even the thought of taking a test causes some people to feel a bit anxious and sends others into a state of sheer panic. Many students dread taking tests, but some actually become physically ill. Symptoms of test anxiety include nervousness, upset stomach, sweaty palms, and forgetfulness. Test anxiety is so acute in some students that they freeze up during exams. Some actually drop the course, and a few even drop out of school. The strategies listed below will help you face the fear, accept it as a challenge, and work through it.

The Critical Thinking Connection

Preparing yourself both mentally and physically, determining what information is important, processing information, linking new material with known information, creating associations, creating a willingness to remember, staying focused, reasoning logically, overcoming fear, and evaluating your progress are all critical thinking skills involved in test taking. Use critical thinking to answer the following questions. Be prepared to discuss your answers in your teams.

1. Describe your test anxiety. Write down your feelings about test taking in general, describing the emotions and thoughts associated with all types of tests.

Do you have different feelings about real-life tests, like a driving test or a vision test, compared to academic tests such as quizzes and exams? Where do you think these differences come from?

What are your memories about your best and worst test-taking experiences? What factors contributed to your ease or discomfort during these tests?

2. List quickly all the reasons, justifications, and rationalizations you have used to avoid studying and reviewing on a regular basis.

3. Create an action plan for overcoming your test anxiety.

4. Look at the common reasons and excuses that some students use for not remembering. Add to this list and use creative problem solving to list strategies for overcoming these barriers.

Reasons   **Strategies**

I don't have a good memory.

I can't concentrate and am easily distracted.

I never study the right material.

There is too much information and I don't know what is important.

My mind goes blank when I take tests.

I get test anxiety and panic.

My instructors ask trick questions.

_____

_____

_____

_____

1. Confront the Myths. There are a lot of myths and misconceptions about grades. Quite simply, tests provide feedback on how well you do at taking tests. They do not measure how much you know. Some students are good at taking tests, and some are good guessers. Tests do not measure your creativity. Remember, many brilliant people did poorly in school. Thomas Edison was one such student, and Albert Einstein was another. Tests do not measure your self-worth, your intelligence, or your ability to contribute to society. Tests provide a chance to learn to face fear and transform it into positive energy. They are an opportunity to show what you have mastered in the course.

2. Distance Yourself. Distance yourself and don't exaggerate the pressure or importance of test taking. The ability to do well on tests is a major factor in getting better grades, and that can cause a lot of pain and hurt feelings. Some common reactions include "I'm a failure," "I'm not very smart," and "If I fail on tests, I won't graduate or be a success in life." These are feelings produced by the myths. You can reprogram your thoughts. Test anxiety can not only be controlled, but can be channeled for your benefit.

3. Be Prepared. The best way to control test anxiety is to be well prepared. If you have gone to every class, previewed chapters, reviewed your notes, and written out, summarized, and studied the material in small chunks of time each day, you will be prepared. Prepare for exams by keeping up and working smarter, not harder. Preparation builds confidence.

4. Practice Taking Tests. Athletes, actors, musicians, and dancers practice for hours. When performers are on stage, their energy is focused. They have walked through, prepared, and rehearsed events so often that the real performance is exciting. They have learned to channel anxiety to work for them, and they don't panic.

You, too, can rehearse taking tests. Make up questions, test yourself, and test classmates. Once you have taken several sample tests, you will find the real one easy. Reducing test anxiety is similar to managing stage fright. Simulate real tests and exams by preparing a full test, timing yourself, and relying upon memory instead of your notes to answer questions. When you rehearse a stressful event, your mind does not see it as a fearful unknown.

5. Exercise. Exercise is great for reducing stress. The day before the test, go for a good walk, jog, or do aerobics. Or, if the test is in the evening, get some exercise during the day. You might try stretching exercises, yoga, jumping rope, or taking a short walk before the test.

6. Keep a Slow Pace on the Day of the Test. Make your test day peaceful by getting prepared the night before. Lay out your clothes, books, supplies, and keys. Review your note cards just before you go to sleep, repeat a few affirmations, and then get a good night's rest. Set an alarm so you'll be up in plenty of time. Before you jump out of bed, relax and visualize your day unfolding in a positive way. Repeat several affirmations. Keep your morning relaxed by getting up early and doing a few exercises and yoga stretches. Eat a light breakfast that includes protein, and keep a piece of fruit and some nuts in your knapsack for energy. A cup or two of coffee is fine, but don't overdo it.

If your test is later in the day or in the evening, make certain you have a light lunch or dinner and pack a high-energy snack in your pack.

Reduce anxiety by relaxing before the test. Last-minute, frantic cramming only creates a hectic climate and increases anxiety.

7. Breathe Deeply. Breathing deeply is calming and increases the oxygen supply. Take a deep breath, hold it for two or three seconds, and then breathe out slowly through your mouth. Concentrate on the air going in and out of your lungs. Fill up your lungs and empty them completely. Relax. Have a clear mind and the self-assurance that you will do well.

8. Relax All Your Muscles. Start at the top of your head and relax your facial muscles. Do several head rolls. Then hunch your shoulders and relax them. Systematically progress down your body, tensing and releasing each muscle group. After you've curled and released your toes, your whole body should be in a relaxed state.

9. Imagine Yourself as Successful. See yourself as relaxed, calm, confident, and recalling information easily. Visualize a peaceful setting. See yourself passing this test with flying colors. See yourself graduating, going across the stage, and receiving your diploma. Rehearse success. Once your mind has re-

▲ Let's take a minute to examine stress as it affects test taking. We all know that stress is part of daily life—in fact, some people think that without stress they couldn't get anything done! This probably isn't the case with most people who want to decrease or control the stress in their lives.

One way to look at the role of stress in your life is to create a 24-hour timeline like the one below and plot the points in your day when stress reaches crazy heights. Try making up a timeline for the next few days; then see if you find any patterns.

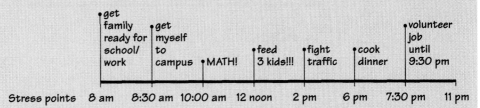

In the case above, you might realize that trying to do too many activities on a test day adds greatly to your stress, and it might help for you to eliminate some activities that day. For example, maybe you could find someone else to take care of your volunteer job on test days.

hearsed events, your body follows through. Athletes use this technique often. Throughout the day, visualize yourself as relaxed, confident, and recalling information.

From the time you wake up until right before the test, it is important to create a positive and supportive state of mind.

10. Use Positive Self-Talk. Use self-talk to program a detached, positive, and focused state: "I have prepared. I know the information. I recall the information easily. I am relaxed and calm. I can do this. This is an opportunity to show what I know." If you start having negative thoughts, tell yourself to stop and take a minute to focus on a pleasant reward. Thoughts are self-fulfilling prophecies, and you can program yourself to succeed. Ask yourself, What am I afraid of? Fear is only in your mind, so try to change any thoughts that make you anxious.

11. Get Involved. Focus on the subject. Get really involved with answering the questions, and be fully in the present. Stop your mind from racing with negative thoughts by being fully in the moment.

12. Put Things in Perspective. This is just a test. Keep things in their proper perspective. Even if the worst happens and you do poorly, you can still pass the class, graduate, and be successful. This will not matter 50 years from now. But facing and conquering fear will be a key factor your entire life.

13. Be Objective. After the test, look objectively at how you did. Evaluate your grade, preparation, anxiety level, and answers. Set your judgmental and negative emotions aside and candidly look at the results. What did you recall easily and what areas gave you problems? Look for obvious mistakes and jot down ideas that can help you next time. What areas confused you? See your instructor if you honestly cannot figure out why you were marked down.

14. Form Study Teams. Form study teams and draw strength, ideas, support, energy, and commitment from each other. Building a sense of team spirit and reviewing with others helps reduce anxiety.

Try all these strategies to overcome test anxiety. If you still are experiencing severe anxiety, seek professional help from a counselor at your school or at a counseling or mental health center.

STRATEGIES FOR TEST TAKING

1. Prepare Early

Preparing from the first day of class is the best way to do well on a test. A lot of studying, thinking, questioning, comparing, and reviewing goes on in your head, and your brain needs time to process information. The obvious tips are to attend all classes, arrive early, and stay until the end. The first day of class is important in that most instructors outline the course and clarify the syllabus and course expectations concerning grading, test dates, and the types of tests given. Keep up with daily reading, homework, and assignments. Consolidate your class notes with your reading notes. Your focus from the first day of class is a major factor in how well you will do on tests.

Just as you wouldn't wait until the night before your performance review to demonstrate competency in your job, you shouldn't wait until the night before to prepare for an examination. Start early by being an active and involved participant in the class. Also, the last thing you need before a test is to be frantic and late. Arrive a few minutes early, practice deep breathing and positive self-talk, and visualize yourself relaxed and successfully completing the test. Sometimes the instructor, while waiting for other students to arrive, will answer questions or explain material to those students who are in class ahead of schedule.

Use anxiety-reducing strategies to stay focused and positive. It's fine to calmly look over your note cards, but don't get into negative conversations. It will just make you feel anxious if someone mentions the length of time they studied. Make certain you have the supplies you need, such as an erasable pen, number 2 pencils, paper, and erasers.

2. Clarify Expectations

A large part of fear and anxiety comes from the unknown. The more you know about what is expected concerning evaluations and exams, the more at ease you will be. Clarify expectations on the first day of class and throughout the term. Most instructors outline the course and clarify the syllabus and course expectations concerning grading, exam dates, and the types of exams given. During class or office hours, ask your instructors about evaluations. Will they give you sample questions or review the material that may be on the test? Is there a study guide available? You are in a partnership with your instructors, and it is important in any relationship to understand expectations. Ask your instructor about the exam format—what kind of questions will be on it, what chapters it will cover, what styles of questions will be used, will examples of questions be available, etc.

As we have learned earlier, active listening is important in doing well on a test. Arrive at class early on the day of the test, and listen carefully as your instructor explains directions and guidelines. Clarify any concerns and make certain you know what is being asked for.

▲ Create another timeline showing your fun or relaxing activities on a typical day. Here's a possible timeline:

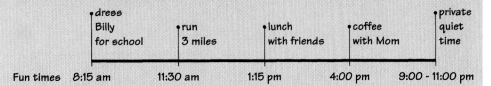

How could you use this information to reduce stress on test days? You may already have reduced some stress-creating activities (as we did in the last box); now how can you build up the amount of stress-reducing activities on test days? Maybe you could run longer or spend a bit more time with your child on a test day if these activities would make you more relaxed.

Remember—when it comes to stress, *balance is all*. If you spend the whole day relaxing and having fun in order to reduce stress, and don't spend any time preparing for the test, you'll be hyperstressed once you sit down to your exam!

3. Observe and Question

Observe your instructors during class to see what they consider important. Every instructor has favorite sections and topics—watch for clues. If your instructors write formulas on the board, repeat dates, stress key words, or illustrate concepts on overheads, you can be fairly certain that these are important. As you listen to lectures or read in your textbook, ask yourself what questions could be on the examination. Notice in class what points and key words are stressed. Ask your instructor questions about important lecture material.

Ask questions in class, as you read, take notes, and review chapter material. Chapter summaries, key concepts, exercises, and discussion and chapter-end questions and exercises can all provide examples of possible text questions. Save all quizzes, course materials, exercise sheets, and lab work. Ask if old tests or sample tests are available at the library. This will give you an idea of the format and possible questions.

4. Review

Start the review process by previewing chapters before classes. (This is such an important point that you will see it in several chapters.) You will get maximum benefit from the lectures if you go to class prepared. Becoming familiar with a new topic opens up the brain to receive new information and links the familiar with the new. This preview is most important with new information.

Take just a few minutes to review your class notes right after class. When information is fresh, you can fill in missing pieces, make connections, and raise questions to look up later. This brief review sets the stage for later reviews. This review is most important for information you have just learned.

Review your notes later the same day, and every day thereafter. Daily review of your notes will increase your recall and transform information into long-term memory. Set up a schedule so that you have time to review daily notes from all your classes. Review time can be short; 5 or 10 minutes for every class is often sufficient. Daily review should also include scanning reading notes and items

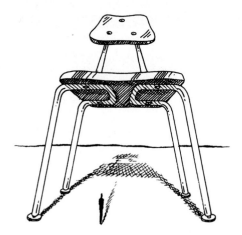

that need memorization. This kind of review should continue until the final exam. Research shows that reviewing often and in short time periods increases learning and recall dramatically.

Weekly review sessions include class notes, reading notes, chapter questions, note cards, mind maps, and study team sessions. Spend about an hour or so for each subject to really dig in and review not only the week's assignments, but what has been included thus far in the course.

A week or so before a test, commit yourself to a major review. This review should include doing practice test questions, comparing concepts, integrating major points, and understanding material that you have studied for the entire course. Remember, long-term memory is dependent upon organizing the information. Fragmented information is difficult to remember or recall. Understanding the main ideas and connecting and relating information kicks the material into long-term memory. The study tools or aids we have discussed in previous chapters can help you get organized.

5. Rehearse with a Pretest

One of the best tips for doing well on tests is to pretest yourself by predicting questions, asking about the test format, reviewing chapter questions, and looking for sample tests.

There are just so many questions that can be asked on course material, and they come from course lectures and reading. You can learn to predict questions. For instance, you can turn key words into test questions. Take each chapter heading and subheading and form questions about them. As you actively read, identify possible questions.

Ask your instructor about the test format—the kind of questions that will be on it, the chapters it will cover, the style and examples of questions. Notice the points and key words stressed in class. Ask your instructor questions about important lecture material if you don't understand it.

Review chapter summaries, key concepts, discussions, and chapter-end questions and exercises. Look for sample tests. Save all quizzes, course materials, exercise sheets, and lab work. Ask if old tests or sample tests are available at the library or from other students. This will give you an idea of the format and possible questions.

Next, summarize in your own words. This is one of the best ways to test yourself. Close your book, and write down everything you know about key topics. Write chapter summaries, and then go back and fill in missing material.

Recite aloud. Go to an empty classroom and give a lecture on the material. Recite notes and questions into a recorder and play them back. Reciting reinforces learning. Reciting summaries to your study group is also very effective. If you want to learn a subject well, teach it to others.

6. Use Your Study Team

You may be tempted to skip studying one night, but not if you know other people are waiting for you and depending upon your contribution. You can learn much more by studying in a team, and it's a lot more fun. You can exchange notes, make up sample test questions, summarize chapters, and grade each other's sample tests. You can actually simulate the test-taking experience by taking, giving, and correcting timed sample tests. Using the classroom where the test will be given would be even better. Come with 10 questions each. Pretend you are the instructor, and come up with questions you would ask if you were putting a test together. Give each other practice tests.

7. Organize Yourself

Write words, facts, formulas, dates, principles, or statistics in pencil on the back of your paper or in the margins as soon as you get the test. If you wait until you are going through each question, you may forget important material under pressure.

Read and listen to all instructions. Scan the entire test briefly. Preview the questions to see which ones you can answer quickly and which will take more time. Some questions may help you answer others. Dates, key words, or related facts may stimulate your memory for another question. Interpret what the question is asking.

Pace yourself according to time. Keep moving through the test according to your plan. Make your time count. Look at points for each question, and determine the importance that should be given to each section. Remember the 80/20 rule of putting the most time into the questions that will give you the most results. For example, you will want to spend more time on an essay worth 25 points than a multiple choice worth 5 points.

8. Move through the Test Quickly

Don't panic if you don't know an answer. Leave it, and answer all the questions you do know. Build upon success and don't block. Rephrase questions that you have difficulty with. It may help for you to change the wording of a sentence if you have trouble understanding it. Use memory strategies if you block: draw a picture, sketch a diagram, or use a different equation. Or you can make a mind map and write down the topic and subtopics. Use association to remember items that are related.

The best order to follow when moving through a test is to answer true/false questions first, then multiple choice, fill-in-the-blank, and short answer questions. Leave essays for last.

9. Reread, Recheck, Rethink, and Reward

Once you have finished, read the test over again and check for careless mistakes and spelling errors. Stay the entire time, and answer extra-credit questions, fill in details, and reread your answers if time permits.

After the exam, reward yourself with a small treat such as a hot bath, walk, or special dinner. Reinforcement is motivation. Always reinforce your successes.

Don't spend a second worrying about how you have done. It's over. Focus on the positive and doing well on the next test.

10. Analyze, Assess, and Reprogram

When you get the test back, analyze and assess it. Be a detached, curious, receptive observer, and view the results as feedback. Feedback is critical for improvement. Ask the following questions:

— Did I anticipate the style, format, and questions?

— What didn't I expect? What did I do right?

— Could I have asked the instructor for more detail—sample questions, etc?

— What should I have studied more?

— How was my recall?

— Did I prepare enough?

— Did I test myself with the right questions?

— Did I handle test anxiety well?

— Would it have helped if I studied with others?

If you honestly don't know why you received the grade you did, see the instructor. Approach the meeting with a positive, "I want to do better" attitude, not a defensive, "Why did you mark me down on this?" attitude. Remember, a test is information and feedback on how you are doing. Information can never hurt you; it can only help you. You cannot change unless you know what you are doing. Learn from your mistakes and go on. Reprogram your self-talk and behavior to be in alignment with your goals.

FOCUS ON STRENGTHS, NOT SHORTCOMINGS

CAREER FOCUS

It may sound strange, but people are often "tested" at work. Of course, pop quizzes and final exams aren't part of most jobs, but testing in the form of job reviews and evaluations is common. Knowing how to predict questions, extract important information, recall facts and details, and overcome the fear of assessment are important job skills.

Luke Bachini, an electrician who was recently promoted to a supervisory position, knows that performance reviews are both part of his job and more than a just tool to determine his salary. They can provide realistic assessment of performance, help pinpoint specific job behaviors that he wants to reinforce or discontinue, are goal-setting tools, and provide an opportunity for his boss to really see Luke perform his job.

To prepare for performance reviews, Luke predicts certain questions that his supervisor is likely to ask. He outlines important information relevant to the job and his company, and keeps this knowledge updated. Rather than wait until the night before his review to cram, Luke keeps his boss informed on a regular basis and, thus, prepares for reviews on a daily basis.

Luke views performance appraisals as a motivational tool. Once he knows how others perceive him and gathers feedback, he can lay out a specific agenda to improve performance. He takes control of his own performance reviews and looks at feedback as valuable information to use for professional growth.

Luke's ongoing preparation for reviews includes:

1. Setting goals.

2. Monitoring his progress.

3. Assessing the results of his efforts.

4. Holding regular meetings with his boss.

5. Watching for nonverbal feedback.

6. Clarifying expectations.

Luke focuses on his strengths, while working to improve his overall performance. He doesn't dwell on setbacks, failures, or criticism, but realizes that mistakes are only temporary stumbling blocks and can be turned into stepping stones to lasting success.

Set the stage for a formal appraisal by taking control of your own review process.

Performance Appraisal

— Write out your job description, including the duties that you actually perform.
— How do you view your job and the working climate?
— What areas do you see as opportunities for improvement?
— What are your strengths and how can you maximize them?
— What are your general concerns?
— What are your advancement possibilities?
— What additional training would be helpful for you?
— What new skills could assist in your advancement?
— How can you increase your problem-solving skills?
— How can you make more creative and sound decisions?
— What can you do to prepare yourself for stressful projects and deadlines?
— What relationships could you develop to help you achieve results?
— What project would be rewarding and challenging this year?
— What resources do you need to do it?

TAKING DIFFERENT TYPES OF TESTS

Although each question on each test is necessarily different, there are often hints to the correct answer hidden in the format or language of the question. Picking up on these hints will give you an extra edge when the next test rolls around. Page 212 gives you concrete tips and strategies for doing your best in all types of tests.

True or False

Stick with your 1st impression. Remember, a question needs to be totally true before you check it true.

Answer all questions— you have a 50/50 chance of being right.

1. In the Robbers Cave experiment, intergroup hostility was reduced by participation of the warring factions in common goals. T or F
2. The language of conflict resolution says, "Be descriptive rather than judgmental." T or F
3. When two people are having difficulty understanding each other, it is always due to conflict assumption. T or F

Multiple Choice

First eliminate poor choices.

Watch for qualifiers such as always.

Answer all questions.

If you haven't a clue, choose "C."

1. If one likes to help people and, as a consequence, assumes that nearly everyone else does too, this is an example of: a. stereotyping; b. self-delusion; c. halo effect; d. projection.
2. Differences in perception between bosses and subordinates may be most directly reduced by: a. motivation hygiene; b. improving maintenance factors; c. communication dialoguing; d. projection.

Fill-in-the-Blank

Focus on key words, definitions and facts.

Look for key words and associations.

1. The one essential ingredient for group think to occur is_____.
2. The best outcome of conflict resolution is_____.

Organize and outline main points.

Essay Questions

The number of blanks is usually a clue to the correct answer.

Use an erasable pen.

Pinpoint exactly what is being asked for.

1. What is the interrelationship among motivation, perception, and communication?
2. Describe the ways that perceptual distortion has been a major problem in organizations.
3. In the handout on conflict resolution, nine conditions of conflict were cited. List as many as possible.

Some words are common to essay questions. Become familiar with them, and make certain you know exactly what is being asked. For example, even if you know the information, if you *describe* rather than *list* the material, you will have missed the point and are not answering the question. Here are just a few common words:

Compare: Emphasize similarities and mention differences. Usually stated as "compare with."
Contrast: Stress the differences and dissimilarities.
Criticize: Discuss limitations, express your views, and evaluate.
Define: Give clear, concise meanings.
Describe: Relate in a story form or sequence.
Discuss: Examine, analyze, and give details.
Explain: Clarify, interpret, and give reasons for opinions and results.
Evaluate: Analyze the problem, list advantages and disadvantages.
Justify: Give reasons, facts, and documentation to prove a point.
List: Itemize statements in list form.
Outline: Organize material into main points, subpoints, and details, and classify in order.
Review: Examine, analyze, and comment on main points.

How to Receive Feedback

Evaluations involve more than just tests and exams. Part of being a student is being on study teams and working with other students on projects, on presentations, in committees, in clubs, on sports teams, in plays, and in a variety of team and group situations. There may be many occasions when you are required to receive feedback from your classmates concerning speeches, case studies, presentations, and performance. You may have conflicts with roommates, co-workers, supervisors, friends, or family that require that you listen to feedback. It hurts to be criticized, and we often feel as if we've been put down and judged. Too often we keep our thoughts and feelings bottled up until we explode and then are forced to deal with the conflict.

Let's begin by looking at criticism as feedback rather than as a judgmental verdict of the truth. When you are working in study teams, lay down the ground rules early and tell the other people that you would like candid feedback if there is a concern. Ask how they would like to deal with resentment and miscommunications, to avoid or reduce conflict. The following strategies may help.

Establish an Open Environment

In Chapter One, we discussed how important feedback is for assessment. We also learned that active listening is required if you are to benefit from constructive, accurate feedback. It is important to listen to the message without overreacting or becoming defensive, but this is not easy—it's always tough to hear negative feedback. This dread may have resulted from our experiences of hearing criticism from parents and teachers. It helps if you can create an open dialogue to invite feedback. This can make criticism easier to hear. For example, say to a new roommate, "I want us to have an open relationship and share expectations. Is it OK if on Tuesday I do my dishes after my evening class? Would you rather we clean the apartment separately during the week, or should we clean together on Saturday?"

Sometimes people have a hard time expressing criticism, so be on the lookout for nonverbal criticism. If the person is aloof, angry, or sad, ask if you did something to offend him or her. If he or she is sarcastic, perhaps there is underlying hostility. You can say something like, "You have been very quiet today. Is there something that I did to offend you?"

Create a supportive climate. People need to feel safe in giving feedback or criticism. Let people know that you like them and you will not get angry if they give you negative feedback. If you just focus on their negative behavior, they will often do the same. Trust that you can both speak your minds, in a calm and nondefensive manner, without destroying your relationship.

There will be times, however, when someone criticizes you and your first reaction is hurt feelings. Reframe the situation and think of it as a way to learn and get information about your behavior. Try these suggestions:

1. Listen. Use the listening strategies discussed in Chapter Five. Don't interrupt or start your defense. Really concentrate on how the person saw the incident, what his or her feelings are, and what he or she wants. Stay calm and detached. Listen for the real message.

2. Don't Justify. Practice saying, "Thank you. I appreciate your viewpoint and your courage in telling me what is bothering you." It's fine if you need to explain a situation, but don't make excuses for your behavior. If the criticism is true, change your behavior. If not, then go on without arguing or being sarcastic.

Some people have difficulty in accepting positive feedback. Accept compliments with a simple "Thank you." Don't undermine a compliment by saying, "Oh, it's really not that good." Don't justify or defend yourself.

3. Ask for Clarification. If you are unclear, ask for specific details, the time of the incident, and clarification. "Can you give a specific incident or time when you think I was rude?" Keep comments in perspective, and ask for clarification. The key is to understand the issue at hand.

4. Calm Down. If you feel anger or defensiveness rise in you, calm down, take a deep breath, and concentrate on the message. Sometimes it helps to pinpoint what is causing your anger. Often anger dissolves when you see that you are expecting others to respond or behave in a certain way or that another person thinks you should live up to a certain standard. If the other person is angry, ask him or her to calm down: "I can see that you are upset and I really want to know what your concerns are. Please talk more slowly."

5. Focus on the Problem, Not the Person. Don't use detours and attack the person. For example, "You think I'm messy? What a joke. Look at your room. You are a real pig." Instead, focus on the problem. "If I do the dishes the same evening I cook, will that make you feel more comfortable?"

6. Ask for Specific Instructive Feedback. "Professor Walker, you gave me a B− on this paper. Could you explain what points you consider to be inadequate? How can I improve it?" Remember, you have a right to ask for clarification.

7. Keep the Criticism in Perspective. Criticism is feedback about how another person views your behavior. It is not necessarily reality, but an interpretation. Relax and put it in perspective. Someone is reacting to a certain behavior at a specific time, not to your whole personality or the way you really are at all times. You might try being more detached and observe your behavior with more awareness or ask others if it is offensive. Keep a solid sense of yourself about you, and view criticism as an opportunity to grow and learn.

8. Be Serious. Be congruent with your words and body language. Don't say that you're "sort of angry" when you are furious. Don't smile and try to make light of an important incident. Don't use sarcasm as a cover-up for anger or as a way to resolve conflict. Be direct, serious, and clear.

9. Value Feedback as a Means for Positive Change. Information can only help you; it can never hurt you. If the information does not seem realistic or sound, disregard it. If, however, you have heard the criticism before from others and know that there is some truth to it, then you are free to choose a different behavior. If it is constructive, however, you can use it for positive change. There is an old saying, "No man is your enemy; all men are your teachers."

10. Accept Yourself. Put criticism in perspective. It is important to like and be yourself. As Fritz Peris said, "The crazy person says, 'I am Abraham Lincoln.' The neurotic says, 'I wish I were Abraham Lincoln.' And the healthy person says, 'I am I, and you are you.'" Be your own best friend, whom you can always depend on. You will succeed in school and in your career when you learn the tools for accepting and using feedback. Being open to feedback shows your willingness to learn and develop new skills throughout your life.

GRID 8.1
Preparing for Tests and Exams

Before you take a test or an exam, use this grid to help you plan your study strategy.

COURSE   **Test #**   **Date**

Format   **Length**   **Importance**

Chapters   **Date reviewed:**

Notes   **Date reviewed:**

Met with instructor   **Date(s) of meeting:**

Study team   **Date(s) of meeting:**

Notecards   **Date reviewed:**

Key words   **Date reviewed:**

Pretest(s)   **Date(s) given and results:**

A. Elizabeth is bright and hardworking. She studies long hours, goes to all her classes, participates, and is a dedicated student. When it comes to taking tests, however, she goes into a total panic. She stays up late cramming, tells herself that she will fail, gets headaches and stomach pains, and sometimes breaks out in a cold sweat. Her mind goes blank when she gets the test, and she has trouble organizing her thoughts. Elizabeth could get much better grades if she could control her stress and apply some test-taking strategies, and she would also enjoy school more. What would you advise Elizabeth to do? What techniques from this chapter may be most useful for her? What one habit could she adopt that would empower her to be more successful?

_____

_____

_____

_____

_____

_____

_____

_____

_____

_____

B. Elizabeth works for a large company as a graphic designer. She likes having control over her work and is an excellent employee; hard working, highly skilled, and willing to learn new skills. There is a great deal of pressure in her job—meeting deadlines, learning new techniques, and competing with other firms. She handles most of these responsibilities well, unless she is being evaluated. Despite her competency, Elizabeth panics when it is time for her performance reviews. She feels under pressure to perform perfectly and does not take criticism or even advice well. What strategies in this chapter would be most helpful to Elizabeth? What would you suggest she do to control "test" anxiety?

_____

_____

_____

_____

_____

_____

_____

_____

_____

_____

A. Nate is a design and technology major at a career school. He is bright, creative, and a self-described "free spirit." He likes to push the limits of art using color and unusual designs. Nate's problem is that he doesn't take negative feedback or suggestions well, and becomes defensive when his instructors suggest ways that his design work could be more effective. He believes that others simply don't understand his creative flair, and that his test results are not a reflection of his talent.

What suggestions could you give Nate for making the most of feedback? How can he use the strategies in this chapter to do better on tests and evaluations?

_____

_____

_____

_____

_____

_____

_____

_____

_____

_____

B. Nate is a jewelry designer at a small jewelry manufacturer, and is known as a talented and creative designer. He has a good relationship with his supervisor and is usually left alone to do his job. His reviews are informal. However, a large manufacturer is about to buy the company Nate works for. Nate is wary of formal performance reviews, because after all, he is an artist, not a production person. Just thinking about being evaluated by the new management makes Nate nervous.

How can Nate approach reviews more positively? What can he learn about evaluations as feedback, rather than criticism?

_____

_____

_____

_____

_____

_____

_____

_____

_____

_____

_____

1. Think of the last time you didn't study in advance and had to cram. How did you feel? How did you do on the test?

2. How can you use your learning style to prepare better for tests?

_____

_____

_____

_____

_____

Pretend you are taking a test on a very personal topic—your life history. Your professor has written the following words on the board: "Write a brief essay on your progress through life so far, covering the highs and lows, major triumphs, and challenges." You take your seat, look at the blank essay form, and pick up your pencil. You want to quickly remind yourself of the areas you want to cover in this essay question. What key words, phrases, events, and dates would you jot down in the margin of your essay paper?

_____

_____

_____

_____

_____

▲ TEST-TAKING STRATEGIES ▲

1. *Prepare early.*

2. *Clarify expectations.*

3. *Observe and question.*

4. *Review.*

5. *Rehearse by pretesting yourself.*

6. *Use your study team.*

7. *Organize yourself.*

8. *Move through the test quickly.*

9. *Reread, recheck, rethink, and reward.*

10. *Analyze, assess, and reprogram.*

EXPRESSING YOURSELF: RESEARCH, WRITING, AND SPEAKING

"Every discourse, like a living creature, should be so put together that it has a body of its own and lacks neither head nor feet, a middle nor extremities, all composed in such a way that they suit both each other and the whole."

Plato, Greek philosopher

"Being good at something is only half the battle. The other half is mastering the art of self-presentation, positioning, and connecting."

Adele Scheele, career counselor, author

Learning Objectives

In Chapter Nine you will learn:

1. The importance of writing and speaking.

2. How to determine your purpose and set a schedule.

3. How to do research and use the library.

4. Strategies for writing effective papers.

5. Strategies for giving effective presentations.

Few things in life are as difficult as writing research papers and speaking before a group. Famed sportswriter Red Smith commented, "Writing is very easy. All you do is sit in front of a typewriter keyboard until little drops of blood appear on your forehead."

Public speaking can cause even more anxiety. To some students, just the thought of speaking in front of a group produces feelings of sheer terror. In fact, research indicates that public speaking is the number one fear of most people, outranking even heights and snakes. For many students, writing not only produces feelings of doubt, but also demands their focused attention, intense thinking, and detailed research. You can't avoid writing or speaking in school or at work, but you can learn strategies that will make it easier and more effective.

WRITING AND SPEAKING YOUR WAY UP THE CAREER LADDER

The ability to communicate clearly—both orally and in writing—is the most important skill you will ever master. Peter Drucker, noted management expert and author, remarked, "Colleges teach the one thing that is perhaps most valuable for the future employee to know. But very few students bother to learn it. This one basic skill is the ability to organize and express ideas in writing and speaking."

You probably won't be asked to write research papers on the job, but most likely you will have to write business letters, memos, and reports—all of which need to be organized and presented clearly. And though you might not have to give a speech before a large group, you may have to preside at a meeting or present ideas to a small group—and those ideas must be presented clearly, concisely, and with an effective style. Writing papers and preparing speeches prepare you for on-the-job reports and correspondence. These skills give you a chance to show initiative, use judgment, apply and interpret information, research resources, organize ideas, and polish your style. Public-speaking skills also help you inform and persuade others at informal meetings and presentations. Good writers and speakers are not born, nor is there a secret to their success. Like any other skill, speaking and writing can be learned with practice and effort.

This chapter won't tell you how to write a great novel or deliver the keynote speech at a political convention, but it will give you strategies for handling every step of the paper-writing and speech-giving process, from choosing a topic to turning in the paper or delivering the speech. Once you master the skills and confidence required for speaking and writing effectively, you will experience a strong sense of accomplishment.

THE LIBRARY: YOUR MOST IMPORTANT RESEARCH TOOL

Work with Librarians. Librarians and their staff are trained to find information about almost every subject. They can often order special materials from other libraries or direct you to other sources. Computer networks are now in many libraries to retrieve information quickly. *Reference librarians can save you hours of time and frustration.* They are there to help, so ask for guidance at the beginning of your research.

Get to Feel Comfortable with the Library. You will have research papers, projects, and reports to complete in school and in your career. Learning how to use a library is essential; you will be using reference and research resources often. Even during your first term in school, you will most likely be asked to do a brief paper. It is important that you have at least an understanding of what resources are available and how to use them. Many libraries have a self-guided tour. Take some time to browse, to get oriented, and to feel comfortable with the facilities. The library is a good source for supplementary textbooks and material for your courses. Look into working part time or volunteering at a library. There is no better way to become familiar with the library, earn extra money, and have it feel like a second home.

The Services. Your research papers or projects will be more effective and you'll save time if you know how to get the information you need. You will want to ask questions about your topic, and creating a mind map may be useful in formulating questions. Next see a librarian for help in finding information on your subject and answering the questions you've outlined.

In designing your research strategy, remember the three basic types of information sources in most libraries: books, articles in periodicals, and reference materials.

Books. Books make up a large part of every library, and even small libraries can get almost any book you want through an interlibrary loan service. Start your research early, as this service may take several weeks (and may also involve a small fee). Books are designed to treat a subject in depth and offer a broad scope. Check the book publication date to make sure the information is as current as other reference material. In your research project, use books to get a historical context for thorough, detailed discussions of a subject, or for varied perspectives on a topic. Use the index in the back of books to search for information.

Periodicals. A periodical is anything published regularly: daily or weekly newspapers, weekly news magazines, professional and scholarly journals, and trade or industry magazines. Periodical articles provide the most current form of printed information. Many current events, issues, and new trends are discussed in periodicals long before a book is written about the subject. For your research strategy, use periodicals when you need the most recent data.

Reference Materials. Reference materials may be books or periodicals, and may be in print, in an electronic format, or on microfilm. Examples of reference materials include encyclopedias, dictionaries, chronologies, abstracts, indexes, and compilations of statistics. In your research strategy, use reference materials when you want to obtain or verify very specific facts. It is also helpful to consult reference material at the beginning of your search to choose a topic, to give an overview of a broad topic, or to identify relevant books or articles.

Most libraries have a *Periodical and Newspaper Locator List* and other periodicals have their own indexes. *The Reader's Guide to Periodical Literature* provides a subject and author index to many general and nontechnical topics. Other guides include the *New York Times* index, the *Wall Street Journal* index, and indexes for business, humanities, social sciences, and other areas of study. Indexes list articles directly under the subject headings.

Other publications that index periodicals include abstracts, annual bibliographies, reviews, and bibliographies. Abstracts separate the subject and author from the abstract itself and include a summary as well as information on where it was published. Many libraries have leaflets describing indexes in a subject area, such as *Psychological Abstracts* or *Fisheries Indexes.* Pamphlets, often stored in file cabinets, are organized by subject and include wonderful ideas for speeches and papers. Almanacs and publications from government departments are also valuable resources for facts and information.

Libraries also have many *dictionaries* and *thesauruses* (a type of dictionary to look up words with similar meanings). Technical disciplines often have their own dictionaries.

Taking Your Research Online

Technology is changing the way people gather information and conduct research. More than 10 million people use the Internet. The Internet is a worldwide network of computers that offers access to people and information. From the *Wall Street Journal* to job listings and music lists, the Internet offers a massive amount of information. Within the Internet, the World Wide Web links you to actual documents using a footnote-like technique called *hypertext.*

The advantage of using the Internet is that it can speed up your research efforts by bringing information to you. You can browse the Library of Congress electronically, review government documents, book reviews, encyclopedias, telephone books, and thousands of articles. Computers on the Internet communicate with each other and share data and information. If you have a specific need, the Internet can provide direct communication and interaction with many files.

The disadvantage to undergraduate students using the Internet for research papers is that your search will provide you with far more data than you need for most college papers. In addition, it takes time to find information, the terminology can be daunting, and it is often difficult to tell what information is current. Many people get sidetracked and find they spend hours "surfing the net" rather than actually doing the research needed for their paper.

There are many books available to help you learn to use the Internet.

BIBLIOGRAPHY OF SOME USEFUL BOOKS

Aboba, Bernard, *The Online User's Encyclopedia: Bulletin Boards and Beyond,* 1993 (ref QA 76.9 B84 A26 1993)

Braun, Eric, *The Internet Directory,* 1994 (ref TK 5105.875 I57 B73 1994)

Cronin, May J., *Doing Business on the Internet: How the Electronic Highway Is Transforming American Companies,* 1994 (HD 30.335 C76 1994)

Farley, Laine, *Library Resources on the Internet: Strategies for Selection and Use,* 1992 (Z 687 L54 1992)

Fraase, Michael, *The Mac Internet Tour Guide: Cruising the Internet the Easy Way,* 1993 (TK 5105.875 I57 F73 1993)

Frey, Donnalyn, *I%@:: The Directory of Electronic Mail Addressing and Networks,* 2nd ed., 1990 (ref TK 5105.5 D57 1990) Provides information on approximately 130 of the world's research, educational, and commercial networks.

Gianone, Christine M., *Using MS-DOS Kermit: Connecting Your PC to the Electronic World,* 2nd ed., 1992 (TK 5105.9 G5 1992) Excellent description of how to use Kermit.

Gilster, Paul, *The Internet Navigator,* 1993 (TK 5105.875 I57 G55 1993)

Hahn, Harley, *The Internet Complete Reference,* 1994 (ref TK 5105.875 I57 H34 1994)

Hardie, Edward T. L., *Internet: Mailing Lists,* 1993 ed. (ref TK 5105.875 I57 I56 1993) Defines and lists available listservers.

Kehoe, Brendan P., *Zen and the Art of the Internet,* 1993 (TK 5105.875 I57 K44 1993) Excellent brief intro to the Internet. It's almost as widely cited as the Krol book and has been available via anonymous FTP.

Kessler, Jack, *Directory to Fulltext Online Resources,* 1992 (ref Z 674.3 K47 1992) Includes basic information on electronic conferences, electronic journals, electronic libraries, etc.

Kochmer, Jonathan, *Internet Passport: NorthWestNet's Guide to Our World Online,* 1993 (TK 5105.875 I57 K62 1993)

Krol, Ed, *The Whole Internet: User's Guide and Catalog,* 1992 (TK 5105.875 I57 K86 1992) The most heavily cited of the Internet guides. You may want to consider purchasing your own copy, because it lists dozens of useful FTP, telnet, and listserve addresses. (now in its second edition, 1994)

Lane, Elizabeth S., *Internet Primer for Information Professionals: A Basic Guide to Internet Networking Technology,* 1993 (TK 5105.875 I57 L35 1992)

LaQuey, Tracy, *The Internet Companion: A Beginner's Guide to Global Networking,* 1993 (TK 5105.875 I57 L37 1993) Brief intro to the Internet and how it works.

Levine, John R., *The Internet for Dummies,* 1993 (TK 5105.875 I57 L48 1993)

Lynch, Daniel C., *Internet System Handbook,* 1993 (TK 5105.875 I57 I58 1993)

Marine, April, *Internet: Getting Started,* 1993 (TK 5105.875 I57 I567 1993)

Quarterman, John, *The Internet Connection: System Connectivity and Configuration,* 1994 (TK 5105.875 I57 Q37 1994)

Quarterman, John, *The Matrix: Computer Networks and Conferencing Systems Worldwide,* 1990 (TK 5105.5 Q37 1990) A useful introduction to how the various networks were created and how they interconnect.

▲ Go to a few parties and don't take any drugs or alcohol. Have a soft drink and just watch people. How do people really act when they are drinking or taking drugs? Do people look cool and "with it" if they smoke or are drunk or high? Are they witty and sophisticated? Be an observer, and when you come home, write a detailed description of the evening.

Rose, Marshall T., *The Internet Message: Closing the Book with Electronic Mail,* 1993 (TK 5105.875 I57 R67 1993)

Sawey, Ronald M., *A Beginner's Guide to VAX/VMS Utilities and Applications,* 2nd ed., 1992 (QA 76.76 O63 S36 1992) Very readable introduction to EDT and other useful information.

Tennant, Roy, *Crossing the Internet Threshold: An Instructional Handbook,* 1993 (TK 5105.875 I57 T46 1993)

Express Yourself: The Basics

1. Determine Your Purpose and Set a Schedule

The first step in writing a paper or speech is to determine the purpose of the message. In doing this there are some factors to consider:

The Audience. Who will read your paper or hear your speech? What is their age group, education level, and knowledge of the topic? For example, a speech on capital punishment would be different if given to a group of legislators versus your class. How large is the audience? How can you create a bond with your audience? Do you want your reader or listener to be moved to take action?

The Situation. What specific points and ideas are you expected to cover? What is the purpose of the paper? Do you want to entertain, inform, explain, persuade, gain or maintain goodwill, gain respect, gain trust, or gather information? How long should the report or speech be? What questions do you want to raise and answer?

Clarify expectations with your instructor. What exactly is the purpose of this paper or speech? What is the expected length, format, and style? What kinds of topics are acceptable? What topics have other students chosen? When is the paper due? Once you have clearly defined your purpose, ideas will start to flow.

A Time Table. In Chapter Three, we discussed the importance of establishing a timetable for projects. This helps in scheduling your time and breaks up a large project into manageable chunks. Estimate how long each step will take and leave plenty of time for proofing. Work backwards from the due date and allow yourself ample time for each step, if possible.

2. Brainstorm Ideas and Choose the Best

Once you have determined your purpose and worked out a time schedule, you can begin to shape your topic. Brainstorm ideas with a friend and make a list of

TERM PAPER FOR CRIMINAL JUSTICE CLASS—DUE APRIL 3

Final review and polish—March 28.

Edit, revise—March 26 (put away for two days).

Complete paper—March 25.

Edit, review, revise—March 24.

Final draft completed—March 22 (review with a good

writer).

First draft completed—March 15.

Research completed—March 12.

Begin research—February 16.

Complete proposal—February 10. Discuss with instructor.

Deadline for outline—February 3.

Choose a topic—January 29.

Brainstorm ideas—January 27.

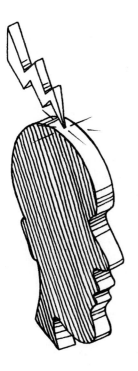

topics that interest you. Thinking out loud and jotting these thoughts down on paper can help to generate lots of ideas. You may want to do initial research at this stage by browsing through magazines, newspapers, books, and pamphlets. This is a good starting point for generating ideas.

Free writing is an effective strategy for producing ideas. Just write without stopping for 5 or 10 minutes. Let the ideas flow and jot down whatever comes to your mind. Don't worry about structure, spelling, or organization. Many students like the creativity of using a mind map for brainstorming ideas. Set a specific deadline for brainstorming ideas, for example, "I will have a list of ideas by 2:00 on Wednesday."

Select and Narrow Your Topic. Students often spend so much time trying to decide on a topic, they have little time to actually prepare. The best way to choose a topic is just to do it. No excuses; just choose a topic from your list of ideas and begin! Close your eyes and point to one if you feel yourself waffling. The choice of your topic is not as important as the amount of energy, time, and thought that you put into developing a good paper. An important factor to consider in choosing a topic is your own interest. Personal interest and the desire to know more about a topic is a good foundation for writing a paper or giving a speech. Besides interest, consider the availability of research material when you select your topic.

First concentrate on the broad area and then narrow it to a specific, concise topic. For example, instead of "Health Problems in America," narrow the subject to "Cigarette Smoking among Teenage Girls," or "Should Cigarette Advertising Be Banned?"

Write a Thesis Statement. A major reason students have problems writing papers is that they lack a clear thesis. The thesis is the main point or central idea of a paper. In one sentence, your thesis describes your topic and what you want to convey. Writing this thesis sentence should help you clarify your topic and your purpose. A good thesis statement is unified and clear. For example, "Smoking among teenage girls is on the rise and will cause serious health problems for them." Of course, you don't have to keep this thesis sentence if your research leads you in a slightly different direction. At this time, it is helpful to do a preliminary outline. A mind map works well at this stage since you have your limited topic. Now you can start to ask a few important questions that you want your paper to answer. What do you already know about the topic? What questions do you want to explore?

This outline will change and grow as you read and complete research, but even a rough sketch will provide you with direction and serve as a guide for your general research. When you've limited your topic, written your thesis statement, and finished a preliminary outline, you will have completed a major and often worrisome phase of your work.

3. Do Reading, General Research, and Analysis

Your initial research is really preliminary reading that will give you an overview of the subject, separate key issues, and help you begin to structure your topic and compile a working bibliography. Begin to research the topic by developing broad questions. These questions will serve as guides for the documentation you will want to support your information. Questions lead you to new directions and further research. Write these questions on 3 × 5 cards and include them later with your research cards. Your initial data collection can include books, brochures, pamphlets, and current magazine and newspaper articles. Go through the card catalogs in the library and discover what is available on your topic. You will also find the *Reader's Guide to Periodical Literature* a helpful source for locating articles. Other standard reference materials that may give you a general understanding and help you to develop questions include *The Encyclopedia Americana* and the *Encyclopaedia Britannica*. Skim the references to see if they contain useful information. If not, cross out the cards and set them aside. Don't discard them, as you may want a quote or specific fact later.

Throughout this book we've discussed the value of 3 × 5 cards. You will find them most valuable at this stage of the research process for organizing your bibliography cards. Write down the author's full name (last name first), exact title (underline books and put articles in quotation marks), full publication data (edi-

Questions to Explore:
1. How many teenage girls start smoking each year?
2. What health complications occur?
3. What health complications may occur later because of this habit?
4. How does advertising contribute to this trend?

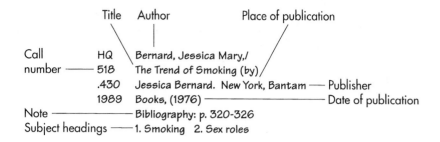

tion, volume, place of publication, name of the publisher, date of publication), and page numbers. Write down each reference on a separate card. You will need exact information for your final bibliography and footnotes and for researching material. Put a rubber band around them and keep them in a small folder. Some students find it useful to color code them. Sorting these cards into natural divisions will help you prepare your outline. Starting your research in an organized and consistent manner will save you hours later.

4. Develop an Outline, Mind Map, or Proposal

An outline is a road map that illustrates your entire project. You already completed a preliminary outline in step 3, so next develop a more detailed outline to give you direction and to ensure that you are including all main supporting data. *A good outline saves time and keeps you focused.* You can do a traditional outline or a mind map. For example, here is a sample outline:

— **Topic:** Smoking.

— **Thesis:** Smoking among teenage girls is on the rise and is causing major health problems.

— **Introduction:** Education has been effective in reducing smoking for the general population. However, one group continues to rise. . . .

— **Body:** Include facts, statistics, and stories.

I. Main point 1—Smoking among teenage girls.
   A. Supporting statement: Smoking has increased by 24 percent.
      1. Supporting information.
      2. Supporting information.

II. Main point 2—Advertising directly targets young girls.
   A. Example of advertising.
      1. Supporting information.
      2. Supporting information.

You can also create a map. This visual model is especially useful for getting a whole picture of your project. In just a few minutes, you can print your topic in the middle of the paper and, with different-colored pens, support this main idea with key words, facts, and ideas. This graphic model stimulates the creative right brain with colors, shapes, associations, and imagination. Mapping is an excellent way to plan, focus, and encourage ideas. A sample map could be:

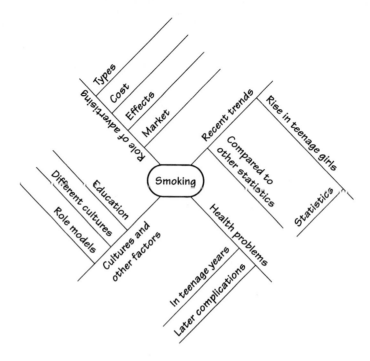

You might also find it helpful to use 3 × 5 cards to arrange main categories. Some students do their outline on a computer, where they can write everything they know about a topic and then rearrange ideas into sections. If you use a computer, check applicable software packages that offer an outline feature. However you do it, brainstorm everything you know about the topic. Ask what, where, when, how, and why. You will be amazed at the free-flowing ideas. After you do your extensive research, you can fill in additional information.

The next step is to write a proposal. Some students do not want to write a proposal, and instead put more energy and time into a detailed outline. That's fine. Many students, however, find it helpful to write a brief one-page proposal from their outline. You may want to include a brief introduction, lead up to your thesis, and add several main points and sources you plan to use. Because the introduction is tentative, you can skip data, illustrations, and quotations. Just get down the substance of the paper, its main points, and the questions you want to raise.

It is an excellent idea to make an appointment with your instructor when you have your proposal and/or outline completed. Most instructors will review it with you, give you suggestions, and discuss what to add and what to revise. Follow these suggestions to the letter.

5. Analyze the Topic

Once you have developed an outline, written a brief proposal, done preliminary reading, and prepared a working bibliography, you can begin research and analysis of the topic. Research the books and articles that you compiled on your bibliography cards. Take down all appropriate data, facts, and information on another set of notecards and number them. At the top of the card write the subject, and below it write a summary in your own words, a brief statement, or a direct quotation. Unless you are quoting for support, write in your own words. If you are quoting, use quotation marks and be sure to write down the words exactly, even if there is an error in the text (use the term *sic,* which means "thus in the original"). If you omit words, indicate this with ellipses points (three dots). Organize and separate information, and be consistent with the format. This process may seem tedious, but will save you hours later on when you start your writing and

▲ PLAGIARISM

▲ Some of the objectives of writing a research paper are to train you to investigate different sources and to give you skills in synthesizing varied information. Some students have a difficult time differentiating between paraphrasing and copying. Plagiarism is a serious ethical offense in school and, along with cheating on tests, can result in a failing grade or even expulsion from school. Plagiarism is the attempt to use another's language or major ideas as your own. It is copying another person's work, sometimes with minor changes. To avoid plagiarism, either paraphrase, assimilate, synthesize, or give credit to the source for major ideas, information, definitions, and quotes. Accuracy is essential. Enclose all quotes in quotation marks and copy word for word. This rule does not include general knowledge. For example, most of us have read that Einstein did poorly in school. This is general knowledge and does not have to be attributed to a specific source.

Paraphrasing is thoroughly rewriting a sentence or paragraph, not just changing a word or two. This requires changing sentence structure, words, and style to reflect your personal writing.

prepare your footnotes. You will want to go back to the library after your first draft to fill in and expand information. With detailed notes, you are well on your way to writing your paper. Use footnotes and the bibliography to show the amount of research that you have completed. Some students prefer to put their rough notes directly on the computer and then rearrange them as needed.

Speeches should also include facts, statistics, quotes, and supporting data. You will lose your audience if you use generalizations or vague points. Most professional speakers use 3×5 cards to compile their data, to keep their speech in order, and to use during the presentation.

6. Refine Your Purpose and Start Writing!

You now have an abundance of cards and information that you have collected. You could be tempted to jump right in and start writing. However, you may find it helpful to set your note cards aside for a day and take time to consider what you are trying to accomplish in writing this paper or giving this speech. This small amount of thinking and planning time will pay off when you actually sit down to write your paper. You cannot write effectively unless you have clearly in mind what your purpose is, the specific topic, your thesis statement, and the main points that you want to present. State your main topic and each subtopic in a complete sentence.

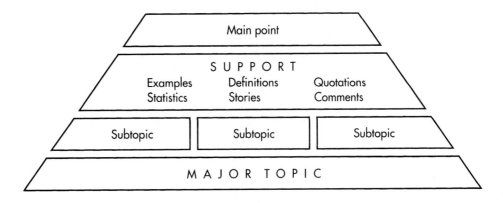

Devise a Strategy. Once you have considered your audience and the situation, you will want to refine your writing strategy by focusing on how best to accomplish your purpose. What is your major topic? What subtopics do you want to include? What form of support (examples, definitions, quotations, statistics, stories, personal comments, etc.) do you want to include? For example, suppose you will be speaking about the increase in smoking and associated health hazards to a group of Campfire Girls, ages 11 to 14. Your purpose is to inform them of the dangers of smoking and persuade them not to start. What information, stories, statistics, and examples would be most interesting to them?

Sort through your note cards and prioritize those that will be most helpful in developing your main points and supporting your subpoints.

Do the First Draft. Now is the time to gather all your notes and generate ideas according to your outline. You have done a lot of the hard work of planning and research. Now let the ideas flow freely. Use a separate sheet of paper for each new paragraph and write quickly from point to point. Some people prefer to write in longhand; others like to type their first draft double spaced and edit with a pencil. Many students swear they write best with the computer so that they can make changes easily. However you do the writing, do it quickly to keep the ideas flowing. It is tempting to put off writing until you have a large block of time. For a quick first draft, give yourself an hour or less. Write it in one sitting, as fast as you can. Don't worry about spelling, grammar, or organization. Don't sit down thinking you will write your final draft. The key is to begin writing and keep the momentum going. If you want, talk into a tape recorder or pretend that you are writing a letter to a friend and explaining the topic.

Check the Draft. Review your "quickie" first draft and rework the structure, giving attention to the introduction and conclusion. Both papers and speeches should have three sections: an introduction, a main body, and a conclusion. The introduction should be a strong opening that captures the audience's attention and sets the stage for the main points. Your purpose is to set tone and style and also outline the main topic briefly. Remember that the thesis statement is the controlling idea and should address the general topic, your opinion, and how you will address it. "Over 300,000 people will die this year from the effects of cigarette smoking" is a stronger introduction than "Tonight (or in this paper) I am going to tell you of the dangers of smoking."

Many people find it easier to write the main body and then come back to the introduction. Don't write lengthy introductions or a story that is unrelated just to get the audience's attention. The introduction should lead the way into the paper or speech and be informative and interesting as well.

The main body is the heart of your paper or speech. Each main point should be presented logically and stand out as a unit. Main points and subpoints should be supported with evidence, quotes, statistics, and interesting stories, and should support the purpose of the paper or speech. Refer often to your outline and your thesis statement. Your research notecards will help you find the support you need. If you find gaps, go back to do more research.

Finally, summarize the main points and write a strong conclusion. Your conclusion should tie together what you have written and leave the reader or listener with an understanding of the topic and an awareness that the purpose has been accomplished. Use a story, a quotation, or a call to action. You may want to relate back to the introduction, reemphasize main points, or rephrase an important position. Keep it brief, interesting, and powerful.

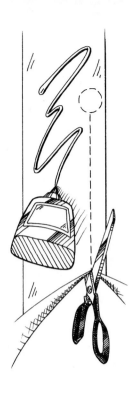

7. Revise and Shine

Now is the time to slow down and take time to revise and strengthen your paper or speech. Review sentence structure, punctuation, grammar, and unity of thought. Rework paragraphs for clarity and appropriate transitions. Throughout the revision process, read your paper out loud and have friends look at it. This gives you new perspective on the paper and helps catch mistakes. Look at the major ideas first. The paper should be concise; information should contribute, not just fill in space. Cut out any excess information—whether it is a single word or an entire page. Revision also involves moving information from one section to another. Go back and check your outline. Have you followed it logically? Have you included supporting information in correct places? If you find something in an inappropriate place, you can literally cut it out with scissors and paste it into a new place with tape. If you are using a computer or word processor, you can "cut and paste" with your word processing program.

Your Second Draft. After you have marked revisions on your first draft, write a second draft. With dictionary in hand, pay attention to sentence structure, spelling, format, grammar, transitions, and style (capitalization, use of abbreviations, and so on). As you write your revisions, make sure your points are clearly and concisely presented with plenty of supporting stories, quotes, and explanations. In a paper, transitions should be smooth and unobtrusive. In a speech, they should be clearly defined so that listeners stay with you. Keep referring to your outline to make sure this revised draft is in logical order.

8. Edit and Proof

Now edit and proofread your second draft. Check carefully for typographical and spelling errors, grammatical mistakes, poor transitions, illogical gaps, and the like. Make a copy for a friend to review. Other people can see errors that you can't and can provide a fresh viewpoint. Pay particular attention to the editing of footnotes, references, and the bibliography, if you have them. Make sure you have styled such references according to your instructor's preferences, and make sure all the information is complete. If you were careful in completing your research note cards, you should be all right. If you're missing an author's name or a complete title, you'll have to return to the library. Often if you're missing only a publisher's name or a date, you can call the library and ask one of the reference librarians to check the information and call you back.

The Finishing Touches. Often the difference between an A and a B paper or speech is that extra polish. If you can set it aside for a day or two before you give it a final polish, you can approach it with a fresh view. Go through your entire paper or speech. Write out your central theme. Is it clear and concise? Give your paper to a friend for another proofing. Read your paper out loud or recite your speech either to a friend or into a tape recorder. Does it flow? Could it use more stories or quotes to add flair? Is it too wordy? Confusing? Can you make it more concise? Does it have an interesting introduction and conclusion?

Following your instructor's guidelines for format and length, prepare your final draft. With a word processor or computer, you need only print out a clean, revised copy. (It's always a good idea to proofread this "hard" copy, though, as sometimes it's easy to miss spelling errors and typos when you proofread on a computer screen.) Whether you use a typewriter or a word processor, be sure to use good-quality paper.

▲ DEALING WITH WRITER'S BLOCK

▲ If you are like most people, you will experience writer's block at one time or another. Perhaps you have been given a term paper assignment and have put it off as long as you can. You stare at the computer or the blank sheet of paper, your mind searching for the right words. Nothing sounds good, so you become more frustrated as the deadline looms closer. You come up with a dozen excuses for not getting started. You can overcome writer's block by brainstorming ideas and setting a strict deadline for choosing a topic and outlining it.

Try these strategies for breaking the writing block:

1. Review Your Purpose

Don't even start to write unless you know what your purpose is. In one or two sentences write down what you want to accomplish. Keep the purpose of the writing and the reader firmly in mind as you establish your purpose statement. As precisely as possible, write the core of what you want to say.

2. Draw a Map Outline

Start with your central purpose and topic. Outline main points, subtopics, etc., and fill in with ideas and topics. A map lets you move around, work on different topics, free flow ideas, and see the connections between topics. Don't feel that you must start at the beginning and work in a linear fashion. In just a few minutes you can have a detailed outline of a speech or paper.

3. Brainstorm Ideas

Using the mapping concept, brainstorm everything you know about the topic and every detail you want to include. Don't worry about putting these ideas in a logical form. The wonderful point of a map is that it allows creative flow of ideas. Your mind will resist writing a paper if you say, "I have to sit down and write this paper." But it willingly will brainstorm ideas and topics. Brainstorming is fun and most effective when done with others. You can use the power of synergy when you brainstorm ideas for each other.

4. Freewriting

After you have completed your map outline, write for 30 or 40 minutes. Don't worry about spelling, organization, or grammar—just keep writing. Timed freewriting is a powerful writing tool to break the writing blahs and get you moving. Freewriting is especially useful if you start early, allow the first draft to sit for a few days, and then go back to it and revise.

5. Write in a Conversational Tone

Write the way you speak. Don't use technical, artificial, or stilted language. Use everyday, common words as if you were talking to someone. You might try using a tape recorder to dictate your paper so it sounds as if you are speaking and not writing.

6. Write a Letter to a Friend

If you continue to block, write a conversational letter to a friend telling about your purpose and conclusion. Come back to it in a day or two and revise it.

7. Write Your Conclusion

After you have finished your first draft, work on your conclusion. Write your conclusion in one sentence to check for clarity. Does it stand out? Is it supported? Is it compelling and clear? Now you can go back and revise the paper in light of supporting your conclusion. Does each paragraph contain just one idea and have a topic sentence? Is it well supported? Make certain you are consistent in your point of view; use of the first, second, or third person; spelling; etc. Break up the narrative with lists if you are presenting a series of data. As you revise, keep focused on your purpose rather than on the ideas that support this conclusion.

8. Keep a Journal

There is no better way to become a writer than to write. Keeping a daily journal encourages you to write down your thoughts and overcome the fear of putting pen to paper. No one need read it, so your ideas, style, and tone are your own. Like everything else, practice makes you a better writer. Write down your experiences, ideas, goals, fears, dreams, emotions, and concerns. If you hear a good story, quote, or joke, keep it in your journal or idea file. You will soon have a file of good material to draw from. Keep a dictionary, thesaurus, handbook of grammar, vocabulary builder, and journal or idea file in your study area. Write letters to friends and family regularly. This is a great way to increase your writing skills and stay in touch. Everyone loves to get letters, and everyone can learn to write interesting, lively, and concise letters and papers.

9. Read Other People's Papers

You will become a better writer by reading other people's papers. Volunteer to proof student's papers and exchange papers when you can. Read novels, classic literature, biographies, and newspapers. Reading helps you to become a better writer.

10. Write in Short Blocks of Time

Write for five minutes before bed, when you first get up in the morning, or between classes. Practice mind maps and freewriting in short snatches of time. Everyone has time to write. You will become a better writer when you stop making excuses and start writing.

Turn in your paper on time and be prepared to give your speech when it's due. Delaying the date just adds to the anxiety and may result in a lower grade. Make a copy of your final paper or speech to file, in case your instructor loses the original.

WRITING STRATEGIES

1. Be Concise. Eliminate unnecessary words. Write in plain language and avoid wordiness.

2. Be Concrete. Emphasize verbs for active, powerful writing. Use vivid action words rather than vague, general terms. The sentence, "Jill wrote the paper" is in the active voice and easy to understand; "The paper was written by Jill" is in the passive voice and sounds weak. Favor familiar words over the unfamiliar. Include stories and quotes for interest and support. Avoid vague adjectives and adverbs such as nice, good, greatly, and badly.

3. Be Clear. Keep in mind the purpose of your writing. Make certain that your message is complete and includes all the information the receiver needs to understand your intent. Never assume that the receiver has any prior information. Use simple words and avoid stuffy, technical terms, cliches, slang, and jargon. If you must be technical, include simple definitions for your audience. Keep in mind the purpose of your writing.

4. Be Correct. Choose precise and grammatically correct words. Make sure your supporting details are factual and that you interpret them correctly.

5. Be Coherent. Your message should flow smoothly. Transitions between topics should be clear and logical.

6. Be Complete. Make certain you have included all necessary information. Will your listeners or readers understand your message? Reread your speech or paper from their point of view. What questions might the audience have?

7. Be Considerate. Use a respectful tone. Don't talk down to your audience or use pompous language. Always write with courtesy, tact, and consideration.

8. Be Interesting. Use variety. Vary the length of sentences for interest and a sense of rhythm. Include stories, examples, and interesting facts.

9. Be Neat. Neatness counts. Papers should always be typed. If you find an error in the final draft, it's okay to use opaquing fluid or pen to make a correction. A word processor or computer, of course, can quickly make the correction and print out a flawless page.

10. Edit and Proofread Several Times. Make certain you use correct grammar, and check spelling and punctuation carefully. It is easy to miss things with only one proofing, so do at least one more.

11. Avoid Biased Language. Language is so powerful that it is important to avoid using words that are biased in terms of sex, disabilities, or ethnic groups. For example:

Instead of	You Can Substitute
mankind	humanity or people
manmade	manufactured, handcrafted
policeman	police officer
fireman	firefighter
housewife	homemaker
crippled	disabled, handicapped
Indian (American)	Native American
Negro	African-American
Oriental	Asian
Chicano	Mexican-American

PUBLIC SPEAKING STRATEGIES

Learning to face and overcome the fear of public speaking is one of life's most confidence-building achievements. You will find that knowing how to give presentations and speeches and lead discussions are skills that are valuable in all areas of your life. Many of the strategies for choosing a topic and organizing a speech are similar to those we just covered for writing papers. Here are a few additional strategies pertinent to public speaking.

The first step is to decide on a topic for your speech. The reference librarian can give you assistance in locating interesting and historic speeches. In addition to the suggestions offered earlier in this chapter, you might also explore the following resources:

1. *Speech Index.*

2. *Index to American Women Speakers, 1828–1978.*

3. *Representative American Speeches, 1937+.*

4. *Facts on File, 1941+.*

5. *Vital Speeches of the Day, 1941+.*

6. *Historic Documents of (Year).*

7. State Department bulletins.

8. Public papers of the presidents of the United States.

> "The more you experience writing, the more writing shapes your experiences."
>
> Dave Kemper

Follow the outline of basic steps for writing papers and giving speeches. Pay special attention to your audience. It is critical to be sensitive and to build rapport with them. Once you have a first draft of your speech, it is important that you practice. A speech needs to be recited many times to get the right sense of timing, gestures, tone, and style. The following strategies may help as you recite, polish, and practice.

1. Be Prepared. Arrive early, so that you can set up visuals if you have them. If you did a dress rehearsal in the actual classroom, that should help you feel prepared. Practice pausing; write "pause" on your notes until this becomes a habit. Bring all your necessary note cards or papers and your visuals with you. If there is a podium and microphone, check to see that they are adjusted for you. If you will be using audiovisual equipment, make sure it is in place and in working order. Even if the overhead projector was working during your rehearsal, turn it on again to make sure it still works. Encountering problems with equipment in the middle of a speech can be distracting to the audience and very stressful for you.

The Critical Thinking Connection

Preparing yourself both mentally and physically, determining the purpose of your paper or speech, deciding on key points, conducting research, reasoning logically, creating an action plan, overcoming writer's block and stage fright, and evaluating your progress are all critical thinking skills involved in writing papers and giving speeches. Use critical thinking to answer the following questions. Be prepared to discuss your answers in your teams.

1. Describe your typical physical reaction to stress when you give a speech. What has helped you control stage fright?

2. Describe the processes of writing that are easiest for you and those that are hardest for you.

3. Look at the common reasons and excuses that some students use for not writing effective papers or giving effective speeches. Add to this list and use creative problem solving to list strategies for overcoming these barriers.

Reasons   **Strategies**

I have panic attacks before I write or give speeches.

I can't decide on a topic.

I don't know how to do research.

I procrastinate until the last minute.

I don't know what my instructor wants.

My mind goes blank when I start to write or give a speech.

_____

_____

_____

_____

2. Be in the Present. Take a deep breath and pause before beginning. Look at your audience and smile. Remember that you are in charge. If you have truly practiced your speech and know the information thoroughly, you can focus on what you are saying, as if you are explaining the subject.

3. Pay Attention to Your Voice. Speak slowly and calmly but louder than usual. Vary the pitch and speed for emphasis. Pause between main points.

4. Use Natural Gestures. If you are a nervous, jittery person, control your gestures. If you are a stiff or laid-back type, add some excitement with relaxed, natural gestures.

When you tell yourself over and over again that you're afraid, nervous, will make a fool out of yourself, and can't get up in front of people, your body will follow your mental orders. Use positive self-talk. What you are doing is hypnotizing yourself with affirmations like the ones on the bottom of page 241.

▲ CHANNEL EXCESS ENERGY

▲ All performers and athletes know they can make stage fright work for them by controlling the fear and harnessing the energy. This energy can give you an edge and add excitement. When you are prepared, you feel confident. Take deep breaths, relax your muscles, and visualize yourself successfully giving a speech. Take a walk before the speech. Practice in the same room where you'll be giving the speech, if you can. Go early and get a feel for the room. Know where you are going to stand, and walk around. Use the excess energy to build confidence. People who suffer from stage fright talk themselves into a state of panic. For example, you have been assigned an oral report to be given in front of your class on Tuesday. Your first response is "Oh no, how will I make this deadline?" This is followed by sweaty palms, shallow breathing, heart racing, and more negative talk. Here are a few examples of negative, stress-producing talk and positive, stress-reducing talk:

Stress-Provoking Talk	Stress-Reducing Talk
I'll never be able to meet that deadline.	I will set priorities.
I am so nervous!	I am calm and in control.
I can't even think of a topic. I am just not good at this sort of thing.	I will use this surge of energy to plan a good report.

I am relaxed, confident, and calm.

I have something important to say.

I am building an essential skill and getting better every day.

My voice is calm, even, and low. I am in control.

I know what I am going to say.

I look people in the eye and pause between points.

▲ Stress adds drama and excitement and gives us a rush of energy. Actors and public speakers say that it is the controlled stress that makes an outstanding performance. How we view a situation triggers a series of responses within us. For many of us, just the thought or expectation of an event can produce an alarm in our body. Many people become anxious just thinking about giving a speech. Typical reactions include sweaty palms, a rush of adrenaline, an increase in breathing and heartbeat, dilated pupils, and tense muscles, and the body prepares to fight or flee. We can learn to use stress productively. This surge of energy provides us with concentration, energy, and the power to perform in crisis. There are many stories of people in a crisis performing beyond their normal physical capacity and behaving with great courage. Besides big crises, there are the normal pressures in everyday life—traffic, waiting in lines, conflicts, frayed tempers, disappointments, and deadlines that can cause stress overload. Successful, well-balanced people learn the signs of burnout and use strategies for controlling their reactions to stress.

Visualize

Let's say you are going to give a speech and you often experience stress, butterflies, and anxiety. Rehearse what you will do, and visualize yourself responding calmly, speaking with confidence and style, and making a positive impact on the audience. Visualize your words and your body language and feel yourself being calm and in control. With practice you can rehearse events and control stress. When you are preparing for a stressful situation such as giving a speech, taking a test, confronting an instructor about a grade, or resolving a problem with a roommate, write a script. Write out the problem, your feelings, and what you want from the other person. Make up a sample test, practice your speech, and rehearse all events before the actual performance.

5. Avoid Unnecessary Words. Get to the point! Use clear, concise words. Don't use pauses as fillers, irritating nonwords, or overused, annoying slang such as "uh," "um," "you know," "stuff like that," "sort of," "like," etc. Use pauses for emphasis; then take a deep breath and go on. Can you imagine a top executive saying, Like, uh, well, you know? Listen to effective speakers and model them. Be aware of how many times people use the term *you know,* and how it sounds. People judge you by your speech. If you sound uneducated or dull, others will assume you are.

6. Look at the Audience. Establish eye contact and speak to people. You are not giving this speech to a brick wall. Smile, develop rapport, and notice when they agree or look puzzled or confused. As you perfect your skill, you will use this feedback to establish contact with the audience. Move your gaze around the room and pretend you are talking with each person.

7. Make a Videotape. Watching yourself on tape can be helpful. Not only can you detect weak points in your speech, but you can assess your voice, gestures, and overall speaking style. If you hate to watch yourself on tape, ask several trusted friends to watch and listen and then give honest assessments. Do you rub your head, play with your hair, click a pen, clear your throat a lot, tap your foot, stand on one foot, or slouch over the podium? Distracted listeners can't concentrate on the message. Make certain you *time yourself,* and have a good watch available during the speech.

▲ CHECKLIST FOR WRITING PAPERS AND GIVING SPEECHES

▲ Appropriate and focused topic?

▲ Attention-getting introduction?

▲ Thesis statement clear?

▲ Word choice appropriate?

▲ Plenty of factual support?

▲ Good examples/visuals?

▲ Sources credited?

▲ Smooth transitions?

▲ Effective summary/conclusions?

Papers	Speeches
Spelling and grammar checked?	Eye contact?
Proofread at least twice?	Appropriate voice level and tone?
Pages numbered?	No slang or distracting words?
Neat?	Relaxed body language?
On time?	Appropriate attire?
Copies made?	Access to watch or clock?

8. Develop Visuals. When it is appropriate, use overheads, slides, and demonstrations. They can add drama, reduce your stress, and reinforce your speech. Just make sure the type is large enough to read, the projector works, and you have practiced working with the visual aids. If you are using handouts, make certain there are enough. Whenever possible, get the audience involved with questions, exercises, and visuals. You are in control, but group involvement takes the focus off you and onto the topic.

9. Prepare Your Prompters. You've probably heard speeches being read, which is different than being given. It's difficult to keep the listeners' interest if you read a speech, because you're looking at your paper all the time. In a class you don't have the benefit of a teleprompter. However, you don't want to actually memorize the speech; instead, you want to be so well versed on your topic that you are comfortable just talking about it. So now is the time to take your paper and prepare notes to prompt yourself. Put key phrases down in large letters. Color code notecards: certain colors contain examples, other colors contain facts, and others, stories.

10. Practice. Think of public speaking in the same way any performer approaches opening night or an athlete prepares for the main event. Rehearsal is everything! The actual event is just your opportunity to shine, because you've already rehearsed many times. Just like any skill, public speaking requires discipline and practice. Practice the speech several times out loud, in front of an empty classroom, and to friends. You don't need to memorize, but you should have your main points firmly in mind, with stories and quotes on note cards. Indicate where you should pause for effect and where you should gesture. You will find that after you become skillful at public speaking, this will come naturally, but until then, you will need to practice.

FOCUS ON CLARITY

CAREER FOCUS

Many times during your career you may have to deal with stage fright, anxiety, and writer's block. Peter Drucker, a well-known management author, has said that the ability to speak and write effectively are two of the most valued and important job skills that people can have in the business world. The higher up the career ladder you go, the more you will use public speaking and writing skills. Employees who can make effective presentations, give clear directions, write short reports, conduct meetings, and write effectively will go far.

Writing and giving presentations are part of most jobs. Even accountants, computer programmers, and forest rangers write memos, letters, annual reports, and proposals, and give short presentations and speeches.

Look at Nancy Kelly, a public relations and academic resources director at a small university. She edits the catalog, news releases, and alumni reports, and prepares letters and memos for the university president. She works with the university's advisory broad to present new marketing ideas, growth trends, lists of alumni making contributions, and academic resources for alumni. Nancy knows it is important to be clear, accurate, and brief. She sets deadlines and allows herself several days to review and polish important material before it is printed. She has other people edit her work to ensure that it is flawless, clear, and to the point. Here's an example of a memo that Nancy wrote to the accounting department:

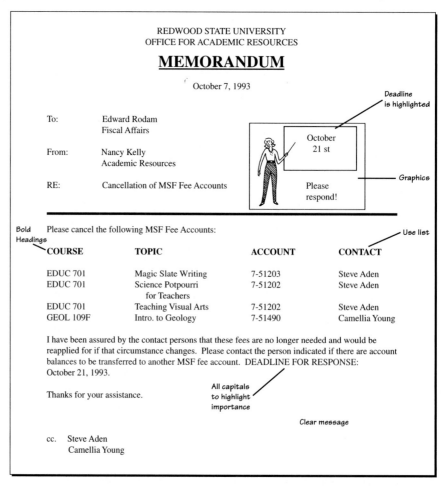

Grid 9.1
Preparing Research Papers

As you start thinking about upcoming research papers, use this grid to get ready and take action.

Topic   **Date Due**

Thesis

Introduction

  Interest and importance

  Introduce thesis in concise statement

Main body

  Background of topic

  Emphasize thesis

  Terminology, facts, data

  Key words

  Main points and arguments

  Supporting points

Conclusion

  Restate thesis

  Summarize key points

  Present clear and strong conclusion

Grid 9.2
Preparing Speech Outlines

For each speech you give, use this grid to prepare a general outline. Avoid the hazards of being unprepared.

Topic   **Purpose**   **Date**

Audience   **Audiovisual/handouts**

Introduction

    Interest

    Background

    Quotes

Body

    Present thesis

    Main points

    Key arguments

Conclusion

    Restate thesis

    Clear, concise, and powerful ending

▲ CASE STUDY 9.1

A. Sarah is a good student but goes blank when she has to write a paper. She has problems choosing a topic and delays the paper as long as she can. Recently Sarah was assigned a paper due in three weeks. This time it is even worse—the paper includes an oral presentation. If there is one thing that is even more difficult for her than writing papers, it is giving speeches.

After changing topics four times, Sarah has finally chosen one. However, she is experiencing writer's block. She sits in front of her computer and her mind goes blank. She is also terrified at the thought of making this formal speaking presentation. What would you suggest to Sarah that would get her started? What are three strategies mentioned in this chapter that would help her most? What could she do to reduce stage fright and anxiety? Suggest one habit that would be very helpful in writing papers and giving speeches.

_____

_____

_____

_____

_____

_____

_____

_____

_____

_____

B. Sarah is a park ranger. She chose this field because of her love of the outdoors and the chance to work with people. She is surprised at the amount of writing and speaking that she has to do. She has to write daily reports, annual reports, brochures, and fliers. She is required to give park tours, presentations, and lead staff meetings. At first the writing demands bothered her, but she is getting better at composing and meeting deadlines. However, Sarah is still experiencing butterflies every time she gives a presentation. She knows she must overcome this terrifying stage fright. What strategies would help Sarah become both a better writer and a more confident public speaker? What tips from this chapter would be most helpful?

_____

_____

_____

_____

_____

_____

_____

_____

_____

_____

A. Steve is a bookkeeping student at a career school. He likes numbers and feels comfortable with order, structure, and right or wrong answers. As a graduation requirement, all students must take classes in speech and writing. Steve becomes nervous about writing reports or giving speeches and doesn't see the connection between the required class and his bookkeeping studies. One of Steve's biggest stumbling blocks is coming up with topics. He experiences writer's block and generally puts off any writing project until the last possible moment.

What strategies in this chapter could help Steve come up with topics and meet his deadlines? What would you suggest to help him see the value of speaking and writing well?

_____

_____

_____

_____

_____

_____

_____

_____

_____

B. Steve is a district manager of an accounting firm and has recently been promoted. He feels very secure with the accounting part of his job. However, with the new promotion comes the responsibility of presenting bimonthly speeches to top management, as well as running daily meetings, and writing dozens of letters, memos, and reports. At least twice a year he must give motivational seminars to his department heads. Steve would like to make his writing and presentations clearer, more concise, and more motivational. What suggestions would you give Steve to help make his presentations more professional and interesting? What strategies could he use to improve his writing?

_____

_____

_____

_____

_____

_____

_____

_____

_____

_____

1. Locate two periodical articles, one on a popular topic and one on a scholarly, technical, or professional topic, and prepare abstracts of both.

2. Identify two or three people who have been (or are) prominent in your particular area of interest. Locate basic biographical information about each and make brief presentations on their lives and why they were (or are) noteworthy.

3. Investigate the on-line resources at your school. Can you get an account number to start exploring the Internet?

_____

_____

_____

_____

▲ Exercise 9.2   Role-Playing

1. Try out new roles. If you tend to be a quiet student in class, practice speaking up and participating in class discussions. Speak out in small groups and volunteer for classroom projects, role-playing exercises, etc. If you tend to speak in class a lot, practice listening to other people, attempt to see their viewpoint, and paraphrase what you hear them saying.

2. After a speaking situation, ask for feedback. What did you do that was effective and what could you improve?

3. Ask five people you know to give you feedback on how you communicate. Be open to suggestions.

_____

_____

_____

_____

▲ STRATEGIES FOR WRITING PAPERS AND GIVING SPEECHES ▲

1. *Determine your purpose and set a schedule.*

2. *Brainstorm ideas and choose the best.*

3. *Do reading, general research, and analysis.*

4. *Develop an outline, map, or proposal.*

5. *Analyze the topic.*

6. *Refine your purpose and start writing!*

7. *Revise and shine.*

8. *Edit and proof.*

TURNING STRATEGIES AND SKILLS INTO LASTING HABITS

"We are what we repeatedly do. Excellence, then, is not an act, but a habit."

Aristotle, Greek philosopher

"All great bosses do one thing: They engage. They capture imagination and energy, and by doing so get people to move mountains."

Nancy Austin, management consultant and co-author, with Tom Peters, of
A Passion for Excellence

Learning Objectives

In Chapter Ten you will learn:

1. The importance of positive habits.

2. The importance of commitment.

3. How to change a negative habit.

4. The best strategies for school and job success.

You've now learned many strategies and techniques for doing well in your school, career, and personal life: how to manage your time, how to take tests well, how to develop good relationships. Making these strategies part of your everyday life will prove rewarding and help you achieve your goals. Knowing that you have the motivational skills to succeed in school and in your career can give you the confidence to risk, grow, contribute, and overcome the setbacks that are part of life. You have what it takes to keep going even when you get stuck, face setbacks, and feel frustrated and unproductive.

This chapter will show you that committing yourself to a positive attitude and good habits is really the foundation for reinforcing the cycle of success.

There is no great achievement without commitment. Look at great athletes. The difference in their levels of physical skill is often not dramatic, but their sense of commitment is what separates the good from the truly great. You can take control of your life and consistently produce excellent results even when faced with setbacks or difficult situations. Successful people know how to create a positive and resourceful state of mind.

Make a Commitment to Have a Positive Attitude

Achieving excellence is a combination of a positive attitude and specific skills. When you commit yourself to being successful, you learn to go with your own natural energy and strengths. You learn to be your own best friend by working for yourself. You begin by telling the truth about who you are: your current skills, abilities, goals, barriers, and habits—both good and bad. You learn to be aware of the common barriers and setbacks that cause others to fail.

Then you set goals to focus your energy on a certain path. Next, you describe the action you intend to take to create the specific thoughts and behaviors that will produce the results you want. Everyone gets off course at times; thus it is important to build in observation and feedback so that you can correct and modify. You will learn to alter your actions until you get back on track. Even when you are equipped with the best skills, self-understanding, and motivated attitude, you will still face occasional setbacks and periods of frustration. At times you may question your decisions, become discouraged, and feel your confidence and self-esteem dip. It would be easy to give in to adversity and see yourself as a victim.

You gain strength, courage, and confidence by every experience in which you really stop to look fear in the face.

Eleanor Roosevelt

The key to being a peak performer is to actually make adversity work for you. Successful people see their failures as temporary setbacks and learning experiences; unsuccessful people see their failures as barriers and dead ends. Use the power of reframing to see your setbacks as stepping stones to your final goal. Learn to integrate specific skills into your everyday life until they become habits.

MAKE A COMMITMENT TO LEARN POSITIVE HABITS

Committing yourself to good habits is really the foundation for reinforcing the cycle of success. Throughout this book you have learned many strategies for getting better grades and the importance of maintaining a resourceful and motivated state of mind.

Answer yes or no to the following:

— Have you created a study area that reflects your learning style and helps you concentrate?

— Do you make learning physical?

— Do you preview each chapter before you read it?

— Do you preview chapters and rewrite your notes before class?

— Do you outline your papers? Do you proofread several times?

— Do you rehearse your speeches until you are confident and well prepared?

— Do you go to every class? Do you sit in the front row?

— Do you actively listen and take good notes? Do you rewrite your notes and review them within 24 hours?

— Do you monitor your work and get help early, if necessary?

— Do you participate in class and ask questions?

— Have you developed a relationship with each of your instructors?

— Have you joined a study team?

— Do you study and review regularly each day?

— Do you complete tasks and assignments first and then socialize?

— Do you review every day? Do you recite and restate to enhance your memory skills?

— Do you take advantage of campus and community activities?

— Are you able to create a motivated and resourceful state of mind?

— Do you know how to creatively solve problems?

— Do you use critical thinking in making decisions?

- Do you exercise daily?

- Do you maintain your ideal weight?

- Do you keep your body free of harmful substances and addictions?

- Do you support your body by eating healthy foods?

- Do you practice techniques for managing your stress?

- Have you developed an effective budget?

- Do you take the time for career planning?

If you find you've answered no to many of these questions, don't be alarmed. When old habits are ingrained, it's difficult to change them. By observing your thoughts, rethinking your beliefs, and reframing your experiences, you can alter your behavior and make lasting changes.

MAKE A COMMITMENT TO CHANGE BAD HABITS

Most people resist change with every fiber of their being. Even when you acknowledge a bad habit, it is difficult to make changes. Some people develop bad habits such as overeating, smoking, drinking, and taking drugs to cover up feelings of social shyness, inadequacy, and low self-esteem. You might start studying with the TV on because it provides a sense of company or read while you're in bed because it's so comfortable. Soon, however, a habit is formed. Thus, you may be finding it hard to integrate into your life some of the skills and strategies that have been presented in this book. Old habits die hard. They become comfortable, familiar parts of your life. Giving them up leaves you feeling insecure somehow. For example, you want to get better grades, and you know it's a good idea to study only in your study area, occasionally while standing up or sitting on the edge of your chair. However, you like to read assignments while watching television or lounging in bed. So you rationalize that you can read and watch TV too, and that you really can concentrate in that comfortable chair or warm bed. You might even try studying at your desk for a few days but then lapse into old habits. Many people give up at this point, rather than acknowledge their resistance. Some find it useful to take stock of what common resistors, or barriers, keep them from meeting their goals. The first step in making a lasting change is acknowledging your fears. Following are a few resistors that may make lasting change difficult.

1. Fear of the Unknown. I may be dissatisfied with my life, but I fear the unknown even more. What would happen if I really did get good grades? Would my friends change? Would I change?

2. Familiarity. I like the sameness of my familiar routine of curling up in a big chair.

▲ WHO MAKES IT? WHO DROPS OUT?

▲ Only about 6 out of 10 freshmen complete the first year of school, and less than half of every 10 students who begin college or advanced education actually graduate in four years. College and professional schools are not just more difficult than high school, they are very different. Very few beginning students are prepared for the academic pressure, the demands, the emotional stress, the distractions, the loneliness, the excitement, and the freedom. You will survive, however, and even do well if you acquire the tools to help you achieve and develop a positive and motivated attitude. Students drop out for many reasons, but often they are confused, bored, afraid, and unprepared. Many students begin their advanced education with poor study habits, deficient study skills, or a negative, immature attitude. It is important to determine if your problem is a lack of prerequisite skills or a negative attitude. Both can be changed if the cause is known. Some students get very frustrated with paperwork, classes, financial problems, roommate conflicts, and juggling of family time and study time. Other students drop out because they are bored with course work that they feel is irrelevant. They want to learn from life instead of a classroom. Other students are overwhelmed with the demands on their time and struggle to work and go to school. Peak performers often have these same fears, problems, and feelings. The difference is that they have decided to empower themselves, to find ways to relate course work to the real world, to get involved, and to postpone immediate satisfaction. Knowing common mistakes made by students can help you avoid them. Here are the top 10 reasons that students fail:

The Ten Most Common Reasons Students Fail

1. Socializing too much.

2. Missing classes.

3. Poor note-taking skills.

4. Failing to get help early.

5. Showing up for class unprepared.

6. Not previewing chapters before reading them.

7. Not taking advantage of daytime study hours.

8. Cramming for tests, rather than having consistent review periods.

9. Failing to review lecture notes within 24 hours.

10. Not realizing the importance of active listening in class.

3. Comfort. It's comfortable and warm in bed. It is not comfortable to study sitting on the edge of a straight-backed chair.

4. Security. I feel safe and secure with my routine and habits. Sometimes I feel so secure that I doze in the chair or fall asleep in bed.

5. Tradition. This is how I've always studied. I never knew anyone who studied standing up or in a straight-backed chair.

6. Embarrassment. I'd feel embarrassed and awkward if I tried to make studying a big deal or studied while standing up. It wouldn't look cool or natural. I'd feel like a nerd. What would my roommates think?

7. Responsibility. It's not my fault how I study. That's how I was raised. My parents always let us study where we wanted to and with the TV on.

8. Expectations. I have certain expectations of myself. I see myself as I am now. I don't see myself as a serious, A student.

9. Environment. I would change, but as long as my roommates watch TV while studying, it's too difficult. Our apartment is just too cramped to have my own study area.

10. Cost. It would cost too much to set up a study area for myself.

11. Giving Up. I tried but I just can't change. I am who I am.

If you are having trouble making changes, realize that habits are learned and can be unlearned. Adapting new habits requires a desire to change; knowledge of the tools, skills, and strategies; and a commitment to change behavior. Try the following strategies for changing old habits and acquiring new ones.

1. You Must Want to Change

You may have thought of a few things you would like to change, such as getting better grades or exercising more. However, most people resist new habits even when they know they want to change. In order to grow, you have to have a real desire and see the value of the change. It helps to identify important goals: I really want to get better grades. I have a real desire to graduate from business college and own my own small retail business. I now see the benefit and value in continuing my education. In order to get you moving, your motivation has to be channeled into constructive action.

2. Break Large Goals into Specific Goals

If the habit you want to change is too foggy or too large, you will become discouraged. Some goals are nothing more than nagging thoughts, vague wishes, or wistful dreams. Setting specific goals gets you off dead center. Statements such as, I wish I could get better grades or I hope I can study more only continue your inertia. State specific goals, such as studying for 40 minutes, two times a day in my study area.

3. Work on One Habit at a Time

You will become discouraged if you try to change too much. When you have listed the habits you want to change, start out by consistently studying for a specific time in your study area for a month. Then work on exercising more; after that, work on giving better speeches; then work on getting up earlier; and so on.

4. Give Yourself Time and Be Persistent

You will regress if you expect too much change too soon. It takes at least 30 days to change a habit. Lasting change requires a pattern of consistent behavior. With time and patience, this new change will eventually begin to feel comfortable and normal. Don't become discouraged and give up if you haven't seen a complete change in your behavior in a few weeks. Give yourself at least a month of pro-

> So few of my prisons are built by others. . . . My sorrows, my loneliness, my despair are all of my own design. If there is confinement in my soul, it is of my own making.
> Bob Samples

gressing toward your goal. If you fall short one day, get back on track the next. Don't expect to get all As the first few weeks of studying longer hours, or become discouraged if you don't instantly feel comfortable studying at your desk instead of lying on the couch.

5. Imagine Success

Imagine yourself going through all the steps to your desired goal. For example, see yourself sitting at your desk in your quiet study area. You are calm, centered, and find it easy to concentrate. You enjoy studying and feel good at completing projects. Think back to a time in your life when you had these same good feelings. Think of a time when you felt warm, confident, safe, and relaxed. Imagine enjoying these feelings, and create that same state of mind. Remember, the mind and body produce your state of mind, and this state determines your behaviors.

6. Observe and Model Others

How do successful people think, act, and relate to others? Do students who get good grades have certain habits that contribute to their success? There are few secrets to being successful. Basic success principles produce successful results. Research indicates that successful students study regularly in a quiet study area. They attend every class, on time, and sit in the front row. Observe successful students. Are they interested, involved, and well prepared in class? Do they seem confident and centered? Now model this behavior until it feels comfortable and natural. Start forming friendships with people who are good students, who are motivated, and who have effective study habits.

7. Observe Yourself

Sometimes just observing your behavior and thoughts can help you to change habits. If you want to study in your study area for about an hour several times a day, observe the thoughts that trigger you to react in a negative or self-defeating way. You may observe, for example, that studying in your bed makes you feel relaxed, warm, and safe. This pattern of thinking may be a clue to reframe the undesirable behavior into a desirable behavior. Ask yourself what you could do instead as a reward that would also make you feel relaxed, warm, and safe. Your reward should fulfill the same need as your undesirable behavior.

8. Reward Yourself

One of the best ways to change a habit is to reward the desired behavior. Increase your motivation with specific payoffs. Suppose you want to reward yourself for studying for a certain length of time in your study area or for completing a project. You might say to yourself, After I outline this chapter and look up the key words, I'll take a 20-minute hot bath or When I finish reading these two chapters, I'll call Brent and talk for 10 minutes. Taking a warm bath and talking with friends may make you feel relaxed, warm, and safe. Of course, the reward should come after the results are achieved and be limited to a specific time.

9. Use Positive Self-Talk

Talking to yourself means that you are reprogramming your thoughts, a successful technique for making change. When you have negative thoughts, say to yourself, Stop! Counter negative thoughts with positive statements. Replace the negative thought, "I can't seem to concentrate. I might as well study in bed," with the affirmation, "I am centered and focused. I have control over my thoughts. When they wander, I gently bring them back. I can concentrate for the next 40 minutes, and then I'll take a short break and have a snack."

10. Write a Contract for Change

Write a contract for overcoming your barriers. State the payoffs for meeting your goals: I agree to take an honest look at where I am now and at resistors, my shortcomings, my negative thoughts, the ways I sabotage myself, and the barriers I experience. I agree to learn new skills, to choose positive thoughts and attitudes, and to try out new behaviors. I will reward myself for meeting my goals. For example:

I most want to change _____

My biggest barrier is _____

The resources I will use to be successful are _____

I will reward myself by _____

The consequences for not achieving the results I want will be _____

_____

Date _____

Signature _____   Witness _____

The Critical Thinking Connection

Stating the problem clearly, exploring alternatives, reasoning logically, looking at your assumptions, choosing the best alternative, creating an action plan, and evaluating your plan are all critical thinking skills involved in making choices and changing habits. Use critical thinking to answer the following questions. Be prepared to discuss your answers in your teams.

1. What are the barriers in your life that keep you from being a peak performer? What are your resistors or bad habits?

2. What do you really want to change?

3. Do you have a commitment to change the habits that keep you from being successful? List three things you can do to begin the process.

4. Look at the common reasons and excuses that some students use for not making a commitment and changing poor habits. Add to this list and use creative problem solving to list strategies for overcoming these barriers.

Reasons   **Strategies**

I really don't have any problems.

I can handle my life without any help from so-called experts.

Even if I study, I still wouldn't get good grades.

I've always done it this way.

My life will be better when _____.

It's not my fault. I blame _____.

It's only school—not a job.

My instructors are too rigid.

I worry that I'll make the wrong decision.

I let time take care of my problems or decisions.

_____

_____

_____

_____

CAREER FOCUS

FOCUS ON RESPONSIBILITY

Career enhancement suggestions are worth little unless you actually change your behavior and develop positive, consistent, and long-lasting work habits. Habits free your mind from constant decisions about daily events. Good habits can transform you into a true professional. Commit yourself to taking responsibility for your career by developing habits that produce results.

Let's look at Laura Learner, sales assistant in a refrigeration plant. As a student, she was undisciplined and never developed effective techniques to make her workload easier. In her new job, Laura was offered the opportunity to take a sales training course. She was told that a great deal would be expected of her, but it was also a tremendous opportunity for advancement. Fortunately, Laura had a boss who was aware of the importance of good habits. She encouraged Laura to assess her strengths and weaknesses and develop goals for better health and energy, better relationships, better work habits, and more effective memory, reading, note taking, listening, problem solving, and decision making skills. Laura

▲ 1. Go to every class.

2. Go early and stay until the end.

3. Sit in the front row, participate, and ask questions.

4. Choose the best instructors and get to know them.

5. Give the first three weeks of classes your all-out effort.

6. Use the power of synergy—form study teams.

7. Preview all reading assignments before classes.

8. Highlight only key words, phrases, and formulas.

9. Write a summary of the chapter in your own words.

10. Study in short blocks of time and take frequent breaks.

11. Abbreviate notes and focus on key words and questions.

12. Review class notes after every class and again within 24 hours.

13. Use note cards for formulas and key words. Carry them with you.

14. Pretest yourself before the actual test. Become an expert test taker.

15. Set goals and daily priorities. Do first things first.

16. Turn in all assignments on time.

17. Create an organized, light, and quiet study space.

18. Eat healthy foods, exercise, get enough rest, and avoid alcohol, cigarettes, and drugs.

19. Study when you are most alert—utilize daytime hours.

20. Use both sides of the brain.

21. Integrate learning styles. Make learning physical and personal.

22. Use a mind map for outlining and brainstorming.

23. Practice speeches until you are comfortable and confident.

24. Read and exchange term papers. Proofread several times.

25. Program your mind with positive affirmations and visualizations.

26. Neatness counts. Focus on details of papers.

27. Negotiate for a better grade *before* grades are sent in.

28. Always do extra credit.

29. Communicate with assertiveness, honesty, and integrity.

30. Use creativity and critical thinking for problem solving and decision making.

31. Keep a journal and write letters to improve your writing skills.

32. Create a resourceful, positive, and receptive state of mind.

33. Empower yourself with play. Make a game out of work.

34. Use an erasable pen for neat, organized essay questions.

35. Reframe your circumstances and see the positive side of life.

36. Make questions out of chapter headings. Read chapter summaries.

37. When taking notes in class, watch for clues from your instructor.

38. Use waiting time for reviewing notes, and use note cards and mind-mapping.

39. Practice memory techniques. Connect information for understanding.

40. Welcome feedback. Use it to monitor your results.

41. Ask for help early.

42. Connect patterns, link concepts, and look for relationships.

43. Summarize chapters in your own words. Recite out loud.

44. Use listening and good communication skills to build rapport.

45. Take control of your time and study habits. Review often.

46. Know the course objectives and the instructor's expectations.

47. Anticipate questions and ask why. Good questions equal good answers.

48. Make information personal, applied, alive, and relevant.

49. Focus on the present and absorb yourself in the moment. Concentrate.

50. Take action, be persistent, and make a commitment to excellence.

also planned to focus on clear communication. Instead of just trying out a few strategies, Laura worked with her supervisor and the training department to develop good habits. She assessed herself often and adjusted her behavior when necessary to get herself on track. Following are 10 habits you can develop that will go a long way toward a successful career. Commit to them!

Ten Habits for Peak Career Performance

1. Be dependable. Strive for perfect attendance and always be on time!

2. Be an active team player. Get involved and contribute your time and talents.

3. Be enthusiastic, motivated, and interested in your work.

4. Be an active learner and continually acquire new skills.

5. Always do more than is required.

6. Be a creative problem solver and use critical thinking to make decisions.

7. Consistently turn in work that is accurate, neat, and on time.

8. Always project a professional, well-groomed image.

9. Consistently use good communication skills—active listening, writing, and speaking.

10. Always act from a point of integrity. Consistently follow high business ethics. Your reputation is your most important asset.

CONCLUSION

You learn that whatever you are doing in life, obstacles don't matter very much. Pain or circumstances can be there, but if you want to do a job bad enough, you'll find a way to get it done.

Jack Youngblood

When knowledge, drive, and experience all come together, it is enormously challenging for the spirit as well as for the mind, body, and emotions. Those students who have mastered basic study skills, developed positive attitudes, learned mature and responsible behavior, set clear goals, and created mindsets are motivated for success. These are the very skills that are fundamental for success throughout life.

Life is about change. Change brings with it problems and choices. You have all the resources necessary to cope with choices and solve problems creatively. Growth begins by having the courage to confront problems directly, to learn tools and strategies, to practice discipline, to take risks, and to practice a lifetime of self-reflection. Commitment to excellence is the foundation of success. The key is to be open to growth and learning and to be willing to risk pain for self-understanding and truth. Once you have the knowledge, understanding, and tools you need, take action. Be a doer. You can take charge of your life by putting your words into action or, as some people say, "walk your talk." It takes a lot of work to be attentive and awareness to live in the present. You have the courage it takes to be a peak performer.

One thing you should have learned from this book is that the best students aren't extraordinarily intelligent, especially lucky, or amazingly talented. Rather, they are average people who have learned to think and act in consistently positive, motivated, and determined ways. They have a mission that inspires them to stay on course most of the time. Regardless of how difficult the path is at times, they know they have the inner resources to empower renewal, call on their inner strength, generate creative ideas, and explore new paths. The best students continuously focus on their mission and set immediate goals to get there. They do not allow adversity to keep them from their goals. You too can learn the necessary skills, create the proper attitude, and find the right resources to handle any task at hand. You have what it takes to inspire commitment and action and create success in your life!

Grid 10.1
Final Exam Schedule

Be sure that you know the exact date, time, and location of each final exam. Good record keeping will pay off

Course	Date	Time	Room	Type of Exam

Grid 10.2
Course Self-Evaluation

After each course ends, take a minute to consider how you progressed through each one. Jot down your personal evaluation for each of the topics below.

COURSE	Interest	Attendance	Projects	Tests	Presentations	Extra Credit

A. Julie is smart, attractive, fun, energetic, and works well with other people. She wants to get better grades, but she is too busy to take a class on study skills. Someone gave her a book of strategies for getting better grades and adjusting to school, but it was pretty thick and she really doesn't have time to read it. Her mother sent her an article about the 10 best habits for being successful, but Julie finds her habits so hard to change. She even tried a few new habits, like going to class on time, but then lapsed back into her old ones. Julie feels powerless to get control over her life and make lasting changes. What strategies would you suggest to Julie that would help her adopt positive habits?

_____

_____

_____

_____

_____

_____

_____

_____

_____

B. Julie is an assistant buyer at a sportswear company. She talks endlessly about the excitement of this field, the opportunities for travel, the contacts with interesting people, and the fun of being around new fashions. Her dream is to become a buyer with a large sportswear company. She knows that she will have to make some major changes. First, she should get additional training in computers, management, and accounting, but when would she find the time? She also knows that she has to follow through on details more carefully, but that part of her job seems boring to her. In addition, Julie has fallen into the habit of coming to work late, being tardy for meetings, and turning in reports that are overdue and incomplete. She also must learn to work with more diverse people, but she finds "different" people so hard to relate to. Clearly, Julie has the desire for advancement, but has a difficult time making real, lasting changes or committing herself to changing poor work habits. What strategies would you suggest to Julie for making changes in her habits and commitment that will produce the results she wants for her career?

_____

_____

_____

_____

_____

_____

_____

_____

_____

A. Cliff is a welding student. He never liked high school, but his natural mechanical ability helped him get into a trade school. He wants to be successful and knows that this is an opportunity for him to get a good job. Cliff's parents both worked, so he and his sister had to get themselves off to school, supervise their own homework, and get many of their own meals. Money was tight and he didn't often receive encouragement for positive behavior. He never learned good study or work habits.

What kind of a study plan would you suggest to Cliff that would build up his confidence and help him to be successful? What strategies in this chapter could help him develop positive, lasting habits?

_____

_____

_____

_____

_____

_____

_____

_____

_____

_____

B. Cliff has just been promoted to general supervisor in charge of welding and plumbing at a large farm equipment manufacturing plant. He has been a valued employee at the firm for several years, and has worked very hard to get promoted. Cliff wants to ensure his success in his new job by getting training in motivation, team building, quality customer service, and communication skills.

What suggestions do you have for Cliff that would help him establish and train his staff in good habits? What strategies in this chapter would help him be more successful?

_____

_____

_____

_____

_____

_____

_____

_____

_____

_____

_____

▲ COMMITMENT STRATEGIES ▲

1. Make a commitment to have a positive attitude.

2. Make a commitment to learn positive habits.

3. Make a commitment to change bad habits.

4. Be persistent.

5. Reward yourself for positive change.

INDEX